Developmental States beyond East Asia

This comprehensive volume reviews recent scholarship regarding the role of the state in economic development. With a wide range of case studies of both successful and failed state-led development, the authors push the analysis of the developmental state beyond its original limitations and into the 21st century.

New policies, institutional configurations, and state-market relations are emerging outside of East Asia, as new developmental states move beyond the historical experience of East Asian development. The authors argue for the continued relevance of the 'developmental state' and for understanding globalization and structural transformation through the lens of this approach. They further this concept by applying it to analyses of China, Latin America, and Africa, as well as to new frontiers of state-led development in Japan and the East Asian developmental states. This book expands the scope of research on state-led development to encompass new theoretical and methodological innovations and new topics such as governance, institution building, industrial policy, and the role of extractive industries.

This book was originally published as a special issue of the journal *Third World Quarterly*.

Jewellord T. Nem Singh is Assistant Professor in International Relations at Leiden University, the Netherlands. He is the recipient of the Japan Society for Promotion of Science (JSPS) Research Award in 2016 and the Alexander von Humboldt Research Fellowship in 2017. His main research lies on the intersection between development and democracy in Latin America and East Asia, with particular interest on state-building and resource-led growth strategies. He is co-editor of *Demanding Justice in the Global South: Claiming Rights* (2017) and *Resource Governance and Developmental States in the Global South: Critical International Political Economy Perspectives* (2013).

Jesse Salah Ovadia is Assistant Professor at the University of Windsor, Canada. Focusing on the political economy of oil, gas, and mining, he writes about local content policies and industrial development. He is the author of *The Petro-Developmental State in Africa: Making Oil Work in Angola, Nigeria and the Gulf of Guinea* (2016) and co-editor of *Energy, Capitalism and World Order: Toward a New Agenda in International Political Economy* (2016).

ThirdWorlds
Edited by Shahid Qadir, *University of London, UK*

ThirdWorlds will focus on the political economy, development and cultures of those parts of the world that have experienced the most political, social, and economic upheaval, and which have faced the greatest challenges of the postcolonial world under globalisation: poverty, displacement and diaspora, environmental degradation, human and civil rights abuses, war, hunger, and disease.

ThirdWorlds serves as a signifier of oppositional emerging economies and cultures ranging from Africa, Asia, Latin America, Middle East, and even those 'Souths' within a larger perceived North, such as the U.S. South and Mediterranean Europe. The study of these otherwise disparate and discontinuous areas, known collectively as the Global South, demonstrates that as globalisation pervades the planet, the south, as a synonym for subalterity, also transcends geographical and ideological frontier.

The most recent titles include:

Class Dynamics of Development
Edited by Jonathan Pattenden, Liam Campling, Satoshi Miyamura and Benjamin Selwyn

Third World Approaches to International Law
Edited by Amar Bhatia, Usha Natarajan, John Reynolds and Sujith Xavier

Fragility, Aid, and State-building
Understanding Diverse Trajectories
Edited by Rachel M. Gisselquist

Rural Transformations and Agro-Food Systems
The BRICS and Agrarian Change in the Global South
Edited by Ben M. McKay, Ruth Hall and Juan Liu

Sustainable Development in Africa-EU relations
Edited by Mark Langan and Sophia Price

New Mechanisms of Participation in Extractive Governance
Between Technologies of Governance and Resistance Work
Edited by Esben Leifsen, Maria-Therese Gustafsson, María Antonieta Guzmán-Gallegos and Almut Schilling-Vacaflor

The Development Dictionary @25
Post-Development and its Consequences
Edited by Aram Ziai

Power and Illicit Drugs in the Global South
Edited by Maziyar Ghiabi

Hybridity in Peacebuilding and Development
A critical and reflexive approach
Edited by Lia Kent, Miranda Forsyth, Sinclair Dinnen, Joanne Wallis and Srinjoy Bose

The Agency of the Governed in the Global South
Normative and Institutional Change
Edited by Anke Draude

Innovations in 'Sport for Development and Peace' Research
Edited by Megan Chawansky, Lyndsay M. C. Hayhurst, Mary G. McDonald and Cathy van Ingen

Global Debt Dynamics
Crises, Lessons, Governance
Edited by Andreas Antoniades and Ugo Panizza

Developmental States beyond East Asia
Edited by Jewellord T. Nem Singh and Jesse Salah Ovadia

Gendering Security and Insecurity
Post/Neocolonial Security Logics and Feminist Interventions
Edited by Navtej K. Purewal and Sophia Dingli

Property Rights and Governance in Artisanal and Small-Scale Mining
Critical Approaches
Edited by Chris Huggins

For more information about this series, please visit:
https://www.routledge.com/series/TWQ

Endorsements

The state isn't taking a backseat. Across the Global South states are taking the lead in driving economic development, looking to East Asian Developmental States as a model. Whether the success of the latter can be replicated is for the future to tell. What matters now is that we have the right theories and concepts to explain what is going on. This timely volume is a move in this direction.

Adam D. Dixon
Associate Professor of Technology and Society Studies
Maastricht University

The global crisis of neoliberalism makes urgent the search for alternatives to market-led economic development. Equally urgent is to find models of economic growth that address the ever-increasing danger of global warming. The two questions cannot be solved by market forces alone. Strong state capacity, working in close partnership with both business and civil society is necessary to achieve ecologically sustainable economic development. By looking at the role of development states across regions in the 21st century and mapping both their successes and their shortcomings, this volume addresses some of the most relevant questions about the future of our planet and of the people that inhabit it.

Francisco Panizza
Professor in Latin American and Comparative Politics
The London School of Economics and Political Science

This collection not only brings together insightful analyses of the transferability of the East Asian developmental state experience to China and African and Latin American states, but also evaluates recent new initiatives among developmental states from the paradigmatic East Asian examples of Japan, South Korea, Taiwan, and, to a certain extent, Singapore. Written in a highly accessible and engaging manner, chapters in this book collectively provide an important addition to the recent academic and policy efforts in rethinking the developmental state increasingly shaped by changing forces in the global political economy. It will serve as a highly relevant guide for our understanding of state-led development in the 21st century.

Henry Wai-chung Yeung
Distinguished Professor
National University of Singapore

Developmental States beyond East Asia

Edited by
Jewellord T. Nem Singh and Jesse Salah Ovadia

Routledge
Taylor & Francis Group
LONDON AND NEW YORK

First published 2019
by Routledge
2 Park Square, Milton Park, Abingdon, Oxon, OX14 4RN

and by Routledge
605 Third Avenue, New York, NY 10017

First issued in paperback 2020

Routledge is an imprint of the Taylor & Francis Group, an informa business

British Library Cataloguing in Publication Data
A catalogue record for this book is available from the British Library

ISBN 13: 978-0-367-72845-8 (pbk)
ISBN 13: 978-0-367-15198-0 (hbk)

Typeset in Myriad Pro
by RefineCatch Limited, Bungay, Suffolk

Publisher's Note
The publisher accepts responsibility for any inconsistencies that may have arisen during the conversion of this book from journal articles to book chapters, namely the possible inclusion of journal terminology.

Contents

Part III: New dynamics for developmental states in the international political economy

Citation Information

The chapters in this book were originally published in *Third World Quarterly*, volume 39, issue 6 (June 2018). When citing this material, please use the original page numbering for each article, as follows:

Chapter 1
Introduction: The theory and practice of building developmental states in the Global South
Jewellord Nem Singh and Jesse Salah Ovadia
Third World Quarterly, volume 39, issue 6 (June 2018), pp. 1033–1055

Chapter 2
Studying the developmental state: theory and method in research on industrial policy and state-led development in Africa
Jesse Salah Ovadia and Christina Wolf
Third World Quarterly, volume 39, issue 6 (June 2018), pp. 1056–1076

Chapter 3
State-owned enterprises and the political economy of state–state relations in the developing world
Jewellord Nem Singh and Geoffrey C. Chen
Third World Quarterly, volume 39, issue 6 (June 2018), pp. 1077–1097

Chapter 4
The developmental state of the twenty-first century: accounting for state and society
Jennifer Hsu
Third World Quarterly, volume 39, issue 6 (June 2018), pp. 1098–1114

Chapter 5
Twenty-first century developmental states? Argentina under the Kirchners
Christopher Wylde
Third World Quarterly, volume 39, issue 6 (June 2018), pp. 1115–1132

Chapter 6
Industrial policy and state-making: Brazil's attempt at oil-based industrial development
Eliza Massi and Jewellord Nem Singh
Third World Quarterly, volume 39, issue 6 (June 2018), pp. 1133–1150

Chapter 7

The Ethiopian developmental state
Christopher Clapham
Third World Quarterly, volume 39, issue 6 (June 2018), pp. 1151–1165

Chapter 8

An extractive developmental state in Southern Africa? The cases of Zambia and Zimbabwe
Richard Saunders and Alexander Caramento
Third World Quarterly, volume 39, issue 6 (June 2018), pp. 1166–1190

Chapter 9

East Asia's new developmentalism: state capacity, climate change and low-carbon development
Christopher M. Dent
Third World Quarterly, volume 39, issue 6 (June 2018), pp. 1191–1210

Chapter 10

Exporting the developmental state: Japan's economic diplomacy in the Arctic
Aki Tonami
Third World Quarterly, volume 39, issue 6 (June 2018), pp. 1211–1225

Notes on Contributors

Alexander Caramento is a PhD candidate in the Department of Politics at York University, Canada. His dissertation research focuses on indigenous capital formation among Zambian mine suppliers and contractors in the Copperbelt and North-Western Provinces. He teaches African History and Political Economy as an Adjunct Lecturer in the Department of History at Trent University, Canada.

Geoffrey C. Chen is Associate Professor of Political Economy in the Department of China Studies at the Xi'an Jiaotong-Liverpool University, China. His recent work has appeared in *New Political Economy* and *China: An International Journal*. His book *Governing Sustainable Energies in China* was published in 2016. His research interests broadly cover environmental politics and comparative political economy.

Christopher Clapham is Professor Emeritus at the Centre of African Studies at Cambridge University, UK. He is a specialist in the politics of Ethiopia and the Horn of Africa and was formerly editor of *The Journal of Modern African Studies*. His books include *Transformation and Continuity in Revolutionary Ethiopia* (1988); *Africa and the International System: The Politics of State Survival* (1996); and, as editor, *African Guerrillas* (1998).

Christopher M. Dent is Professor of East Asia's International Political Economy at the University of Leeds, UK. His research interests centre on the international political economy of East Asia and the Asia-Pacific, particularly issues relating to energy, trade, development, climate change strategy, and regional economic co-operation and integration. He has acted as a consultant advisor to multiple governments, as well as the Asian Development Bank, European Commission, ASEAN Secretariat, APEC Secretariat, Secretariat for Central American Economic Integration and Nike Inc.

Jennifer Hsu is Visiting Fellow in the Department of Social Policy at the London School of Economics and Political Science, UK, and a Non-Resident Senior Fellow of the China Policy Institute at the University of Nottingham, UK. Her research broadly covers state–society and state–NGO relations, and the internationalisation of Chinese NGOs. Her monograph *State of Exchange: Migrant NGOs and the Chinese Government* was published in 2017.

Eliza Massi works as a heavy industry and oil and gas analyst for the Department of Trade and Investment, Embassy of Brazil in London, UK. Her research focuses on industrial policy, the role of development banks, and mobilisation of finance for development in Latin America and East Asia.

Jewellord T. Nem Singh is Assistant Professor in international r elations at Leiden u niversity, the Netherlands. He is the recipient of the Japan s ociety for Promotion of s cience (JsPs) r esearch Award in 2016 and the Alexander von Humboldt r esearch Fellowship in 2017. His main research lies on the intersection between development and democracy in Latin America and east Asia, with particular interest on state-building and resource-led growth strategies. He is co-editor of *Demanding Justice in the Global South: Claiming Rights* (2017) and *Resource Governance and Developmental States in the Global South: Critical International Political Economy Perspectives* (2013).

Jesse Salah Ovadia is Assistant Professor at the u niversity of Windsor, Canada. Focusing on the political economy of oil, gas, and mining, he writes about local content policies and industrial development. He is the author of *The Petro-Developmental State in Africa: Making Oil Work in Angola, Nigeria and the Gulf of Guinea* (2016) and co-editor of *Energy, Capitalism and World Order: Toward a New Agenda in International Political Economy* (2016).

Richard Saunders is an Associate Professor in the Department of Politics at York u niversity, Canada, where he teaches African political economy. His current research focus is the role of the Zimbabwean minerals sector in that country's political transition. His most recent book is *Facets of Power: Politics, Profits and People in the Making of Zimbabwe's Blood Diamonds* (edited with t inashe Nyamunda, 2016).

Aki Tonami is Associate Professor in international r elations and economics at the u niversity of t sukuba, Japan. in her research, she works on the theory and practice of economic diplomacy with a particular emphasis on foreign investment, science and technology, development aid, and environment. Her publications include *Asian Foreign Policy in a Changing Arctic: The Diplomacy of Economy and Science at New Frontiers* (2016).

Christina Wolf is Lecturer in economics at Kingston u niversity, u K. Her research interests include late-industrialisation in Africa with special focus on demand-side dynamics as well as China's emerging role in the African construction sector. s he is particularly interested in how structural transformation is shaped by the state and spending patterns in the economy as well as external or systemic influences, such as the intensification of s outh–s outh economic ties and financialisation.

Christopher Wylde is Associate Professor of international r elations at r ichmond, the American international u niversity in London, u K, and is a Visiting r esearch Fellow at the institute of Latin American s tudies (iLAs), u niversity of London, u K. He is also a Fellow of the s alzburg s eminar American s tudies Association. His publications include *Latin America after Neoliberalism* (2012), *Argentina Since the 2001 Crisis* (with Cara Levey and Daniel o zarow, 2014), and *Emerging Markets and the State* (2017).

Dedication

To the matriarchs of our family, *Natividad Bautista and Maria Corazon Reyes*, thank you for being the pillars of our migratory family. This book is a token of appreciation for your strength and love for us.

Jojo Nem Singh, Amsterdam, January 2019

To Diana, whose love and support sustains me, who accompanies me on all my journeys, and makes me feel like I can do anything.

Jesse Salah Ovadia, Toronto, January 2019

Acknowledgements

This project was borne out of the editors' shared interest in understanding how state agency can be theorized at a time when developing countries are often understood as rule takers and weak amidst the changes occurring in the global political economy. It was, like many other research projects, a long collective thought process that involved communicating and organizing calls across continents and time zones. The early stages of our research were made possible through the support of our mentors and colleagues at Sheffield and Newcastle University. We held a workshop entitled "Developmental States beyond East Asia", hosted by the Politics Department at Newcastle University and the PSA Development Politics Group on the 5th June 2015, which brought together a diverse group of senior and junior academics to discuss and rethink whether 'developmental state' was an appropriate conceptual and methodological lens to explore a wide range of policy instruments, new institutions, and emerging policy practices outside of East Asia. We were convinced that developmentalism was indeed on the rise in Africa and elsewhere, but that it needed more conceptual precision in order to make sense of the similarities and differences in the design of development strategies at the turn of the millennium.

We took on the challenge of reviving this concept and brought together a collection of papers that would capture the essence of the East Asian developmental states – its historical idiosyncrasies, geopolitical conditions, and policy instruments – as many industrializing countries beyond this region find novel ways to respond to economic globalization. Fortunately, *Third World Quarterly* was interested in this idea and our special issue proposal became part of a wider research agenda in development studies to include politics in the analysis of development strategies. We are extremely grateful to the anonymous reviewers for the journal. We also wish to thank our authors who painstakingly accepted our editorial interventions as each paper undergoes the review process.

The success of collective undertakings like a special issue requires energy and massive amounts of time. Jojo was very fortunate to have been awarded two fellowships that provided time and space to devote to this project. He would like to thank Professor Jin Sato who served as host in his stay at the University of Tokyo, Japan in 2016–2017 and Dr. Bettina Engels who remains a good friend and colleague during his time as an Alexander von Humboldt Research Fellow in Freie Universität Berlin in 2017–2018.

Finally, we would like to thank our family and circle of friends in the Philippines, Europe and North America who have always been understanding about the difficulties in making time for them while being committed to our academic careers.

Jojo Nem Singh, Amsterdam, January 2019
Jesse Salah Ovadia, Toronto, January 2019

OPEN ACCESS

The theory and practice of building developmental states in the Global South

Jewellord Nem Singh and Jesse Salah Ovadia

ABSTRACT
Reviewing decades of thinking regarding the role of the state in economic development, we argue for the continued relevance of the concept of the 'developmental state'. With reference to Argentina, Brazil, Ethiopia, Rwanda and China, we contend that new developmental states are evidence of a move beyond the historical experience of East Asian development. Further, we argue for the applicability of the developmental state framework to key questions of governance, institution building, industrial policy and the extractive industries, as well as to a wide variety of cases of successful and failed state-led development in the early twenty-first century.

Development is essentially a record of how one thing leads to another.

Albert Hirschman[1]

Development, often understood in economic terms as the structural transformation of the national economy, has been an elusive objective for many outside the advanced industrialised countries of the West. Despite the multitude of reforms rooted in the economic modernisation paradigm of the 1950s, very few countries have succeeded in realising sustained, rapid industrial development. The intellectual history of this debate stems from questions around which policies can deliver economic growth and why countries failed to take off and experience similar economic transition.

The exceptionalism of East Asia's success, therefore, generated a vibrant debate centred on the extent to which policy choices, institutional dynamics and external circumstances have shaped economic development. As our special issue collectively suggests, the *politics* underpinning development planning is a key determinant of the outcomes of policy-making. Without understanding the political basis of development, one becomes excessively focussed on policy design as the explanation to the success of East Asia.

The collection builds on long-standing debates on state transformation and contributes to a richer understanding of the politics of growth in the context of global market integration.

Jewellord Nem Singh http://orcid.org/0000-0002-5216-4408;
Jesse Salah Ovadia http://orcid.org/0000-0002-5010-8269

While high export prices translate into greater rents and new competitive advantages are crafted with strong state support, a lacuna exists in explaining how and why some governments are able to craft development strategies that create and sustain new sources of growth. Owing to disillusionment from international financial institutions (IFIs) that advised or insisted upon structural adjustment programmes (SAPs) and counselled against state interference, the post-2000 period was marked by profound inspiration to emulate – if not replicate – the development strategies of East Asia, which led to rapid, sustained industrialisation in less than 50 years.[2] We provide some tentative answers through several cases, for example Brazil under Lula da Silva's Workers' Party (PT), Argentina under Nestor Kirschner and Ethiopia under the Ethiopian Peoples' Revolutionary Democratic Front (EPRDF), whereby new developmentalist thinking has shaped policy choices in the twenty-first century.[3] Beyond country cases, we likewise identify non-traditional pathways of growth, particularly through natural resources, which require new ways of managing the national economy. We suggest that important lessons can be drawn from those who appear to be succeeding, those who may have succeeded for a time and those who have tried and failed.

Our special issue directly engages the 'transferability' debate: that is, the extent to which the developmental state (DS) model(s) can be adapted beyond East Asia's geographical, socio-political and historical conditions to provide alternative ways of doing development in the Global South. We carefully selected papers to answer three inter-related questions:

(1) Given that the DS model(s) emerged within specific conditions, what *generic* policies and state institutions can inform contemporary governing elites to address the challenge of economic and social development?
(2) In states with weak capacity and legacies of inequality, oppression and colonial rule, what theoretical and methodological approaches will enable scholars to examine states with *political intent* and *institutional capacity* to promote industrialisation?
(3) In reflecting the evolution of development paradigms and the movement beyond old models of 'developmental authoritarianism', what lessons arise from how do political elites in East Asian developmental states face rising challenges to economic governance and to what extent have they been successful in managing economic globalisation and addressing sustainable development?

Each paper interrogates one or two key aspects of the DS model(s), then critically engages with the theory and builds new insights either through new empirical evidence or re-appraisal of conventional wisdom regarding DS theory. Collectively, we examine economic and political development in the Global South in the context of economic globalisation; consequently, the case studies reflect on how old models of developmental authoritarianism remain compatible with global democratisation. Our introduction offers an overview of the debates and arguments put forward in the collection. We begin with a reflection on the 'state of the art' of developmental state theory, outlining its key tenets and a brief summary of the main arguments. We then proceed with an analysis of emerging conceptual frameworks aimed at how these tools might provide the foundations for different theories and methods of studying state governance and development. Finally, we synthesise some common themes across the papers, stressing two important findings from our collection: (a) *new institutions and policies* are needed to understand emerging responses to globalisation; and (b) the *political base of development* must be examined to contextualise how strategies are crafted. Our approach deploys sectoral/industry-specific, country by country and policy-focused analyses to highlight the features, prospects and challenges for twenty-first century developmental states.

1. Thirty years of research on developmental states

Chalmers Johnson[4] first proposed the concept of a 'developmental state', using the term to describe strong interventionist policies implemented by Japan that led to sustained, rapid industrialisation and long-term economic development. The term became a shorthand for the successful rise of the newly industrialised countries (NICs) of East Asia, or the 'Asian Tigers' – Japan, South Korea, Taiwan and Singapore.[5] In the period that began with the Second World War and continued up to the 1980s, their developmental strategies were shaped by a political ideology that privileged raising income levels and sustaining industrial growth (or 'GNP-ism'). This paradigm asserts the state as key to the development process, with the capability and intent to resolve market failures, capital scarcity and lack of coordination between governments and industrial elites.[6]

The DS framework offers important analytical tools to understand the East Asian 'miracle'. However, national industrialisation was, and remains, elusive in the rest of the developing world. Table 1 confirms what many scholars[7] have argued – that Southeast Asia (notably Indonesia, Malaysia, Thailand and Vietnam) – is the region that came closest to the growth rates and capital accumulation experienced by East Asia. This is particularly evident when examining GDP at nominal values, growth rate averages (although these are significantly lower when comparing 1980s–1990s and 2000s–2015), poverty gaps and poverty headcount ratio using a higher threshold for poverty.[8] Latin America's record likewise confirms established wisdom regarding its high levels of inequality but also impressive poverty reduction during the 2000s – mainly a direct outcome of the Left's social investments during the commodity boom. Nevertheless, remarkable progress is discernible in Argentina, Brazil, Ethiopia, Rwanda and China – all of which are newer examples of developmentalist thinking with varying success. Ethiopia and Rwanda are particularly impressive due to their fourfold increase in GDP between 2005 and 2015, average growth rates at 9.7 and 8%, and fairly respectable shares of income for the lowest 20% of the population (see Table 1). Their performance is especially notable when compared to Botswana and Kenya, which also experienced growth spells over the past decades. The growth strategies of Argentina, Brazil, Ethiopia, Rwanda and China involve centralising rent management, strengthening political ties between government and domestic capitalists and adapting industrial policy and state-backed finance to create new competitive advantages.[9]

This introduction seeks to synthesise emerging literatures on the political economy of state transformation to examine the institutions and policies on the one hand, and the political bases of developmental states in the Global South on the other. As a departing point, we identify the *necessary* political conditions that brought forth the economic miracle in East Asia: (1) state transformation through the creation of a professionalised, meritocratic bureaucracy alongside a fairly insulated group of technocrats, which overall constitutes the historical development of state capacity widely referred to as 'pockets of state efficiency';[10] (2) a pro-business orientation in policy-making that created a mutually-beneficial alliance between states and big business, notably referred to as 'embedded autonomy';[11] and (3) the presence of exceptionally difficult circumstances, which then creates a structural condition in which national elites must deal with their 'systemic vulnerability' and hence focus on

Table 1. Social and economic performance of selected developing countries.

Selected Countries	Gross Domestic Product (1)			Adjusted net national income (2)		Gross Capital Formation (average annual % growth) (3)		GINI Index (4) (5)	Percentage Share of Income or Consumption		Broader Measures of Domestic Savings		Poverty Rates at International Poverty Line		
	US$ Billion (2005)	US$ Billion (2015)	Average annual % growth (2000–2015)	US$ Billion (21,015)	Average annual % growth (2000–2015)	1990–2000	2000–2016		Lowest 20% (5) (6)	Highest 10% (5) (6)	Consumption of Fixed Capital as % of GNI (2015) (7)	Education expenditure as % of GNI (2015) (8)	Reference Year	Population below US$3.10 a day (9)	Poverty gap at US$3.10 a day (10)
East Asia															
China	2,286.00	11,064.70	10.1	8,361.10	..	11·6	12.5	42.2	5.2 (2012)	31.4 (2012)	23	1.8	2013	11.1	2.5
Singapore	127.4	296.8	5.9	237.6	5.5	7	6.6	..	..	..	14.8	2.8	..	..	..
South Korea	898.1	1,382.80	3.9	1,113.90	3.2	4.3	2.9	..	..	..	19.5	4.1	..	..	..
Latin America															
Argentina	198.7	584.7	3.9	510.1	5	7.4	5.9	42.3	4.8	30.6	10.3	5.1	2014	4.3	1.7
Brazil	891.6	1,803.70	3.5	1,590.10	4	4.4	4.2	52.9	3.3	41.8	8.6	5.5	2014	7.6	3.1
Chile	123	242.5	4.3	188.1	5	..	..	50.5	4.6	41.5	13	4.6	2013	2.1	0.8
Colombia	146.6	291.5	4.5	242.9	5.1	2.1	9.1	53.5	3.4	41.9	12.4	3.5	2014	13.2	5
Mexico	866.3	1,151.00	2.3	986.6	2.3	4.1	2.7	48.1 (2012)	4.9 (2012)	38.9 (2012)	11.4	5			
Southeast Asia															
Indonesia	285.9	861.3	5.5	760.9	5.2	–0.6	6.3	39.5	7.2	31.9	7.5	3	2014	36.4	9.6
Malaysia	143.5	296.3	4.9	234.2	6.3	..	12	46.3 (2009)	4.6 (2009)	34.6 (2009)	17	6.1	2009	2.7	0.5
Philippines	103.1	292.8	5.1	324.3	5	2.1	5.9	43 (2012)	5.9 (2012)	33.4 (2012)	7.4	1.8	2012	37.6	11.7
Thailand	189.3	399.2	4	298.7	3.7	–4.2	4	37.9	6.9	29.2	19.2	4.2	2013	0.9	0.1

Vietnam	57.6	193.2	6.4	159.2	6.4	19.8	8.6	38.7 (2012)	6.5 (2012)	30.1 (2012)	12.3	5.4	2014	12	3.1
Africa															
Botswana	9.9	14.4	4.7	10.8	4.5	4.6	6.4	60.5 (2009)	2.8 (2009)	49.6 (2009)	21.9	9.5	2009	35.7	14
Ethiopia	12.4	64.5	9.7	44.9	..	..	..	33.2 (2010)	8 (2010)	27.4 (2010)	14.1	2.9	2010	71.3	26.5
Kenya	18.7	63.8	4.9	47.7	5.7	6.1	9.2	48.5 (2005)	4.7 (2005)	38.8 (2005)	21	4.9	2005	58.9	25.5
Nigeria	112.2	481.1	7.9	402.9	7.9	−1	12.4	43 (2009)	5.4 (2009)	32.7 (2009)	10.7	0.9	2009	76.5	39.1
Rwanda	2.6	8.3	8	..	7.6	3.8	14.1	50.4	5.2	43.2	13.8	4.3	2013	80.6	42.5
Tanzania	16.9	45.6	6.7	40.8	7.1	−1.1	9.7	37.8 (2011)	11.1 (2011)	31 (2011)	7.4	3.7	2011	76.1	33.6

Source: Compiled by authors from World Development Indicators. http://wdi.worldbank.org/tables

(1) GDP at purchaser's prices is the sum of gross value added by all resident producers in the economy plus any product taxes and minus any subsidies not included in the value of the products. It is calculated without making deductions for depreciation of fabricated assets or for depletion and degradation of natural resources. Data are in current US dollars. Dollar figures for GDP are converted from domestic currencies using single year official exchange rates. For a few countries where the official exchange rate does not reflect the rate effectively applied to actual foreign exchange transactions, an alternative conversion factor is used.

(2) Consumption of fixed capital represents the replacement value of capital used up in the process of production.

(3) Gross capital formation (formerly gross domestic investment) consists of outlays on additions to the fixed assets of the economy plus net changes in the level of inventories. Fixed assets include land improvements (fences, ditches, drains and so on); plant, machinery and equipment purchases; and the construction of roads, railways and the like, including schools, offices, hospitals, private residential dwellings and commercial and industrial buildings. Inventories are stocks of goods held by firms to meet temporary or unexpected fluctuations in production or sales and 'work in progress'. According to the 1993 SNA, net acquisitions of valuables are also considered capital formation. Data are in constant 2010 US dollars.

(4) Gini index measures the extent to which the distribution of income (or, in some cases, consumption expenditure) among individuals or households within an economy deviates from a perfectly equal distribution. A Lorenz curve plots the cumulative percentages of total income received against the cumulative number of recipients, starting with the poorest individual or household. The Gini index measures the area between the Lorenz curve and a hypothetical line of absolute equality, expressed as a percentage of the maximum area under the line. Thus, a Gini index of 0 represents perfect equality, while an index of 100 implies perfect inequality.

(5) Unless the reference year is indicated, the default year is 2013.

(6) Percentage share of income or consumption is the share that accrues to subgroups of population indicated by deciles or quintiles. Percentage shares by quintile may not sum to 100 because of rounding.

(7) Consumption of fixed capital represents the replacement value of capital used up in the process of production.

(8) Education expenditure refers to the current operating expenditures in education, including wages and salaries and excluding capital investments in buildings and equipment.

(9) Poverty headcount ratio at US$3.10 a day is the percentage of the population living on less than US$3.10 a day at 2011 international prices. As a result of revisions in PPP exchange rates, poverty rates for individual countries cannot be compared with poverty rates reported in earlier editions.

(10) Poverty gap at US$3.10 a day (2011 PPP) is the mean shortfall in income or consumption from the poverty line US$3.10 a day (counting the nonpoor as having zero shortfall), expressed as a percentage of the poverty line. This measure reflects the depth of poverty as well as its incidence. As a result of revisions in PPP exchange rates, poverty rates for individual countries cannot be compared with poverty rates reported in earlier editions.

economic development as the principal source of their political legitimacy.[12] We discuss these elements in detail below.

The study of the East Asian miracle was associated with the impressive transformation of state institutions aimed at generating rapid, sustained industrialisation throughout the post-war years. Indeed, the developmental capacities of states – defined in terms of the creation of a Weberian rational bureaucracy – and the choices in economic state-crafting were deemed pivotal in directing economic growth in the region. State capacity is oftentimes linked to economic growth and poverty reduction,[13] political legitimacy[14] and nation-building.[15] In Latin America, political corporatism emerged as a way of reconfiguring state–business alliances and, almost coincidentally, as a platform for integrating social actors into political structures.[16] Taking a broader view, we find that an intellectual history exists surrounding the centrality of political states – and particularly developmental states – in enhancing productivity, creating comparative advantages for export promotion and driving policy cohesion through a relatively insulated cadre of bureaucrats and pilot agencies. In so doing, the state could deploy a variety of instruments, such as government-backed financing and state-owned enterprises acting as direct producers, to seek new areas for competitiveness.

The second tenet of a developmental state involves the crafting of a mutually beneficial state–business alliance, whereby the state implements a series of incentives and rewards to persuade domestic capitalists to undertake investments in targeted sectors in the economy. This relationship partly underpins the justification for national ownership. National ownership opens a developmental space for domestic firms to compete with multinational companies through state protectionism. Because foreign firms can crowd out nationally-owned firms in mid- and high-tech industries, national enterprises can only catch up with the brand name recognition and technological finesse of foreign firms through market protectionism under a limited time period.[17] Crucially, state–business relations are embedded in a political framework, in which the centralised management of rents enables states to impose political stability, reduce transaction costs for private actors to motivate entrepreneurship and create further opportunities for productivity-driven rent-seeking.[18] For East Asian states, *the ways states organise their support for various business groups* determined the high levels of institutional capabilities to push for industrialisation.[19]

Finally, developmental states that are capable of mobilising financial resources to pursue ambitious industrial policy had motivations linked to national security and survival of the political ruling class. That elites saw economic growth as the main source of regime legitimacy stems from existential threats and immense vulnerability brought about by structural conditions and historical contexts.[20] Specifically, the Cold War rivalry, the threat of communism and the constant threat of war were critical factors that drove national elites in Singapore, South Korea and Taiwan to undertake economic reforms that would otherwise be impossible during 'normal times'.[21] In effect, the geopolitical situation forced elites to build robust, developmentally-oriented states with industrialisation as the answer to state insecurity.

These three conditions have become the basis for several path-breaking studies on the origins, prospects and limits of developmental states. Further research has interrogated several new themes in lieu of the 'transferability' question of the East Asian experience, namely: (1) the importance of colonial legacies and historical path dependence in shaping growth regimes towards a developmentally-oriented state;[22] (2) the rise of welfare regimes and social democracy as a 'Third Way' between neoliberalism and state intervention[23] (3) the role of industrial policy and value chain upgrading as a development strategy towards economic globalisation;[24] and (4) the significance of political alliances among contending elites and important fractions of society in the context of weak state capacity as a means to promote economic growth.[25] This burgeoning literature on state governance is crucial if we are to further take the DS as an analytical framework beyond the East Asian context.

2. A new research agenda for the DS theory

To take the DS model as homogenous and as a blueprint for development would be a mistake. Indeed, reflecting on his work over a decade after *Embedded Autonomy*, Evans forcefully argues for the need to build pragmatic, flexible states that can respond to new challenges and changing international contexts and avoid *institutional mono-cropping* and one-size fits all approaches to development policy.[26] If the 'developmental state' concept is to travel beyond East Asia, we need to build new scholarship that takes the diversity of the Global South as a starting point. There have been several calls to move 'beyond' the developmental state.[27] But, the concept has remained popular in scholarly discourses – particularly regarding African development in the post-Washington Consensus era. In Latin America, from 2000 onwards, the intellectual fashion stressed the return of state-led approaches to development, oftentimes understood as governance strategies aimed at creating 'globalisation with a human face'.

In order to understand the moves towards embracing and then re-embracing state-led development, we need to explore the unique challenges and nature of post-neoliberal experiments in Africa, Latin America and Asia and their respective positions in the world economy. There are two key challenges in doing this: first, addressing theoretical and methodological debates between and within development economics, comparative political economy and area studies; and second, finding empirical evidence of both success and failure that lends credibility to the DS approach. In the contemporary contexts of Latin America and Africa in particular, this involves and coincides with a re-examination of the role of natural resources in structural transformation.

The first challenge is to chart a course between overlapping – sometimes competing – conceptual frameworks that explore development processes rooted in localised experiences of capital accumulation while also considering the theoretical innovations within area studies. In this context, conceptual debates offer new possibilities to expand the scope of the DS framework. In particular, we would like to draw similarities and differences across four concepts: *post-neoliberalism*, *neo-structuralism/neo-developmentalism*, *developmental patrimonialism*, and *neo-extractivism*. As Table 2 summarises, there are shared assumptions across these frameworks and they provide fresh starting points for further elaboration. With the exception of developmental patrimonialism, most conceptual tools from these debates have rarely referenced the DS model, despite their shared interest in analysing state intervention and industrial policy-making. We briefly outline some of these debates below.

In Latin America, scholars have recently coined 'post-neoliberalism' as a reference to the return of state capitalism in the region while calling for a 'new kind of politics that place citizenship, rights and inclusive politics' in governance and development.[28] Built on political economy and comparative area studies, this school reflects and critically explores how regional governments can deepen democratic engagement and practices to go beyond simply calling for state renewal and activist policies in economic governance. Complementing this approach, political economy and development economics have a long-standing tradition

Table 2. Key conceptual frameworks in development politics.

	Key Authors / Publications	Analytical Focus	Theoretical Foundations
Post-Neoliberalism	Grugel and Riggirozzi 2012, 2017; Wylde 2012.	State–market relations and state–society relations, with specific references to welfare and social policies, poverty reduction and citizenship claims-making; emphasis on Latin American Left (2002–2012).	Political science and sociology
Neo-Structuralism / Neo-Developmentalism	Key documents: Bárcena and Prado 2015; ECLAC's *Changing Production Patterns with Social Equity* (1990) and *Structural Change for Equality* (2012).For scholarly work, see Ffrench Davis 1988, 2010, 2015; Leiva 2008; Ocampo 1998, 2005; Ocampo and Bértola 2012; Ocampo et al. 2000.[+]For neo-developmentalism: Boito Jr. 2012; Boito Jr. and Berringer 2013; Bresser-Perreira 2011, 2012; Castelo 2012; Gezmis 2017.Famous structuralists include Celso Furtado (1920–2004); W. Arthur Lewis (1915–1991), Raúl Prebisch (1901–1986), Juan Noyola Vázquez (1922–1962); Aníbal Pinto Santa Cruz (1919–1996); Osvaldo Sunkel (1929–) and Ignácio Rangel (1914–1994).	Building on structuralist thought in Latin America and the Caribbean in the 1950s and 1960s, neo-structuralism opposes the Washington Consensus based on stabilisation, privatisation and liberalisation. Instead, the paradigm reflects on how to deal with the consequences of greater liberalisation in trade and finance, how to overcome productive heterogeneity and how improve income distribution.Neo-developmentalism builds on developmentalist thinking in Brazil, which focusses on sectoral development through industrial policy, governing through state-owned enterprises and state-backed financing, exchange rate management to improve export competitiveness and policies avoiding the Dutch disease. Some important work in political sociology also examines the role of class politics and the changing political base of development in Brazil.	Development economics; political economy
Developmental Patrimonialism	Booth 2011; Kelsall 2011; see also Clapham and Saunders & Caramento, this volume for critical engagement.	State–business relations, principally understood as how the state as a cohesive actor shapes interest groups. Emphasis on state power and role of political elites in managing economic rents to produce export sectors rather than predatory capitalism. A re-appraisal of how neo-patrimonial relations in African regimes can be conditioned to produce better developmental outcomes.	Comparative politics; political economy

Neo-Extractivism	Burchardt and Dietz 2014; Veltmeyer and Petras 2014; Gudynas 2010, 2016. For alternative but similar viewpoints, see Haslam and Heidrich 2016; Ocampo 2017.	Linked to debates on structural transformation, neo-extractivism is critical of possibilities for natural resource-led growth. Building on Latin America's recent policy innovations, these authors examine the causes, processes and shortcomings of resource-linked development policy. Emphasis on social investments, poverty reduction and participatory forms of governance in the mining sector. Some critical views on the ability of developing states to manage the resource curse and move away from rentier politics.	Political science and sociology

+Selected works only.

of understanding Latin American (under)development from a structuralist point of view, whereby systemic factors and structural conditions that undergird regional and national political economies limit the capacity of states and firms to reposition themselves in a globally integrated economy. There appears to be less nuance between 'new structuralism' as applied to Spanish-speaking Latin America[29] and 'new developmentalism'[30] in Brazil, although recent attempts to connect these debates have begun.[31] These frameworks recognise the tensions between structural transformation through renewed state activism and inclusive politics as neoliberal reforms constrained more meaningful forms of democratic participation. Crucially, social policies and civil society activism are novel features of these models, whereby the scope of state capacity goes beyond the notion of *infrastructural capacity*, or the 'capability of governmental institutions to implement public goals through a professional bureaucracy',[32] but instead includes the ability of the political classes to generate political legitimacy through acceptance and negotiation with social forces and organised civil society.

By contrast, in Africa, recognising the pervasiveness of corruption, money politics and rent-seeking, David Booth, Tim Kelsall and others have utilised 'developmental patrimonalism' as a framework to explain the political conditions which can produce *incremental* state transformation and renewed growth strategies based on natural resource-based industrialisation.[33] Given the divergent developmental outcomes amongst neo-patrimonial regimes and the failure of 'good governance' approaches to African development, Booth suggests that 'we should at least consider the possibility that there are forms of the neo-patrimonial state that combine patronage politics with quite a high degree of developmental effectiveness' and that 'in Africa just as in Asia, patronage politics and corruption can work in ways that block provision of the public goods that are essential to reasonably inclusive economic growth and human development'.[34] The underlying condition here, as Kelsall notes, is not only the presence of long-term development visions (or developmental roles in Vu's language) but the *state capacity* to make autonomy decisions over how economic rents can be transformed into productive assets. What distinguishes the economic performance of Ethiopia and Rwanda from other East African states is the immense capability of states to *centralise rent management*, enabling political elites to expand participation in key sectors, though concerns remain about the growing concentration of power and wealth within a small group, increasingly less accountable to the public.[35]

As in the East Asian experience, economic growth becomes the primary motivation for state intervention; centralisation of patrimonialism and rent-seeking becomes a form of *disciplined* capital accumulation. Growing authoritarianism notwithstanding, the ability of political elites at the apex of power to generate a consensus or 'political settlement' is the glue that holds together the relationships between contending elites – and between states and social forces – that consequently provides an enabling environment for national elites to secure political stability and policy consensus over the trajectory of development planning.[36]

These debates have advanced our understanding of localised capital accumulation and the importance of the changing bases of production in a globalised world economy. However, one emergent debate in political economy of development involves the extent to which new forms of capital accumulation – principally through natural resources – can generate sustained, rapid industrialisation. These development projects were underpinned by a commodity boom and a return to old debates about resource-led growth. In Latin America, neo-extractivism has become a conceptual framework to connect intensive and extensive resource extraction to the politics of redistribution.[37] The 'commodity supercycle' of the early 2000s was a catalyst for new thinking about the role of the state in economic development. Moving from an overview of new developmentalism in Latin America to studies of more and less successful extractivism in Africa, the papers in this special issue will address the new possibilities for new developmental states that leverage natural resource wealth before returning to consider alternative configurations and alliances that might lead to developmental states beyond East Asia.

Across these conceptual debates, some necessary conditions can be identified, which explains the relative success of Brazil (2002–2010) and Argentina (2002–2007), the partial success of Rwanda under Paul Kagame and Ethiopia under the EPRDF and the significantly more limited success or outright failure of other states who have articulated a vision of state-led development and may or may not have made real moves to realise it. We summarise this in Table 3. As a starting point, state-led high growth systems and those which feature partial success are underpinned by the creation of a group of 'economic technocrats' who were more or less able to steer the political economy relatively insulated from external pressures of rent-seeking and profiteering – a highly politicised process that governments historically partook to establish the political capacity to implement public policy and provide goods conducive for private sector expansion.[38] One distinction between Argentina and Brazil, for example, is the presence of coordinating councils, presidential advisory committees and other intermediary institutions which enable states to establish formal and informal lines of communications with business firms and state-owned enterprises. These 'developmental spaces' are crucial for industrial policy and for the government to maintain discipline over capital, which could prevent rent-seeking that leads to predatory capitalism. Furthermore, there have been significant reforms in the state-owned enterprise (SOE) sector in Brazil and China, according states managers with greater autonomy and isolation from political processes. Conversely, increasing political interventions in Brazil under Dilma Rousseff and in Argentina under Cristina Kirchner led to the erosion of state autonomy, which is consequential to the performance of domestic firms. Their success is also underpinned by favourable external conditions that allowed unconventional approaches to development to be implemented.

These institutional conditions are only one part of the story; policy choices and the ways economic reforms are implemented in the wider political context equally matter. As the first wave of DS theorists argued, state intervention was implemented to deliberately 'get the prices wrong' and, in response to changing market conditions, governments were able to switch from import substitution industrialisation (ISI) towards export orientation of capital goods.[39] In so doing, the fiscally-expensive industrial policy in Asia was mediated through mutually-agreed targets between the conservative government and business leaders towards the internationalisation of their exports. Finally, states were pragmatic in adjusting to the international context. For East Asian states, the geopolitical context of the Cold War fortunately provided the much-needed support through US military aid and development assistance to mobilise financial resources for development, but it also created an immediate export market through demands for infrastructure and heavy capital goods as the US government ventured into proxy wars and opened its domestic market for imports from its allies. To put it crudely, there is undoubtedly a security imperative that drove developmental states from rapidly industrialising and for the conditions for its emergence to materialise.[40]

In moving forward, the collection places special emphasis on how global rules and the changing patterns of production and consumption are reshaping spaces of development

Table 3. Comparative evidence on new developmental states.

	Brazil (2002–2015)	Argentina (2002–2008)	China (2003–present)	Ethiopia (2005–present)	Rwanda (2000–present)
State capacity	Presence of 'leading agencies' like Itamary (Foreign Ministry), Ministry of Planning, state-backed financing through BNDES and state-owned enterprises	Independent Central Bank although clear absence of 'leading pilot agencies' similar to East Asia	National Development and Reform Commission (NDRC) as the 'leading pilot agency' of national strategic industries. State-owned Assets Supervision and Administration Commission (SASAC) as shareholder and supervisor of Central state-owned enterprises	Capacity boosted by war and revolution. Efficient state-owned enterprises. Ministry of Finance and Economic Development balances domestic rent extraction with encouraging foreign investment	Ministry of Agriculture heavily involved in promoting the sector and working with donor agencies and cooperatives. Rwandan Development Board modelled on Singapore's EDB
Sources of growth	Dependence on domestic savings, generated from windfall profits and export earnings; consumption-driven growth	Consumption and export-led growth mainly from agricultural products (e.g. soya)	Foreign-direct investment in manufacturing industry and the development of both state and private sectors	Agricultural development-led industrialization (ADLI) giving way to policies that privilege private entrepreneurs	Agricultural development leading to increased output; concentration of manufacturing in a small number of domestic and foreign-owned firms
Industrial policy	Macro-economic fundamentals were in place through reforms in the 1990s. PT government promoted the internationalisation of Brazilian firms, such as construction, food processing and extractives, while attempting to create new sectors, such as ship-building and expansion of petrochemicals	Macroeconomic management through trade and exchange rate policies; government subsidies in strategic sectors and relative high spending on infrastructural development	Strategic positioning to support infrastructure. Upgrading the selected manufacturing industry with the support of export-led policy incentives. Heavy state investment in research and development for state-owned enterprises. Internationalisation of state-owned enterprises	Heavy investment in infrastructure (roads and rail, communications network and hydroelectricity as well as human capital formation). Promotion of the agricultural sector through assistance with technology and access to credit. Promotion of labour-intensive manufacturing with subsidies for textiles and agro-processing	Implementation of successive Programme for the Strategic Transformation of Agriculture (PSTA) plans and Vision 2020; heavy state investment in agriculture and successful implementation of an upgrading strategy; use of parastatal companies with ties to the RPF and military

Poverty reduction record	Consolidation of conditional cash transfer (CCT) programmes into *Bolsa Familia* targeted towards poorer regions and communities	*Jefes y Jefas, AUH* and policies towards minimum wage increases	Most successful poverty reduction as an outcome of sustained growth. Universal compulsory education, the minimum standard of living system and the system of land ownership in rural areas	Significant poverty reduction and improved food security since the mid-1990s	Resettling of refugees and IDPs from the genocide; 2004 PRSP has led to some poverty reduction. Heavy investment in social services and cash transfers
Political base of development	Political coalition led by Lula da Silva's Workers' Party (PT) with side payments made to minor parties to support its policy reforms; acquiescence from regional elites especially agricultural elites who benefited from state support	*Frente para la Victoria* Party (PJ coalition): continuity with changes in terms of state compact with various labour unions and social groups; 'segmented corporatism' where formal, urban-based unions negotiate with state while informal labour and agricultural elites excluded in the coalition	Support from the Politburo of the Communist Party of China to conduct the planning of the economic policies	EPRDF as dominated by Tigray region but also a composite party that has created a new political settlement in a federal system allowing it to run a 'single-party state in all but name'	Legitimacy of RPF bolstered by strategy of growth and transformation. Political control maintained through high levels of state violence against critics
External environment	Commodity boom that drove export earnings from agriculture and mining; Brazil as a growing regional power and emerging market	Commodity boom with export taxes as fiscal base	Competition and cooperation with international trade partners; rising importance of China in the global economy	Importance of external development aid and concessional loans for investment capital	Supportive donor community post-genocide; possibility of aid dependency

Source: Authors' elaboration with help from special issue participants.

and the degree to which new industrial strategies might succeed. For instance, since the heyday of neoliberalism in the 1990s, trade rules have banned the use of traditional industrial policy instruments like export credits, trade subsidies and tariffs to support domestic producers in competing with technologically-advanced multinational companies which dominate high value-added segments of global production networks.[41] At the back of a debt crisis, hyperinflation and macroeconomic instability, during the 1990s global governance institutions pushed developing countries to adopt market liberalisation in textile, manufacturing and even natural resources, arguing that monopolistic markets and previously state-controlled sectors need competition to create dynamism and recover from economic decline.

This is an important context for the 'return of the state' debate. In 2003, the commodity boom opened up the question of state intervention as a policy strategy to maximise rents and to pursue structural transformation. For example, new developmentalism brought in structuralist thinking into the analysis of natural resources as a strategic sector for renewed industrialisation for developing countries. Given that Africa and Latin America are historically raw materials producers for the world economy, changing the fiscal, exchange rate and monetary policies towards more heterodox principles in economics were perceived as acceptable in order to capture windfall profits. Accordingly, oil, gas and mineral rents have become a potent force in financing industrialisation in the Global South. From a linkages perspective, industrial policy through natural resources can generate the big push for African and Latin American countries to capture more value in the global supply chain. As Nem Singh and Massi detail, natural resources have the potential to generate production, fiscal and consumption linkages that can generate spill-over effects and, consequentially, technological learning between global and national firms while gradually supporting the development of a network of domestic suppliers.[42] In developing countries with relative industrial capabilities, notably in Brazil, Argentina and Mexico, natural resources can only be harnessed as a key revenue contributor if an explicit developmental strategy exists. In a resource-intensive, commodity-based economy like Brazil, the Workers' Party (PT) government under Lula da Silva (2003–2010) pursued a state-driven industrial policy aimed at the internationalisation of Brazilian firms, even if the leading sectors are export agriculture, mining and oil and gas. Brazil implemented interlinked economic policies aimed at sector-specific industrial growth, with state subsidies acting as economic rents distributed in the domestic sector.[43] Examining the potential for a 'petro-developmental state', Ovadia cogently argues that African oil producers should follow suit, organising a range of trade, investment and industrial policies across the economy around natural resource-based development and the creation of linkages between the oil and non-oil sectors in order for the slow move towards economic diversification and eventually a transition away from fossil fuels to take place in the region.[44] Such industries with the potential for value-added production, in other words, is how industrialisation might look like for the rest of the developing world.

3. The collection of articles

The special issue is organised in three sections. Part 1 'Rethinking the developmental state concept' begins with some theoretical and methodological concerns in studying state intervention and development capacity-building. We emphasise the need for new approaches and finding new elements in the DS model(s) to unpack how development strategies are formulated. Ovadia and Wolf argue that we need to start at unconventional sectors as a place to look for developmental state-making while Nem Singh and Chen suggest unpacking the state-owned enterprises as the black box to capacity-building. Hsu, in examining East Asian countries, explicitly challenge the 'development as industrialisation' narrative as sufficient to explore social development in the twenty-first century; instead, she draws inspiration from Amartya Sen's human capabilities approach as a more holistic approach to development. Part 2 'National experiences of building developmental states' offers critical engagement with the DS theory by way of examining country case studies from traditional lens of developmental states. In contrast to standard case studies, each paper carefully draws out the utility of insights from the DS model, such as state capacity, developmental corruption and geopolitical contexts as a means of understanding how complex patterns of state–society and state–market relations emerge as Africa and Latin America face the need to find new sources of growth in the contemporary world economy. In our Latin American cases, Wylde, Massi and Nem Singh draw from Argentina and Brazil to critically reflect on the equally important role of developmental ideology in industrial policies. In Africa, Clapham writes an insightful compendium of the political bases and the changing developmental state in Ethiopia. By contrast, Saunders and Caramento uses Zimbabwe and Zambia as an example to show the historical relevance of 'developmental structures' and a state–business alliance that is committed to a developmental vision. Finally, Part 3 'New dynamics for developmental states in the international political economy' revisits the original East Asian developmental states by examining how their economic success has been limited in engaging with new challenges, notably in climate change and economic diplomacy. Dent focusses on Singapore and South Korea to demonstrate how East Asian states have combined growth targets with environmental concerns while Tonami demonstrates the importance of political continuity in the Japanese developmental state as contemporary elites engage with economic diplomacy in the Arctic Circle.

Part 1 discusses new conceptual and methodological ways to understand the proliferation of state-led development in the Global South. Ovadia and Wolf explicitly engage with methodological debates that area studies and political economists must consider when comparing the nascent process of African industrialisation with other regions and in the context of economic globalisation. The paper argues that quantitative and qualitative approaches can mutually reinforce each other in using the case study approach to development and structural transformation. This observation sets the scene for the papers that follow with their breadth of case studies across Africa, Asia and Latin America. Taking from the best of the burgeoning literature on African state-led development, Ovadia and Wolf demonstrate how mixed methods can be applied not only to state policy, but also to the study of specific sectors and even specific firms. Crucially, this paper convincingly argues for bringing in the demand side in political economy debates, suggesting that successful industrial policy hinges as much on the demand for productivity as on the supply. The authors substantiate this argument through illustrations from Nigeria and Tanzania's construction and oil and gas sectors, emphasising state agency and state–business relations as the key to identify successful, partial and unsuccessful examples of developmental states.

In the second paper, Nem Singh and Chen continue the focus on state–business relations but shift the analytical focus towards state-owned enterprise as potential bearers of efficiency and competitiveness rather than vessels of rent-seeking and corruption. The paper examines SOEs and their relationship with centralised governments, or what they refer to as 'state–state relations', as one way to understand how novel institutions and policies are crafted to generate new comparative advantages. Giving emphasis to the recent experience of China and the resource sector, the focus on state–state relationships across countries and sectors can enable scholars to identify elite motivations for institutional change as well as how states choose 'winners' and 'losers' in the industrialisation race – an issue to which Nem Singh and Massi provide further empirical depth through the case study of Petrobras and Brazil's oil-led industrial policy.

Hsu complements our exploratory approach to theory by bringing into conversation tenets of developmental state theory and Amartya Sen's human development approach (HDA), with an emphasis on how new forms of social protection and investments in poverty reduction and social welfare are changing the motivations behind state action in China, Japan and South Korea. As a departing point, Hsu argues that the DS concept, and indeed the study of state–business relations, must be expanded to incorporate other types of coalitions that allow for human development and social welfare provision. Given the realignment of the Japanese and South Korean developmental states around the HDA, Hsu suggests that Chinese development is gradually moving towards the political inclusion of civil society actors when responding to a broader range of development priorities. The interventionist perspective of DS theory can help understand how socially inclusive developmental states are being constructed in order to mitigate the negative consequences of social inequality and economic globalisation.

Part 2 brings out the case studies that demonstrate institution-building and state capacity formation in the context of economic globalisation. We have been fortunate to include Brazil and Argentina – two economically important economies in Latin America – as examples of how developmental states evolve over time and space. Nem Singh and Massi critically explain the successes and failures of Brazil's approach, i.e. utilising sector-specific development through local content policy, Keynesian style infrastructure-spending and building inter-sectoral linkages, in sustaining industrialisation as policy elites identify new sources of growth and inspiration for industrial policy-making. As in East Asia, the Brazilian state was key to the country's industrialisation, characterised by a slow-moving process of state centralisation and consolidation of political corporatism to create a structured relationship with domestic capitalists and organised labour. What is new, however, is the PT government's intent to utilise the natural resource sector, especially its oil and gas industry, to further deepen the process of structural transformation in Brazil. While the policy was, by and large, well-designed, rent-seeking and clientelism have weakened the autonomy of Petrobras, which meant losing its ability to deliver public policy goals and profit-making for its shareholders.

In Argentina under the Kirchners, and in the context of the 'Pink Tide' more generally, Wylde argues that such a vision was part of building a hegemonic project – a project that ultimately went into decline. Given the importance of reforming and transforming both the state and its defining social relations, the DS concept retains analytical purchase regardless of the eventual outcome. This is a message repeated in Saunders and Caramento's analysis of Zambia and Zimbabwe and the prospects of developmentalist projects in 'deviant' extractive developmental states. The authors argue that Zambia and Zimbabwe have sought to link resources and development and move beyond the context of resource curse, yet they have been unsuccessful using the developmental state paradigm for the same reason they were unable to develop using the rents from natural resources – low levels of state capacity and a lack of commitment to democratically-driven state restructuring.

Saunders and Caramento suggest limits on 'developmental patrimonialism' in resource-rich but otherwise weak states due to a lack of incentive for elites to engage in meaningful reform. Still, in Sub-Saharan Africa it is Ethiopia that, along with Rwanda, is most often considered developmental. In his article reflecting on the development experience of Ethiopia, Clapham suggests the country has achieved undoubted successes despite its patrimonial character. Its heavy investment in infrastructure and agricultural development-led industrialisation provides 'one of the clearest examples of a developmental state in Africa'. At the same time, the top-down and autocratic tendencies of its leaders present challenges for a long-term transition of the economy led by the private sector and a political system that is truly democratic and accountable.

Part 3 brings us back to East Asia, where the DS concept was born but has been abandoned as a model of state governance. Aki Tonami and Christopher Dent offer an overview of how East Asian developmental states have begun to move beyond the confines of their historical models of development in the twenty-first century. Tonami's examination of the Japanese developmental state focuses on Japan's external relations, exploring how the country leverages development assistance, science and technology to bolster its economic success and to expand its economic diplomacy into the Arctic. Her paper details the vital role of Japan's historically strong and professionalised bureaucracy in order to achieve a new policy objective: to export the Japanese DS model as a means of promoting Japan's own economic security and to revive a model that was clearly in decline since the 1990s as the country entered a period of prolonged economic stagnation. Meanwhile, Dent turns his attention to the East Asian approach to low-carbon development. The East Asian region has moved beyond original conceptions of developmental statism with new and evolving forms of state capacity to respond to the global challenge of climate change. Using South Korea and Singapore as case studies, Dent shows that the region has embraced new developmentalism and 'climate interventionism' in order to pursue sustainable 'green growth'.

Taken together, these papers bring us full circle toward new and expanded relevance for the developmental state in the twenty-first century in which the original interventionist model of a developmentally-oriented state works toward structural transformation and sustainable growth. Beyond its origins in East Asia's export-led industrialisation, the DS framework continues to offer a useful approach to analysing the role of the state in economic and social development. Its deployment in this special issue underscores the continued importance of the state and of development politics in global political economy.

Disclosure statement

No potential conflict of interest was reported by the authors.

Notes

1. Hirschman, *Essays in Trespassing*, 75.
2. Stiglitz, *Globalization and its Discontents.*
3. Clapham, "The Ethiopian Developmental State"; Nem Singh & Massi, "Industrial Policy and State-making"; Wylde, "Twenty-first Century Developmental States?"
4. Johnson, *MITI and the Japanese Miracle.*
5. Haggard, *Pathways from the Periphery.*
6. Amsden, *The Rise of "The Rest"*; Evans, *Embedded Autonomy*; Kohli, *State-Directed Development.*
7. Henley, *Asia–Africa Development Divergence*; Jomo, *Southeast Asia's Misunderstood Miracle*; Kuhonta, *The Institutional Imperative*; Macintyre, "Funny Money"; Teichman, *Social Forces and States*; Vu, *Paths to Development in Asia.*
8. Henley, *Asia–Africa Development Divergence.*
9. Kelsall, *Business, Politics and the State.*
10. Chu, "The Asian Developmental State"; Evans, *Embedded Autonomy*; Soifer, "The Development of State Capacity."
11. Evans, *Embedded Autonomy.*
12. Doner, Ritchie and Slater, "Systemic Vulnerability"; Yeung, *Strategic Coupling.*
13. Brødsgaard and Young, *State Capacity in East Asia*; Kuhonta, *The Institutional Imperative.*
14. von Hau, "State Infrastructural Power and Nationalism."
15. Centeno and Ferraro, *State and Nation-Making.*
16. Collier, "Trajectory of a Concept"; Schneider, *Business Politics and the State*; Yashar, "Contesting Citizenship"; Yashar, *Contesting Citizenship in Latin America.*
17. Amsden, *Escape from Empire*, 143–6.
18. Khan and Jomo, *Rents, Rent-Seeking, and Economic Development*; Kelsall, *Business, Politics and the State in Africa.*
19. Weiss, "Government–Business Relations in East Asia."
20. Doner, Ritchie and Slater, "Systemic Vulnerability."
21. Yeung, "Rethinking the East Asian Developmental State."
22. Chibber, *Locked in Place*; Kohli, *State-Directed Development.*
23. Sandbrook et al., *Social Democracy in the Global Periphery*; Segura-Ubiergo, *Political Economy of Welfare State.*
24. Sanchez-Ancochea, "States, Firms and the Process"; Whitfield et al., *The Politics of African Industrial Policy.*
25. Hickey et al., *Politics of Inclusive Development*; Mosley, *Fiscal Policy and Natural Resources Curse.*
26. Evans, "Development as Institutional Change".
27. Chan, Clark and Lam, *Beyond the Developmental State*; Saraswati, Fine and Tavasci, *Beyond the Developmental State.*
28. Grugel and Riggirozzi, "New Directions in Welfare"; Grugel and Riggirozzi, "Post-Neoliberalism in Latin America; Ruckert, Macdonald & Proulx, "Post-neoliberalism in Latin America."

29. Leiva, *Latin American Neostructuralism*; Nem Singh, "Reconstituting the Neostructuralist State."
30. Bresser-Pereira, "From Old to New Developmentalism."
31. Gezmis, "From Neoliberalism to Neo-Developmentalism?"
32. Mann, "Autonomous Power of the State"; Mann, "Infrastructural Power Revisited."
33. Kelsall, *Business, Politics and the State in Africa*; for a critical view, see Saunders & Caramento, "An Extractive Developmental State."
34. Booth, "Introduction," 1–4.
35. Mann and Berry, "Understanding the Political Motivations"; Behuria, "Centralising Rents and Dispersing Power"; Clapham, "The Ethiopian Developmental State."
36. Nooruddin, *Coalition Politics and Economic Development*; Saylor, *State Building in Boom Times*; Whitfield and Buur, "Politics of Industrial Policy"; Whitfield et al., *Politics of African Industrial Policy*.
37. Gudynas, *New Extractivism*; Veltmeyer and Petras, *New Extractivism*.
38. Soifer, "Development of State Capacity"; Vu, "Studying the State."
39. Amsden, *Asia's Next Giant*; Wade, *Governing the Market*.
40. Yeung, "Rethinking the East Asian Developmental State."
41. Wade, "Rethinking Industrial Policy for Low Income Countries"; Wade, "What Strategies are Viable?"
42. Massi and Nem Singh, "Industrial Policy and State-making."
43. Massi, *Political Economy of Development Finance*; Musacchio and Lazzarini, *Reinventing State Capitalism*.
44. Ovadia, "Local Content and Natural Resource Governance"; Ovadia, "Local Content Policies and Petro-Development"; Ovadia, *The Petro-Developmental State*.

Bibliography

Amsden, Alice. *Asia's Next Giant: South Korea and Late Industrialization*. New York: Oxford University Press, 1989.

Amsden, A. *Escape from Empire: The Developing World's Journey through Heaven and Hell*. Oxford: Oxford University Press, 2007.

Amsden, Alice. *The Rise of "The Rest": Challenges to the West from Late-Industrializing Economies*. Oxford: Oxford University Press, 2009.

Bárcena, Alicia, and Antonio Prado, eds. *Neoestructuralismo y Corrientes Heterodoxas en América Latina y el Caribe a Inicios del Siglo XXI*. Santiago de Chile: CEPAL Publications, 2015.

Behuria, Pritish. "Centralising Rents and Dispersing Power while Pursuing Development: Exploring the Strategic Uses of Military Firms in Rwanda." *Review of African Political Economy* 43, no. 150 (2016): 630–647. doi:10.1080/03056244.2015.1128407.

Boito Jr., Armando. "As Bases Políticas do Novodesenvolvimentismo." Paper presented in the Fórum Econômico da FGV, São Paulo Brazil, 2012. http://bibliotecadigital.fgv.br/dspace/bitstream/handle/10438/16866/Painel%203%20-%20Novo%20Desenv%20BR%20-%20Boito%20-%20Bases%20Pol%20Neodesenv%20-%20PAPER.pdf?sequence=1.

Boito Jr., Armando, and Tatiana Berringer. "Classes Sociais, Neodesenvolvimentismo e Política Externa nos Governos Lula e Dilma", *Revista de Sociologia e Política*, 21 no. 47 (2013): 31–38.

Booth, David. "Introduction: Working With the Grain? The Africa Power and Politics Programme." *IDS Bulletin* 42, no. 2 (2011): 1–10.

Bresser-Periera, Luiz Carlos. "From Old to New Developmentalism in Latin America." In *The Oxford Handbook of Latin American Economies*, edited by José Antonio Ocampo and Jamie Ros. Oxford: Oxford University Press (2011): 108–129.

Bresser-Periera, Luiz Carlos. "Structuralist Macroeconomics and the New Developmentalism." *Brazilian Journal of Political Economy* 32, no. 3 (2012): 347–366.

Brødsgaard, Kjeld, and Susan Young, eds. *State Capacity in East Asia: Japan, Taiwan*. China and Vietnam. Oxford: Oxford University Press, 2000.

Burchardt, Hans-Jürgen, and Kristina Dietz. "(Neo-) Extractivism – A New Challenge for Development Theory from Latin America." *Third World Quarterly* 35, no. 3 (2014): 468–486.

Castelo, Rodrigo. "O Novo Desenvolvimentismo e a Decadência Ideológica do Pensameno Econômico Brasileiro," *Serviço Social e Sociedade*, 112 no. Oct-Dec. (2012): 613–636.

Centeno, Miguel, and Agustin Ferraro, eds. *State and Nation-Making in Latin America and Spain: Republics of the Possible*. Cambridge: Cambridge University Press, 2013.

Chan, Steve, Clark, Cal, and Lam, Danny. *Beyond the Developmental State: Asia's Political Economies Reconsidered*. Basingstoke: Palgrave MacMillan, 1998.

Chibber, Vivek. *Locked in Place: State-Building and Late Industrialization in India*. Princeton, NJ: Princeton University Press, 2003.

Chu, Yin-Wah. "The Asian Developmental State: Ideas and Debates." In *The Asian Developmental State: Reexaminations and New Departures*, 1–25. New York: Palgrave Macmillan, 2016.

Clapham, Christopher. "The Ethiopian Developmental State." *Third World Quarterly* (2017): doi:10.1080/01436597.2017.1328982.

Collier, David. "Trajectory of a Concept: 'Corporatism' in the Study of Latin American Politics." In *Latin America in Comparative Perspective*, edited by Peter Smith, Chapter 6, 135–162. Westview Press, 1995.

Doner, Richard, Bryan Ritchie, and Dan Slater. "Systemic Vulnerability and the Origins of Developmental States: Northeast and Southeast Asia in Comparative Perspective." *International Organization* 59, no. 2 (2005): 327–361.

Economic Commission for Latin America and the Caribbean. *Changing Production Patterns with Social Equity: The Prime Task of Latin American and Caribbean Development in the 1990s*. Santiago de Chile: ECLAC Publications, 1990.

Economic Commission for Latin America and the Caribbean. *Structural Change for Equality: An Integrated Approach to Development (34th Session of ECLAC. San Salvador, August 27-31)*. Santiago de Chile: ECLAC Publications, 2012.

Evans, Peter B. *Embedded Autonomy: States and Industrial Transformation*. Princeton, NJ: Princeton University Press, 1995.

Evans, Peter B. "Development as Institutional Change: The Pitfalls of Institutional Monocropping and the Potentials of Deliberation." *Studies in Comparative International Development* 38, no. 4 (2004): 30–52.

Ffrench Davis, Ricardo. "An Outline of Neo-structuralist Approach." *CEPAL Review* 34 (1988): 37–44.

Ffrench Davis, Ricardo. "Macro-economics for Development: From 'Financierism' to 'Productivism'." *CEPAL Review* 102 (2010): 7–26.

Ffrench Davis, Ricardo. "Neoestructuralismo y Macroeconomía para el Desarollo." In *Neoestructuralismo y Corrientes Heterodoxas en América Latina y el Caribe a Inicios del Siglo XXI*, edited by Alicia Bárcena and Antonio Prado, 128–154. Santiago de Chile: CEPAL Publications, 2015.

Gezmis, Hilal. "From Neoliberalism to Neo-developmentalism? The Political Economy of Post-crisis Argentina (2002-2015)." *New Political Economy* 23, no. 1 (2018): 66–87. doi:10.1080/13563467.2017.1330877.

Grugel, Jean, and Pia Riggirozzi. "Post-neoliberalism in Latin America: Rebuilding and Reclaiming the State after Crisis." *Development and Change* 43, no. 1 (2012): 1–21.

Grugel, Jean, and Pia Riggirozzi. "New Directions in Welfare: Rights-based Social Policies in Post-neoliberal Latin America." *Third World Quarterly* (2017): 1–18. doi:10.1080/01436597.2017.1392084.

Gudynas, Eduardo. *The New Extractivism of the 21st Century: Ten Urgent Theses about Extractivism in Relation to Current South American Progressivism*. Americas Programme Report. Washington, DC: Americas Policy Programme, 2010.

Gudynas, Eduardo. "Beyond Varieties of Development: Disputes and Alternatives." *Third World Quarterly* 37, no. 4 (2016): 721–732.

Haggard, Stephen. *Pathways from the Periphery: The Politics of Growth in the Newly Industrializing Countries*. Ithaca: Cornell University Press, 1990.

Haslam, Paul, and Pablo Heidrich, eds. *The Political Economy of Natural Resources and Development: From Neoliberalism to Resource Nationalism*. London: Routledge, 2016.

Henley, David. *Asia–Africa Development Divergence: A Question of Intent*. London: Zed Books, 2015.

Hickey, Sam, Kunal Sen, and Badru Bukenya. *The Politics of Inclusive Development: Interrogating the Evidence*. Oxford: Oxford University Press, 2014.

Hirschman, Albert O. *Essays in Trespassing: Economics to Politics and Beyond*. New York: Cambridge University Press, 1981.

Johnson, Chalmers. *MITI and the Japanese Miracle: The Growth of Industrial Policy, 1925–1975*. Stanford: Stanford University Press, 1982.

Jomo, K. S. *Southeast Asia's Misunderstood Miracle*. Boulder: Westview Press, 1997.

Kelsall, Tim. "Rethinking the Relationship between Neo-Patrimonialism and Economic Development in Africa." *IDS Bulletin* 42, no. 2 (2011): 76–87.

Kelsall, Tim with David Booth, Diana Cammack, Brian Cooksey, Mesfin Gebremichael, Fred Golooba-Mutebi, and Sarah Vaughan. *Business, Politics, and the State in Africa. Challenging the Orthodoxies on Growth and Transformation*. London: Zed Books, 2013.

Khan, Mushtaq and Jomo KS, eds. *Rents, Rent-seeking, and Economic Development: Theory and Evidence in Asia*. Cambridge: Cambridge University Press, 2000.

Kohli, Atul. *State-Directed Development: Political Power and Industrialization in the Global Periphery*. Cambridge: Cambridge University Press, 2004.

Kuhonta, Erik. *The Institutional Imperative: The Politics of Equitable Development in Southeast Asia*. Stanford: Stanford University Press, 2011.

Leiva, Fernando. *Latin American Neostructuralism: The Contradictions of Post-neoliberal Development*. Minneapolis, MN: University of Minnesota Press, 2008.

Macintyre, Andrew. "Funny Money: Fiscal Policy, Rent-seeking and Economic Performance in Indonesia." In *Rents, Rent-seeking, and Economic Development: Theory and Evidence in Asia*, edited by Mushtaq Khan and Jomo KS, 248–273. Cambridge: Cambridge University Press, 2000.

Mann, Laura, and Marie Berry. "Understanding the Political Motivations That Shape Rwanda's Emergent Developmental State." *New Political Economy* 21, no. 1 (2016): 119–144. doi:10.1080/13563467.2015.1041484.

Mann, Michael. "The Autonomous Power of the State: Its Origins, Mechanisms, and Results." *Archives Europeénes de Sociologie* 25 (1984): 185–213.

Mann, Michael. "Infrastructural Power Revisited." *Studies in Comparative International Development* 43, no. 3 (2008): 355–365.

Massi, Eliza. *The Political Economy of Development Finance: The BNDES and Brazilian Industrialisation*. PhD diss., School for Oriental and African Studies, University of London, 2014.

Massi, Eliza, and Jewellord Nem Singh. "Industrial Policy and State-making: Brazil's Attempt at Oil-based Industrial Development." *Third World Quarterly* (2018). doi: 10.1080/01436597.2018.1455144

Mosley, Paul. *Fiscal Policy and Natural Resources Curse: How to Escape from the Poverty Trap*. London: Routledge, 2017.

Musacchio, Aldo, and Sérgio G. Lazzarini. *Reinventing State Capitalism: Leviathan in Business, Brazil and Beyond*. Cambridge, MA: Harvard University Press, 2014.

Nem Singh, Jewellord. "Reconstituting the Neostructuralist State: The Political Economy of Continuity and Change in Chilean Mining Policy." *Third World Quarterly* 31, no. 8 (2010): 1413–1433.

Nooruddin, Irfan. *Coalition Politics and Economic Development: Credibility and the Strength of Weak Governments*. Cambridge: Cambridge University Press, 2011.

Ocampo, Jose Antonio. "Más allá del Consenso de Washington: una visión desde la CEPAL." *Revista de la CEPAL*, 66 (1998): 7–28.

Ocampo, Jose Antonio, ed. *Beyond Reforms: Structural Dynamics and Macroeconomic Vulnerability*. Palo Alto: Stanford University Press, ECLAC and World Bank, 2005.

Ocampo, Jose Antonio. "Commodity-led Dependence in Latin America." In *Alternative Pathways to Sustainable Development: Lessons from Latin America. International Development Policy Series* 9 (2017): 51–76. http://journals.openedition.org/poldev/2354.

Ocampo, Jose Antonio, and Luis Bértola. *The Economic Development of Latin America since Independence*. Oxford: Oxford University Press, 2012.

Ocampo, Jose Antonio, Enrique Cárdenas, and Rosemary Thorp, eds. *Industrialisation and the State in Latin America: The Post War Years. An Economic History of Twentieth Century Latin America, Volume Three*. Houndmills: Palgrave, 2000.

Ocampo, Jose Antonio, Stephany Griffith-Jones, and Joseph E. Stiglitz, eds. *Time for a Visible Hand: Lessons from the 2008 World Financial Crisis*. New York: Oxford University Press, 2010.

Ocampo, Jose Antonio, Lance Taylor, and Codrina Rada. *Growth and Policy in Developing Countries: A Structuralist Approach*. New York: Columbia University Press, 2009.

Ovadia, Jesse Salah. "Local Content and Natural Resource Governance: The Cases of Angola and Nigeria." *Extractive Industries and Society* 1, no. 2 (2014): 137–146.

Ovadia, Jesse Salah. "Local Content Policies and Petro-Development in Sub-Saharan Africa: A Comparative Analysis." *Resources Policy* 49 (2016): 20–30.

Ovadia, Jesse Salah. *The Petro-Developmental State: Making Oil Work in Angola, Nigeria and the Gulf of Guinea*. London: Hurst, 2016.

Ruckert, Arne, Laura Macdonald, and Kristina Proulx. "Post-neoliberalism in Latin America: A Conceptual Overview." *Third World Quarterly* 38, no. 7 (2017): 1583–1602.

Sanchez-Ancochea, Diego. "States, Firms, and the Process of Industrial Upgrading: Latin America's Variety of Capitalism and the Costa Rican Experience." *Economy and Society* 31, no. 1 (2009): 62–86.

Sandbrook, Richard, Marc Edelman, Patrick Heller, and Judith Teichmann. *Social Democracy in the Global Periphery: Origins, Challenges, Prospects*. Cambridge: Cambridge University Press, 2007.

Saraswati, Jyoti, Ben Fine, and Daniela Tavasci, eds. *Beyond the Developmental State: Industrial Policy into the Twenty–first Century*. London: Pluto Press, 2013.

Saunders, Richard, and Alexander Caramento. "An Extractive Developmental State in Southern Africa? The Cases of Zambia and Zimbabwe." *Third World Quarterly* (2017): doi:10.1080/01436597.2017.1409072.

Saylor, Ryan. *State Building in Boom Times: Commodities and Coalitions in Latin America and Africa*. Oxford: Oxford University Press, 2014.

Schneider, Ben Ross. *Business Politics and the State in Twentieth Century Latin America*. Cambridge: Cambridge University Press, 2004.

Segura-Ubriego, Alex. *The Political Economy of the Welfare State in Latin America: Globalization, Democracy, Development*. Cambridge: Cambridge University Press, 2007.

Soifer, Hillel. "The Development of State Capacity," In *The Oxford Handbook of Historical Institutionalism*, edited by Orfeo Fioretos, Tulia Falleti, and Adam Sheingate, 181–194. Oxford: Oxford University Press, 2016. doi:10.1093/oxfordhb/9780199662814.013.10.

Stiglitz, Robert. *Globalization and its Discontents*. New York: W.W. Norton, 2002.

Teichman, Judith. *Social Forces and States: Poverty and Distributional Outcomes in South Korea, Chile and Mexico*. Stanford: Stanford University Press, 2012.

Veltmeyer, Henry, and James Petras. *The New Extractivism: A Post-Neoliberal Development Model or Imperialism of the 21st Century?* London: Zed Books, 2014.

von Hau, Matthias. "State Infrastructural Power and Nationalism: Comparative Lessons from Mexico and Argentina", *Studies in Comparative International Development*, 43 no. 3–4 (2008): 334–354.

Vu, Tuong. "Studying the State through State Formation." *World Politics* 62, no. 1 (2010): 148–175.

Vu, Tuong. *Paths to Development in Asia: South Korea, Vietnam, China, and Indonesia*. Cambridge: Cambridge University Press, 2011.

Wade, Robert. *Governing the Market: Economic Theory and the Role of Government in East Asian Industrialization*. Princeton: Princeton University Press, 1990.

Wade, Robert. "What Strategies are Viable for Developing Countries Today? The World Trade Organization and the Shrinking of 'Development Space'." *Review of International Political Economy* 10, no. 4 (2003): 621–644.

Wade, Robert. "Rethinking Industrial Policy for Low Income Countries." *African Development Review* 21, no. 2 (2009): 352–366.

Weiss, Linda. "Government-business Relations in East Asia: The Changing Basis of State Capacity." *Asian Perspective* 18, no. 2 (1994): 85–118.

Whitfield, Lindsay, and Lars Buur. "The Politics of Industrial Policy: Ruling Elites and their Alliances." *Third World Quarterly* 35 (2014): 126–144.

Whitfield, Lindsay, Ole Therkildsen, Lars Buur, and Anne Mette Kjar. *The Politics of African Industrial Policy: A Comparative Perspective*. Cambridge: Cambridge University Press, 2015.

Wylde, Christopher. *Latin America after Neoliberalism: Developmental Regimes in Post-Crisis States*. New York: Palgrave Macmillan, 2012.

Wylde, Christopher. "Twenty-first Century Developmental States? Argentina Under the Kirchners." *Third World Quarterly* (2017). doi:10.1080/01436597.2017.1333418.

Yashar, Deborah. "Contesting Citizenship: Indigenous Movements and Democracy in Latin America." *Comparative Politics* 31, no. 1 (1998): 23–42.

Yashar, Deborah. *Contesting Citizenship in Latin America: The Rise of Indigenous Movements and the Postliberal Challenge*. Cambridge: Cambridge University Press, 2005.

Yeung, Henry Wai-chung. *Strategic Coupling: East Asian Industrial Transformation in the New Global Economy*. Ithaca: Cornell University Press, 2016.

Yeung, Henry Wai-chung. "Rethinking the East Asian Developmental State in its Historical Context: Finance, Geopolitics and Bureaucracy." *Area Development and Policy* 2, no. 1 (2017): 1–23.

Studying the developmental state: theory and method in research on industrial policy and state-led development in Africa

Jesse Salah Ovadia and Christina Wolf

ABSTRACT

This paper examines theoretical and methodological issues in the study of African developmental states. We argue that applying this concept beyond East Asia must take into account changes in the global economic context – in particular systemic tendencies towards deficient consumer demand – to uncover the conditions under which demand for commodity production remains or becomes expansionary. We further argue for a mixed methods case study approach to structural transformation, blending quantitative and qualitative evidence at multiple levels of analysis. The examples of concrete manufacturing and oil and gas in Nigeria and Tanzania illustrate our approach to researching state-led development in Africa.

Introduction

East Asia's developmental states structurally transformed their economies from largely agrarian subsistence to achieve high levels of industrial development, high income status and technological market leadership. While there was no one strategy followed by Japan, South Korea and other East Asian developmental states, many have argued the core tenets of their approach represent an 'East Asian model'.[1] More recently, several African states are attempting to emulate this approach to industrialization and structural transformation, albeit under very different political and economic circumstances.

Yet, the new era of 'Africa rising' has so far failed to deliver significant developmental benefit to the continent. Economic growth has not raised standards of living or reduced poverty.[2] Despite the new interest in African developmental states, no African state meets the supposed criteria of the East Asian model, which is not surprising given ongoing debates about whether any East Asian states ever had the ideal type of Weberian bureaucracies suggested in the literature on developmental states.[3] For Whitfield et al.,[4] the insight that East Asian developmental states had varied experiences, made numerous improvised decisions and ad hoc policy changes and never followed a grand strategy suggests that the entire developmental state concept must be abandoned in the search for a general theory

Jesse Salah Ovadia http://orcid.org/0000-0002-5010-8269

on what makes successful industrial policy. This debate involves two separate but interlinked issues: which economic policies ought to be implemented to achieve high rates of growth in the productive sectors of the economy, and under which political conditions they are adopted.

With the other papers in this special issue, we continue to hold that the language of developmental states is useful in describing what is being attempted by and what are the developmental outcomes of state-intervention. Rather than seek general conditions/pre-conditions for structural transformation, we raise some important theoretical and methodological issues about how to advance the understanding of state-led structural transformation in Africa. At the theoretical level, we stress the necessity to broaden conceptually the dimensions of economic policy and agency relations that research on state-led development ought to dissect in order to understand patterns of success and failure.

In particular, we argue that recent research on industrial development neglects demand for profitable production as one among other determinants of investment under the assumption of a potentially unlimited export-market. Rethinking economic policies in support of demand is all the more relevant for Sub-Saharan African (SSA) economies today when considering the shrinking space for export-led industrialisation exposed by Asian drivers and systemic global demand deficiencies stemming from the financialisation of developed and developing economies. By extension, we argue that, when trying to understand the extent to which and the reasons why the growth of demand is supported or not by domestic policy, greater weight must be given to the study of agency relations beyond state–business relations. In terms of methodology, we show that descriptive quantitative analysis can help in the contextualisation and therefore generalisation of focused firm-level qualitative research, which in many cases is the only way to understand the dynamics of particular sectors and clusters of firms.

In Part 1, we discuss in greater depth the above-mentioned theoretical issues. In Part 2, we explore selective examples of Tanzania and Nigeria, looking at the national economy, chosen sectors and key firms to explore the scope for and limitations to domestic sources of demand and show how qualitative and descriptive quantitative analysis can be blended at the level of the macro-economy, specific sectors and (clusters of) firms to gain new insight into African developmental states. While neither Tanzania nor Nigeria would fit any definition of a classical developmental state, the theoretical extensions and empirical approach proposed can contribute to gain further insights into the reasons for (partial) success and failure of structural transformation.

Theoretical and methodological issues

Case study method and theoretical inference

For research on state-led development, the case study method[5] has the advantage of producing the context and time dependent knowledge needed to trace complex multi-dimensional, path-dependent and path-shaping processes such as structural change. Yet, case studies have been criticised for their inability to produce generalizable conclusions. Some case study researchers maintain that this should not be our aim in the first place;[6] instead case studies are to build 'naturalistic generalisations' through a wealth of detail derived from a multitude of concrete cases that build a tacit understanding of causal processes which can be subjectively and intuitively applied.[7] Alternatively, case studies are said to help formulating transferable working hypotheses if there are sufficient similarities between source and target cases.[8]

Yet, even the concepts of 'transferability' and 'naturalistic generalisation' imply that the findings of one case can be extrapolated to a wider, however defined, set of cases. Gomm et al.[9] point out that sound induction needs to be both theoretically informed and systematically tested across large numbers of cases. That is, theoretical induction first relies on a process of conceptual thinking in formulating what is to be explained and the factors explaining it. Second, researchers have to seek a large number of cases where the explanatory factor is present so as to check whether and under which conditions it has the effect predicted.[10] While this paper cannot offer systematic testing across a large number of cases, we seek to broaden conceptually the dimensions of economic policy and agency relations that research on state-led development ought to dissect to add to our understanding of patterns of success and failure; arguing in particular that research on developmental states needs to uncover the reasons why demand for manufacturing output becomes expansionary or fails to do so.

The extent to which the specific case is symptomatic for a wider phenomenon needs to be established empirically. Gomm et al. advocate collecting and presenting information about the case and the population by way of extensive analysis of secondary data.[11] For research on structural change, the characterisation of a case with respect to a broader population of cases can be done at the economy level, sector level or firm level depending on the focus and scope of the study but faces problems of availability and quality of data in the SSA context, where even basic indicators of economic activity like National Accounts data are subject to considerable margin of error and reliable sector or firm-level data are even more difficult to obtain.[12] Jerven argues, however, that even imperfect data can produce useful analysis to the extent that their limitations are clearly documented and descriptive quantitative analysis is complemented with qualitative analysis.

For our purposes, the cases of concrete manufacturing and oil and gas are useful for studying state-led development because they are not normally emphasised as sectors that can drive structural transformation. The oil and gas industry is more associated with capital intensive enclave development while construction is generally not thought to lead to increased productivity. However, by studying these sectors in two prominent cases at the level of the national economy, strategic sectors and clusters of firms, we are able to suggest possible approaches for African developmental states.

African manufacturing activities and systematic global demand deficiencies

Hirschman[13] starts from the observation of *frustrated savings*, i.e. mobilisable savings not invested in productive activities but, instead, showing up in luxury consumption or capital flight. To find an answer to the question what constrains investment demand, Hirschman distinguishes between autonomous and induced demand. Correspondingly, we can distinguish between two types of demand constraints on industrial output growth: *Keynesian-type* or *Kaldorian-type* demand constraint. The former concerns entrepreneurial expectations about the level of aggregate demand. Rosenstein-Rodan's[14] shoe factory argument, for instance, relies on the observation that mass production requires mass consumption. An important constraint thereto is income distribution: if income distribution is very narrow then manufactured goods can only be sold to the relatively few rich who, given their small numbers, cannot sustain demand for mass production.[15]

Regarding induced demand, mass production of Good A *induces* demand for inputs to the production of Good A (technical complementarity) or consumed with Good A (consumption complementarities).[16] These 'linkages' constitute an in built investment multiplier process that does not require an anticipation of demand in the Keynesian sense.[17] However, backwardly-linked industries can still face demand constraints to the extent that there are differences in the rates of growth of the value of output and therefore purchasing power along the demand chain. In the Kaldorian growth literature it is the growth of agricultural purchasing power which limits the growth of manufacturing output growth and later the growth of export demand.[18]

Studying the causes of the demise of African manufacturing industries starting in the mid-1970s, research produced by the Washington institutions at the height of the neoliberal policy reversal, surprisingly, points to stagnating domestic and global demand.[19] Yet these issues are interpreted as problems of overproduction caused by distorted market signals,[20] which are best corrected through free-market supply-side reforms and trade liberalisation.

To reassert the legitimacy of state intervention against the free-market paradigm, the critical scholarship on the East Asian Developmental States (DS) emphasised market failures in technology acquisition.[21] To debunk the free-trade paradigm, critical scholarship on the East Asian DS stressed that export-led industrialisation does not result from 'neutral trade regimes' as purported by the Washington Consensus.[22] Instead, import-substitution and export-oriented industrialization are dependent on each other and rely both on market distorting state intervention,[23] though a key factor explaining successful industrial policy in East Asia was 'how vigorously and rapidly exportables were extracted from a sequentially rising number of import substitution sectors'.[24]

Taken together, the critical scholarship on the East Asian DS challenges the *type* of supply-side policies necessary to achieve (industrial) output growth but largely sidelines the demand-side conditions necessary to sustain manufacturing production under the assumption of a potentially unlimited export market.[25] Even in models of structural change incorporating demand,[26] the only (relevant?) component of aggregate demand is export demand. This conceptually circumscribes the scope and nature of macroeconomic policies in support of industrial development, by and large to incentivising exporters through a depreciated exchange rate.[27]

Export demand is specific in that it links the Keynesian and Kaldorian type of demand problems. Export demand is a component of aggregate demand and, as such, affects entrepreneurial expectations in the Keynesian sense. Beyond providing market outlets, export demand constrains imports necessary for (ongoing) production processes.[28] The expansion and gradual upgrading of manufacturing exports has therefore unsurprisingly and rightly been singled out as a key to successful industrialisation but the assumption of unlimited export markets is untenable. At least for certain manufacturing sectors, there is excess capacity relative to world demand leading to intense price and wage competition between developing countries and ultimately a race to the bottom ('fallacy of composition').[29] The terms of trade for low value added manufacturing products are declining and the concurrent attempt of each country to boost its competitiveness through wage depression further undercuts a vital source of domestic purchasing power and further contributes to the deflation in world demand.[30] In fact, sub-Saharan African economies today face a global economic context marked by systematic demand deficiency. While aggregate export earnings of many SSA economies increased since the turn of the century,[31] manufacturing exports face displacement by Chinese products.[32] In addition, the financialisation of developed and developing economies crowds out production in the real economy and tends to worsen income distribution thereby depressing consumer demand.[33]

Against this context, one key challenge of developmental policy will be to mobilise domestic consumer and inter-sectoral demand. This has a number of implications for policy-making located at the macro- and inter-sectoral level. If demand growth is a function of income distribution, then supporting manufacturing sector development will involve policy choices on the distribution side, notably with respect to the regulation of labour compensation and wage-bargaining institutions, income redistribution through taxation or measures increasing the disposable income of households like the provision of affordable housing. Government expenditure being a component of aggregate demand also implies a central role for fiscal policy in sectors with a strong potential for linkages and government procurement of manufacturing output.

On the intersectoral level, agricultural productivity acts as a pace-setting factor for backwardly linked manufacturing industries like fertilisers and machinery, which finds ample empirical support in the development experiences of newly industrialised countries.[34] Yet, the intersectoral dimension of policy-making in support of industrial development is not limited to agriculture. Construction activities are considered by Hirschman as an important source of linkages (induced investment demand):

> An example … is cement and reinforcing steel rods in the construction, say, of downtown office buildings … the existence of new office buildings strengthens demand for a great variety of goods and services: from modern office furniture and equipment … to parking and restaurant facilities, stylish secretaries and eventually perhaps to more office buildings.[35]

The examples of the concurrent growth of the construction, mining and manufacturing sectors in Tanzania and Nigeria show that government fostered linkages between those sectors can spur inter-sectoral demand driven growth and even contribute to the formation of a final consumer demand base via employment generation.

State–business relations and beyond

Political science research on developmental states emphasises that the state has to stand apart from the market and vested interests found within it. Evans[36] coined the term 'embedded autonomy', or a state autonomous from – yet constrained by – the society it represents, to exclude self-serving bureaucratic elites that appropriate surplus from the ideal type developmental state. However, conceiving vested interests as a deviation from the ideal-type norm conceals how specific economic, political and ideological interests come about, what sustains them (materially and ideologically) and how they change over time.[37]

The embedded autonomy framework therefore remains too general. For subsidy schemes to work, the threat of removing the subsidy has to be credible as otherwise firms do not have the necessary incentives to achieve learning by doing.[38] The feasibility of eliminating losers depends on the *nature* of patron–client networks not their absence. Hence, industrial strategies have to be adapted to the organisational and structural distribution of economic and political power within specific countries.[39] Whitfield et al.[40] is helpful in showing that 'pockets of efficiency' in productive sectors can emerge in different 'political settlements' whether marked by vulnerable authoritarian, weak dominant party, strong dominant party or competitive clientelist coalitions. A key political challenge lies in the mediation of interests in competition with one another, for instance along a supply–demand chain where processors interest to pay the lowest price on inputs collides with producers' objective to obtain the highest price for their output.

The embedded autonomy framework remains too narrow in the sense that it assesses the DS through state–business relations alone. Amsden maintains: 'Labour repression is the basis of late industrialization everywhere ... Developmental differences among late industrializers are best explained in terms of the discipline imposed on big business, not labour'.[41] However, structural transformation is also a process of social transformation and invariably associated to distributional conflicts over a growing pie. Disentangling those is important not least because they shed light on the spending behaviour of different social strata and the state.

Taken together, understanding the nature of the accumulation process requires an understanding of what motivates investment (for domestic and export markets), what constrains the growth of demand and supply and to what extent savings are mediated into productive investment. The following agency relations therefore must be dissected by research on developmental states. Firstly, state–business relations to understand how a state can discipline businesses within a particular political settlement. Secondly, capital–labour relations to shed light on distributional conflicts occurring in the growth process and how these affect the spending behaviour of different social strata. Thirdly, industry–finance relations to understand under which conditions savings are channelled into productive sector investment.

Lessons from Tanzania and Nigeria

The previous section aimed at broadening conceptually the dimensions of economic policy and agency relations that research on state-led development ought to dissect, while arguing that, at the empirical level, case study research should rely on a mix of qualitative and extensive descriptive quantitative analysis. While the scope of this paper does not allow for all of these issues to be discussed at sufficient depth empirically, we consider them important foundations on which future case study work can build. In what follows, we discuss selective examples from Tanzania and Nigeria to illustrate the possibilities for and limitations of demand-driven linkage formation across sectors, the formation of a consumer demand base and distributional conflict in the process of structural change.

The African construction boom and cement production in Tanzania and Nigeria

Average real annual GDP growth rates in SSA (excluding South Africa) had been picking up since the turn of the century, averaging 6.5% in the period 2001–2013 against 2.5% over the 1990s. The agricultural and manufacturing sectors realised higher growth rates than over the 1990s but fell slightly short of overall GDP growth rates. The construction sector is the only sector of the real economy which realised higher growth rates than total GDP in all developing regions. Yet, growth rates of the construction sector in SSA are highest across developing regions with 9.6% over the period 2000–2013, even ahead of the BRICS (9%) (Table 1).

The slower than average increase in output of manufacturing goes together with slow increases or even decreases in indicators of structural change, real manufacturing value added (MVA) per capita increasing only from US$68.4 in 1990 to US$78.1 in 2013. By

Table 1. Evolution of the manufacturing sector in the developing world.

		Manufacturing VA*		Average real annual growth rates by sector					
		per capita (2005 USD)	% of GDP	agri.	manuf.	constr.	mining	non-mining	GDP total
Asia (excluding China)	1990–2000	188.1	19.3%	1.9%	4.5%	1.9%	3.7%	3.7%	3.7%
	2001–2013	379.3	20.1%	3.4%	5.0%	6.2%	3.5%	5.4%	5.2%
BRICS	1990–2000	188.1	19.9%	2.6%	5.7%	1.8%	2.7%	4.2%	4.0%
	2001–2013	758.8	27.6%	3.7%	8.8%	9.0%	5.2%	7.5%	7.3%
Latin America (excluding Brazil)	1990–2000	587.9	19.8%	2.0%	3.3%	2.4%	3.6%	3.2%	3.3%
	2001–2013	796.7	17.5%	2.5%	2.6%	5.0%	2.1%	3.7%	3.5%
SSA (excluding South Africa)	1990–2000	68.4	11.8%	3.1%	0.2%	3.7%	2.0%	2.6%	2.5%
	2001–2013	78.1	8.7%	5.6%	5.9%	9.6%	3.9%	7.0%	6.5%
Tanzania	1990–2000	23.2	7.0%	4.3%	4.4%	7.8%	8.5%		4.1%
	2001–2013	48.3	8.2%	4.4%	7.7%	10.5%	8.5%		6.7%
Nigeria	1990–2000	80.3	9.0%	3.5%	−0.4%	4.0%	1.0%		2.5%
	2001–2013	158.1	8.6%	9.6%	10.8%	10.2%	−1.7%		8.7%

Calculations based on UN National Accounts.
*shares calculated for 1990 and 2013 respectively.
**shaded areas are the sectors whose growth rates exceed average GDP growth rates.

comparison, in 2013 MVA per capita in China amounts to US$1267 and as much as US$8013 in high income countries like Germany. Relative to GDP, manufacturing value added even decreased in SSA from 11.8% in 1990 to 8.7% in 2013 (Table 1).

Tanzania and Nigeria are two SSA economies that show more dynamic manufacturing sectors than the SSA average, with MVA per capita doubling in both countries relative to 1990 and growth rates of manufacturing exceeding average aggregate output growth. The data on sectoral growth, analysed alongside state intervention in those sectors, can deepen our understanding of developmental activities of the state and their relative success. In Tanzania, sectors leading output growth are manufacturing, construction and mining. In Nigeria, these are agriculture, manufacturing and construction (Table 1), raising the question about the link and policy mediation between these sectors.

One of the most noteworthy linkages forming between the construction and manufacturing sectors in Nigeria and Tanzania is cement production. Increased cement production is an Africa-wide trend; cement production per capita in SSA increasing by a factor of more than five since 1990. Tanzania's small but above SSA average production base in 1990, doubled by 2014 but increased slower than the SSA average. By contrast, Nigeria's production base emerged from zero in 1990 to becoming SSA's biggest cement producer (excluding South Africa) with a production base substantially above SSA average in 2014 (Table 2).

Comparing cement production in both countries, we find in both countries efforts to support domestic cement production through industrial policy but it is government spending on infrastructure which makes the production of building materials profitable in the first place. In Nigeria we observe a particular conjunction of forces, in which the anticipated growth of the final consumer demand base supports the reinvestment of cement profits domestically. The Tanzanian case illustrates how a comprehensive development strategy, aiming at building backwardly linked supply chains and supporting the growth of a domestic consumer demand base, can face obstacles at various levels. In the cement industry,

Table 2. Cement production Tanzania, Nigeria, SSA (selected years).

		1990	2000	2014
Tanzania	per capita	26.6	26.9	53.5
	Total	0.7	0.9	2.9
Nigeria	per capita	0.0	20.3	115.2
	Total	0.0	2.5	20.0
SSA (excluding South Africa)	per capita	15.6	27.9	79.2

Compiled based on Global Cement Report Database.

Table 3. Nigerian cement production base in 2015.

Company	Capacity (Mta)	No. of Plants
Dangote Cement	29.00	3
Lafarge Africa	9.00	5
Cement Company of Northern Nigeria (BUA)	0.60	1
Purechem	0.1	1

Source: Global Cement Report 11th edition.

competing interests of producers of energy inputs and the cement producers make the use of domestically produced energy inputs difficult, despite comprehensive government plans. The domestic consumer demand base, while growing, faces the dominance of low income generating activities and illustrates the need to study distributional conflict beyond state–business relations.

Cement manufacturing: Nigeria

Still a major importer of cement in 2007, the build-up of the Nigerian production base started following successful lobbying of local cement importers (mainly the Dangote Group) and subsequent government protection in the form of licences, tax breaks and import duties imposed by the Obasanjo Government. Phasing out import licences since 2012, those with existing licences could only import under the condition of developing further domestic production. Over the course of just few years, Nigeria has become the largest cement producer in SSA, second only to South Africa. What is more, Nigeria's Dangote becomes a major investor in other African countries – successfully competing with the South African Pretoria Cement Corporation (PCC) and the major European multinationals over the rapidly expanding African cement market.[42]

Two major producers control the huge Nigerian production base of 39Mta installed capacity in 2014 (Table 3). Starting out as a cement import business in 1981, Dangote Cement, as of 2014, has a market share of about 60% spread over five plants. Lafarge, controlling about 32% of the Nigerian market, has undertaken efforts to consolidate its position against Dangote by way of progressing its ownership in the Ashaka and Unicem cement plants to 100% and consolidating Lafarge Nigeria and Lafarge South Africa into a joint stock exchange listing.[43]

As of 2015, Dangote operates cement plants in eight SSA countries and has reported a 25.6% rise in revenues in 2015 (US$2.47bn).[44] Apart from further planned expansions of its African cement operations, the company has reported plans to expand beyond Africa into Asia and Latin America.[45]

Pushed by the Obasanjo government to move from cement import into cement production, Dangote can be considered an important catalyst for manufacturing in Nigeria not only because the group has successfully accumulated capital in the lucrative cement business and even expanded abroad but more importantly, because this capital has been reinvested domestically in labour intensive agro-alimentary (including fruit juice, dairy, bottled water and pasta production) as well as petro-chemical activities (oil refinery and a fertiliser project). Quoted in the *Financial Times*, Dangote maintains that Nigeria's growing population and, by extension, 'demand for basic supplies' was a driving force behind his decision to reinvest in Nigeria.[46] Other African owned companies and Western multinationals without links to cement production tap into this emerging market for fast-growing consumer goods as well. Beloxxi Biscuits and Leventi Foods are among the largest bakery and snack producers in Nigeria. The food processing company Zambeef is market leader in Zambia, now expanding into Nigeria. Expecting to triple sales to US$2.2 billion by 2023, Nestlé Nigeria invested US$446 million between 2003 and 2014 and plans another US$635 million before 2023. Diageo and Heineken also increase their footprint, the former selling by now more Guinness in Nigeria than in Ireland.[47]

Construction and building materials manufacturing in Tanzania

There are two key aspects of recent industrial policy-making in Tanzania. First, there is a clear recognition of the importance of the domestic market in supporting manufacturing growth. Government strategy documents published following the Tanzanian Development Vision 2025 (TDV) emphasise that a viable export sector forms on the basis of growth in domestic demand in critical mass to allow for economies of scale:

> the best scenario would be that of having domestic demand in critical mass that will amortize and absorb all the investment costs with an acceptable rate of return on the capital employed, such that manufactured goods for export trade would be competitively priced on the basis of marginal cost of producing the surplus for export trade over and above the requirements to supply domestic demand.[48]

To build on existing demand in Tanzania's 'vibrant and captive consumer market', government efforts focus on expanding capacity in food and beverage industries.[49]

Second, policy documents such as Tanzania's Five-Year Development Plans (FYDPs) for 2011–2016 and 2016–2021 clearly recognise the need to build manufacturing activities backwardly linked to other sectors of the economy, identifying fertilisers and building materials as key strategic sectors. Both aspects are in line with the key economic issues of building a consumer and intersectoral domestic demand base discussed at the theoretical level in section 1.

The government's sectoral priorities are well reflected in subsectoral output figures. Output data from the Tanzanian 2013 census of industrial production show that the biggest sectors are the food processing and beverages sectors followed by non-metallic minerals (cement) production, producing 55% and 7% of total gross output respectively and employing 40% and 4% of the manufacturing workforce respectively (Table 6). The strong growth of output in food and beverage production is primarily driven by soft drinks and bottled beer (increasing by 122% and 67% respectively since 2004), while many food processing industries such as polished rice or canned fruit saw their output reduced relative to 2004. Output of 'chemicals, petroleum and plastics' increased by 29% relative to 1985, yet a number of fast-growing subsectors exist especially for building materials like paints and basic consumer goods like soap and detergents or plastics products. Similarly, while output growth in 'basic metals' remains somewhat below average, corrugated iron sheets and rolled steel are both among the five fastest growing industries in Tanzania (Table 5).

Government spending on infrastructure has surely increased demand for a range of building materials, in particular cement and steel.[50] Contrary to most other African countries, Tanzania provides active policy support for its construction industry.[51] However, the only building material specifically targeted in the most recent FYDPs is cement production. While the cement sector provides employment and offers high wages, the entire sector is foreign owned. Dangote has opened Tanzania's largest cement plant with an installed capacity of 3Mta in 2015; 62.5% of the shares of Tanzania's third largest producer Tanga Cement are owned by AfriSam a South Africa based company owned by the Black Economic Empowerment Consortium; 15% of AfriSam remains, however, under the ownership of Holcim. The remaining shares of Tanga are held by pension funds and local stock exchange listings. The Kenyan owned ARM plant which opened in 2012 is another, albeit much smaller, African investor. The remainder of the Tanzanian cement production base are under majority ownership of the major European multinationals; 69% of Tanzania's second largest producer – the Tanzania Portland Cement Company – are owned by Scancem International, a Norwegian subsidiary of Heidelberg Cement. The smaller Mbeya plant is wholly owned by Lafarge. Some smaller Asian players control Lee Cement and Lake Cement (Table 4).

The case of Tanzania's cement industry illustrates the predicaments that can arise from competing interests. Both the establishment of domestic cement manufacturing and the promotion of backwardly linked inputs rests on conflicting interests between capitalists and bureaucrats. Tanzania's last government led by President Kikwete, for example, offered generous incentives for Dangote to invest in Tanzania, including tax exemptions on the import of diesel, tax waivers on machinery, government provision of land for Dangote's factory and the facilitation of permits and contracts for expatriate staff. At the same time, the Ministry of Energy and Minerals aimed at developing the supply chain by incentivising the procurement of Tanzanian energy inputs. The ban on coal imports in 2016, however, increased Dangote's production costs.[52] In addition, current regulations force Dangote to buy gas through middle companies at inflated prices instead of directly from the state-owned Tanzania Petroleum Development Company (TPDC). Dangote's recent shutdown is therefore an attempt to exert pressure on the new government led by President Magufuli to relax these measures: Dangote has been awarded its own coal mining licence after a government report confirmed that Tancoal, the only active coal producer in Tanzania, was unable to guarantee the quality and quantity demanded by the market.[53]

Existing research on Tanzanian manufacturing firms point to supply-side constraints like technological capabilities, infrastructure, access to finance[54] and to industrial land, as well as the high concentration of exporting firms[55] and contending factions of intermediate classes within the state.[56] As in Nigeria, Tanzania has experienced increased demand for

Table 4. Tanzania cement production base in 2015.

Company	Capacity (Mta)	No. of Plants
Dangote Industries (Tanzania) Ltd.	3.00	1
Tanzania Portland Cement Co. Ltd (Scancem)	1.40	1
Tanga Cement Co. Ltd (Afrisam)	1.20	1
ARM Cement	0.75	1
Lake Cement	0.50	1
Mbeya Cement Co. Ltd (Lafarge)	0.35	1
Lee Cement	0.30	1

Source: Global Cement Report 11th edition.

industrial goods from a growing consumer class.[57] Domestic entrepreneurs tap into these gaps: Azam Cola, a family owned business, entered the market in 2011 and gained 30% market shares in just 18 months.[58] However, a closer look at output and employment figures by sectors and firm sizes suggests hindrances to growth in the final consumer demand base, namely the small scale of production of the majority of manufacturing establishments and correspondingly low levels of productivity, wages and purchasing power. The Tanzanian 2013 census of industrial production reveals that more than 53% of those employed in manufacturing work in firms with less than 10 employees. These firms produce merely 5% of total gross output. Output per worker in firms with less than 10 employees is on average merely 5.2% that of firms with more than 10 employees, ranging from 1.6% in the tobacco industry to 34.3% in machinery and equipment manufacturing. This productivity differential is also reflected in wages and, by extension, purchasing power of those employed in the manufacturing sector (wages per worker in firms with less than 10 employees are on average 14.2% of those in bigger firms). The problem of small-scale and comparatively unproductive manufacturing activities becomes particularly apparent in the production of wearing apparel, textiles and furniture, employing together 31% of the total manufacturing workforce but contributing merely 9% of total gross output (Table 6).

The problem of small-scale, low productivity production generating few consumption multipliers is more far-reaching and concerns large parts of the agricultural sector, which employs 75% of the Tanzanian workforce but only produces about 21% of total output in 2010.[59] To understand why these issues are not readily addressed by policy despite well-drafted policies on paper requires dissecting distributional conflicts. For instance, initiatives to support output growth in the production of food crops like rice through extensive irrigation systems were poorly implemented due to half-hearted political support. The political influence of the predominately black and small-scale rice producers was scattered and unorganised while capitalists in the rice import business dominated by Asian-Tanzanians were important financiers of the ruling party and able to resist the introduction import tariffs against their immediate interests.[60]

The oil and gas industry in Tanzania and Nigeria

Petroleum resources are at the centre of a number of African states' strategies for industrialization. In Nigeria, oil and gas are fundamental to the economy, accounting for over 75% of exports and 60% of government revenue in 2014 prior to the oil price shock. By 2016, oil was closer to 30% of exports and revenues, with revenues also down 30% from 2014.[61] Tanzania is an emerging gas producer with minimal current production but large plans for gas-based development. The following sections argue, that contrary to resource curse arguments, the mining sector does not have to remain an enclave in the economy but can directly and indirectly support manufacturing production by way of generating revenues for the government and by widening the consumer demand base through job generation in mining-related services.

The rebasing of Nigeria's GDP in 2014 not only made Nigeria SSA's largest economy but also indicated that petroleum resources were much less important for Nigeria's economy than previously thought. Adding industries not accounted for in the previous base year of 1990 made manufacturing grow from 1.9% of GDP under the old calculation to 9% and Services from about 25% to roughly 50% of GDP. However, as anyone even casually familiar with Nigeria's political economy would immediately note, the growth of these sectors does not necessarily have anything to do with state policy and is more likely in fact to have occurred despite the Nigerian government. The country remains however one of the most developed in SSA in terms of its industrial base and workforce skills. This is important for understanding its future potential.

Combined with renewed militancy in the Niger Delta cutting into production, the fall in oil prices has left the country in a major economic crisis. Foreign direct investment has been falling and the economy has begun contracting while inflation has returned to double digits. Exports were down 40% in 2015, 'decimating government revenues'.[62] Despite facing a budget deficit of US$11 billion, the 2016 budget represented a 20% increase over the previous year, reflecting the new president's desire to spark further industrial transformation through investment in national quality infrastructure. There are other indications that the Buhari administration is seeking to play a larger role in fostering structural transformation. A core of highly competent cabinet ministers has been led by Vice-President Osinbajo in their efforts to revive economic planning and direct state investments more effectively toward national development priorities. Osinbajo is Chairman of the National Economic Council, an advisory group of state governors, key ministers and others. The committee has taken on new importance and an implementation steering committee has been formed with high-profile governors and members of cabinet. A six-point implementation plan for the 2016 budget focuses on diversifying the economy by fast-tracking industrialization, agriculture and agro-processing. The plan aims to increase Nigeria's food output of basic commodities like rice, tomato paste, wheat, maize, soya, poultry and livestock.[63] There has also been a focus on solid minerals with an eye toward reviving Nigeria's long-dormant steel industry.

As Ovadia[64] argues, structural transformation of the economy can also be rooted in petroleum resources, despite Nigeria being seen as a prime example of the 'resource curse' or 'paradox of plenty'.[65] After decades of no discernible benefit to the majority of citizens, Nigeria began to embrace local content in the mid-2000s. The effort to promote the employment of Nigerians, use of Nigerian companies and value addition in Nigeria was boosted by the 2010 Nigerian Oil and Gas Industry Content Development Act. The agency it created, the Nigerian Content Development and Monitoring Board (NCDMB), is now leading a set of initiatives that very much resemble the interventionist strategies of East Asian developmental states. They have been involved in promoting infant industries such as steel pipe and subsea equipment manufacturers, spurred the building of new fabrication and yards and led other initiatives that have created thousands of jobs and, as of late 2015 prior to a change in executive leadership, were spearheading three industrial parks in the Niger Delta states of Imo, Cross River and Bayelsa that will specialise in manufacturing of low-cost equipment, component parts, spare parts and chemicals.

The above sector-level analysis can be complemented with case studies of specific firms, as Ovadia demonstrates with profiles of 10 indigenous oil and oil services firms in Nigeria. Quantitative and qualitative research at all three levels of analysis reveal a developmental project that has very real aspirations but many challenges ahead. While this paper cannot fully go into those, we maintain that the success or failure of Nigerian content and of the Buhari government's recent efforts toward economic diversification can best be researched through an extended developmental state framework and adaptation of theory and methodology to researching developmental states in the African context.

Tanzania discovered natural gas in 2012. Since then, a vigorous debate has begun over how best to take advantage of these resources to help the country achieve its development objectives. Several separate but interrelated support programmes have launched since 2012 to link investment in the industry to a broader strategy of structural transformation. Working with the African Development Bank,[66] the EU, UNDP and other international organisations, the National Economic Empowerment Council (NEEC) has taken the lead on local content promotion – in extractives and throughout the economy. The updated Petroleum Act of 2015 and Draft Local Content Regulations of 2017 encourage local participation in the emerging gas industry with an aim to increasing in-country value addition and promoting local linkages.

The World Bank has funded a multi-year study on the potential opportunities for industrial development and linkages promotion through the planned Tanzania Liquid Natural Gas (TLNG) facility, which will (due to government intervention) process gas from both the Statoil and BG/Shell gas projects. The World Bank study[67] concludes that by providing goods and services to the TLNG project in three areas, Tanzania could capture as much as US$2 billion of the total US$15–17 billion investment, creating as many as 80,000 direct and indirect jobs. The three categories alone account for US$12 billion of the US$17 billion of spend on the project. They are general construction, LNG project-specific industries and key supporting services. The first category is important because building these industries, which operate both inside and out of oil and gas and are crucial to structural transformation, leaves a lasting benefit to the Tanzanian economy. The second category is important because this is where the majority of spend is located for their TLNG project. Capturing even a few percent of the spend would be significant for developing heavy industry. Finally, the third category represents 'low-hanging fruit', services that Tanzanian companies should be able to provide (catering, security, cleaning and low-skilled labour) that may not capture significant value but will generate significant employment and purchasing power.

Crucially, the World Bank study demonstrates a significant difference between a 'base case' in which minimal intervention is carried out prior to the final decision to invest in the TLNG project (now not expected before 2020) and a 'success case' that assumes government and donor intervention to integrate supplier and workforce development interventions. Under the success case, local value capture increases from US$1.4 billion to US$2 billion, while employment generated increases from around 60,000 to 80,000. These figures bolster the argument of Ovadia and others[68] about the significance of local content in oil and gas.

Conclusions

We have argued that one factor largely sidelined by research on development states concerns the conditions under which demand for commodity production remains or becomes expansionary. This is of particular relevance to SSA economies today as they face a global economic context tending towards systemic deficient demand. Financialisation in developed economies crowds out long-term productive investment and tends to worsen the distribution of income and wealth thereby depressing consumer demand. What is more, intense competition from China has been shown to displace African manufacturing exports.

Against this context of shrinking space for export-led industrialisation, domestic developmental policy has to mobilise and support the growth of domestic consumer and intersectoral demand. Disentangling the conditions under which this occurs or the reasons why it does not can provide important additional insights into patterns of growth and stagnation of manufacturing activities in SSA. The article draws on selective examples from Tanzania and Nigeria to show how certain manufacturing activities in both countries emerged on the basis of domestic sources of demand and investigates limitations thereto.

Large-scale building materials manufacturing in both countries was assisted by the strong growth of construction activities, which created a profitable market for building materials. Of particular relevance here is not just the emergence of mutual interest between capitalists and bureaucrats but also the mediation of conflicting interests. Data on ownership structures in the Tanzanian and Nigerian cement industries serve to take account of tendencies towards monopolisation and gauge bargaining positions in situations of competing interest. For instance, Tanzania's government actively pursued efforts to build cement and other manufacturing industries backwardly linked to the construction sector. Yet, these efforts, while in the mutual interest of suppliers and bureaucrats may clash, as they have in Tanzania with the interests of foreign investors – even African ones. What is noteworthy is that government support for building materials manufacturing in both countries primarily extends to the capital-intensive cement sector. The developmental potential of linkages between the construction and building materials sector could be enhanced by targeting the production of less capital-intensive building materials more systematically.

In Nigeria, the anticipated growth of the large domestic consumer market has favoured the re-investment of profits generated inside and outside of the cement sector. Qualitative evidence, for instance, suggests that Dangote's expansion into other sectors is based on the anticipation of growing consumer demand base. In Tanzania, manufacturing output and ownership data revealed an enormous differential in wages and productivity between small-scale and medium- to large-scale manufacturing enterprises with corresponding ramifications for the consumption multiplier processes. Future research will have to uncover the dynamics of redistributive and capital–labour relations in greater detail to understand the factors that further or constrain the broadening of the domestic consumer demand base.

The case of petroleum and natural gas production in Nigeria and Tanzania shows that these sectors do not have to remain enclaves if mutual interest forms to support linkage formation to forward- and backward-linked manufacturing activities, and local content policies supports domestic employment generation.

Disclosure statement

No potential conflict of interest was reported by the authors.

Acknowledgements

The authors would like to thank the journal editors and two anonymous reviewers for their very helpful feedback. Jesse Ovadia would also like to thank Jewellord Nem Singh, co-guest editor for this Special Issue, as well as the other authors and participants in the 'Developmental States Beyond East Asia' workshop held in Newcastle upon Tyne in June 2015 with the support of the Development Politics Specialist Group, Political Studies Association (UK) and School of Geography, Politics and Sociology, Newcastle University (UK).

Notes

1. Chang, *East Asian Development Experience*; Arrighi, *Adam Smith in Beijing*.
2. Whitfield et al., *Politics of African Industrial Policy*; Taylor, "Dependency Redux."
3. Moon and Prasad, "Beyond the Developmental State."
4. Whitfield et al., *Politics of African Industrial Policy*.
5. Whitfield et al., *Politics of African Industrial Policy*; Williams, *End of the Developmental State?*; Kanyenze et al., *Towards Democratic Developmental States*.
6. Lincoln and Guba, "The Only Generalization Is."
7. Stake, "Case Study Method in Social Inquiry."
8. Lincoln and Guba, "The Only Generalization Is."
9. Gomm, Hammersley, and Foster, "Case Study and Theory."
10. Ibid., 249.
11. Gomm, Hammersley, and Foster, "Case Study and Generalisation."
12. Jerven, *Poor Numbers*.
13. Hirschman, *Strategy of Economic Development*.
14. Rosenstein-Rodan, "Problems of Industrialisation."
15. Dutt, "Stagnation, Income Distribution."
16. Hirschman, *Strategy of Economic Development*.
17. Ibid.
18. Thirlwall, "General Model of Growth."
19. Steel and Evans, "Industrialization in Sub-Saharan Africa," 50; Meier and Steel, *Industrial Adjustment in Sub-Saharan Africa*, 87.
20. Meier and Steel, *Industrial Adjustment in Sub-Saharan Africa*, 87.
21. Khan, "Technology Policies and Learning."
22. World Bank, "Accelerated Development in Sub-Saharan Africa."
23. Zhu, "Rethinking Import-Substituting Industrialization."
24. Amsden, *The Rise of the "Rest,"* 161; Shafaeddin, "Industrial Policy Relevant," 36.
25. Amsden, "Third World Industrialization," 11; Monga, "Winning the Jackpot," 154.
26. Cimoli and Porcile, "Accumulations of Capabilities"; Astorga, Cimoli, and Porcile, "Role of Industrial and Exchange."
27. Cimoli and Porcile, "Accumulations of Capabilities."
28. Thirlwall, "Reflections on the Concept."
29. Palley, "The Economic Case."
30. Razmi and Blecker, "Developing Country Exports of Manufactures."
31. Bagnai, Rieber, and Tran, "Sub-Saharan Africa's Growth."

32. Giovannetti and Sanfilippo, "Do Chinese Exports Crowd-out African Goods?"
33. Wade, "Choking the South."
34. Ikpe, "Lessons for Nigeria from Developmental States."
35. Hirschman, *Strategy of Economic Development*, 68.
36. Evans, *Embedded Autonomy*.
37. Fine, "Beyond the Developmental State."
38. Khan, "Technology Policies and Learning."
39. Ibid.
40. Whitfield et al., *Politics of African Industrial Policy*.
41. Amsden, "Third World Industrialization," 18.
42. White, "The Case of Cement."
43. Armstrong et al., *The Global Cement Report*.
44. ICR Newsroom, "Dangote Cement Full-Year Boosted."
45. ICR Newsroom, "Dangote Asian Expansion?"
46. Wallis, "Aliko Dangote – Africa's Richest Man."
47. Games, "Fast-Moving Consumer Goods."
48. URT-ERB, "15 Years of Implementation," 10.
49. URT, "Tanzania Five Year Development Plan," 2.
50. The Business Year, "Construction - Hammer Time."
51. URT-MOW, "Construction Industry Policy."
52. IPP News Media, "Dangote Saga Continues."
53. Mtulya, "Report Backs Cement Firms."
54. Wangwe et al., "Performance of the Manufacturing Sector."
55. Sutton and Olomi, "An Enterprise Map of Tanzania."
56. Gray, "Industrial Policy and Political Settlement."
57. URT-ERB, "15 Years of Implementation," 22.
58. Games, "Fast-Moving Consumer Goods."
59. Whitfield et al., *Politics of African Industrial Policy*.
60. Ibid.
61. IMF, "Nigeria," 34.
62. Ibid., 1.
63. For example, an import ban on rice has increased prices by 60%, fuelling local demand and drawing new investment into the sector; Fick, "Nigeria's Rice Farmers."
64. Ovadia, *The Petro-Developmental State*.
65. Auty, *Sustaining Development in Mineral Economies*; Karl, *The Paradox of Plenty*; Ovadia, "The Nigerian 'One Percent.'"
66. Jesse Ovadia has worked as a consultant for the African Development Bank in their programme of support for NEEC on local content.
67. World Bank, "Leveraging a Large Capital," 9.
68. Ovadia, "Local Content and Natural Resource Governance"; Ovadia, *The Petro-Developmental State*; White, "Regulating for Local Content."

Bibliography

Amsden, Alice H. *The Rise of the 'Rest' - Challenges to the West from Late-Industrializing Economies*. New York and Oxford: Oxford University Press, 2001.

Amsden, Alice H. "Third World Industrialization: 'Global Fordism' or a New Model?" *New Left Review* 182, no. July-August (1990): 5–31.

Armstrong, Thomas, Muriel Bal, Peter Bell, Jolyne Fernandes, and Suzanne Starbuck, eds. *The Global Cement Report*. 11th ed. Dorking: Tradeship Publications Ltd, 2015.

Arrighi, Giovanni. *Adam Smith in Beijing: Lineages of the 21st Century*. London: Verso, 2007.

Astorga, Rodrigo, Mario Cimoli, and Gabriel Porcile. "The Role of Industrial and Exchange Rate Policies in Promoting Structural Change, Productivity and Employment." In *Transforming Economies*, edited by José Manuel Salazar-Xirinachs, Irmgard Nübler and Richard Kozul-Wright, 79–111. Geneva: International Labour Office, 2014.

Auty, Richard. *Sustaining Development in Mineral Economies: The Resource Curse Thesis*. London: Routledge, 1993.

Bagnai, Alberto, Arsène Rieber, and Thi Anh-Dao Tran. "Sub-Saharan Africa's Growth, South–South Trade and the Generalised Balance-of-Payments Constraint." *Cambridge Journal of Economics* 40, no. 3 (May 2016): 797–820. doi:10.1093/cje/bev020.

Chang, Ha-Joon. *The East Asian Development Experience: The Miracle, the Crisis and the Future*. London: Zed Books, 2006.

Cimoli, Mario, and Gabriel Porcile. "Accumulations of Capabilities, Structural Change, and Macro Prices: An Evolutionary and Structuralist Roadmap." In *The Industrial Policy Revolution II - Africa in the 21st Century*, edited by Joseph E. Stiglitz, Justin Yifu Lin, and Ebrahim Patel, 73–113. Basingstoke: Palgrave Macmillan, 2013.

Dutt, Amitava Krishna. "Stagnation, Income Distribution and Monopoly Power." *Cambridge Journal of Economics* 8, no. 1 (März 1984): 25–40.

Evans, Peter. *Embedded Autonomy: States and Industrial Transformation*. Princeton, New Jersey: Princeton University Press, 1995.

Fick, Maggie. "Nigeria's Rice Farmers Enjoy Growth amid Economic Crisis." *Financial times*, September 3, 2017. http://www.ft.com/content/79bea9fa-0279-11e7-aa5b-6bb07f5c8e12.

Fine, Ben. "Beyond the Developmental State: An Introduction." In *Beyond the Developmental State - Industrial Policy into the Twenty-First Century*, edited by Ben Fine, Daniela Travasci, and Jyoti Saraswati, 1–32. London: Pluto Press, 2013.

Games, Dianna. "The Fast-Moving Consumer Goods and Retail Sectors." In *Africans Investing in Africa - Understanding Business and Trade, Sector by Sector*, edited by Terence McNamee, Mark Pearson, and Wiebe Boer, 147–176. Houndmills: Palgrave Macmillan, 2015.

Giovannetti, Giorgia, and Marco Sanfilippo. "Do Chinese Exports Crowd-out African Goods? An Econometric Analysis by Country and Sector." *European Journal of Development Research* 21, no. 4 (September 2009): 506–530. doi:10.1057/ejdr.2009.20.

Gomm, Roger, Martyn Hammersley, and Peter Foster. "Case Study and Generalization." In *Case Study Method*, edited by Roger Gomm, Martyn Hammersley, and Peter Foster, 98–115. London: Sage, 2000.

Gomm, Roger, Martyn Hammersley, and Peter Foster. "Case Study and Theory." In *Case Study Method*, edited by Roger Gomm, Martyn Hammersley, and Peter Foster, 234–258. London: Sage, 2000.

Gray, Hazel. "Industrial Policy and the Political Settlement in Tanzania: Aspects of Continuity and Change since Independence." *Review of African Political Economy* 40, no. 136 (June 2013): 185–201.

Hirschman, Albert O. *The Strategy of Economic Development*. Reprinted by Norten 1978. New Haven, CT: Yale University Press, 1958.

ICR Newsroom. "Dangote Asian Expansion?" *International Cement Review*, October 18, 2016. http://www.cemnet.com/News/story/160329/dangote-asian-expansion-.html?source=b3efe8984a522baf9004706a13907f79.

ICR Newsroom. "Dangote Cement Full-Year Boosted by New African Plants." *International Cement Review*, March 2, 2016. http://www.cemnet.com/News/story/158683/dangote-cement-full-year-boosted-by-new-african-plants.html?source=62441870629c74f8a4e16ff1410010b9.

Ikpe, Eka. "Lessons for Nigeria from Developmental States: The Role of Agriculture in Structural Transformation." In *Beyond the Developmental State - Industrial Policy into the Twenty-First Century*, edited by Ben Fine, Jyoti Saraswati, and Daniela Tavasci, 187–215. London: Pluto Press, 2013.

IMF. *Nigeria: 2016 Article IV Consultation*. Washington, DC: International Monetary Fund, 2016. http://www.imf.org/external/pubs/ft/scr/2016/cr16101.pdf.

IPP News Media. "Dangote Saga Continues." *IPP News Media*, 2016. http://www.ippmedia.com/en/news/dangote-factory-saga-continues-now-man-himself-coming-tanzania?utm_campaign=shareaholic&utm_medium=twitter&utm_source=socialnetwork.

Jerven, Morten. *Poor Numbers: How We Are Misled by African Development Statistics and What to Do about It*. Ithaka and London: Cornell University Press, 2013.

Kanyenze, Godfrey, Herbert Jauch, Alice D. Kanengoni, Masego Madzwamuse, and Deprose Muchena. eds. *Towards Democratic Developmental States in Southern Africa*. Harare: Weaver Press, 2016.

Karl, Terry Lynn. *The Paradox of Plenty*. Berkeley: University of California Press, 1997.
Khan, Mushtaq Hussain. "Technology Policies and Learning with Imperfect Governance." In *The Industrial Policy Revolution I. the Role of Government beyond Ideology*, edited by Justin Yifu Lin and Joseph E. Stiglitz, 79–115. London: Palgrave Macmillan, 2013.
Lincoln, Yvonna S., and Egon G. Guba. "The Only Generaliztion is: There is No Generalization." In *Case Study Method*, edited by Roger Gomm, Martyn Hammersley, and Peter Foster, 27–44. London: Sage, 2000.
Meier, Gerald M., and William F. Steel. *Industrial Adjustment in Sub-Saharan Africa*. Oxford: Oxford University Press, 1989.
Monga, Celestin. "Winning the Jackpot: Jobs Dividends in a Multipolar World." In *The Industrial Policy Revolution II - Africa in the 21st Century*, edited by Joseph E. Stiglitz, Justin Yifu Lin, and Ebrahim Patel, 135–172. Houndmills: Palgrave Macmillan, 2013.
Moon, Chung-in, and Rashemi Prasad. "Beyond the Developmental State: Networks, Politics and Institutions." *Governance: An International Journal of Policy and Administration* 7, no. 4 (1994): 360–386.
Mtulya, Athuman. "Report Backs Cement Firms' Outcry on Coal." *The Citizen*, December 7, 2016. http://www.thecitizen.co.tz/News/Report-backs-cement-firms–outcry-on-coal/1840340-3477740-kq7fbnz/index.html.
Ovadia, Jesse Salah. "Local Content and Natural Resource Governance: The Cases of Angola and Nigeria." *Extractive Industries and Society* 1, no. 2 (2014): 137–146.
Ovadia, Jesse Salah. "The Nigerian "One Percent" and the Management of National Oil Wealth through Nigerian Content." *Science & Society* 77, no. 3 (2013): 315–341.
Ovadia, Jesse Salah. *The Petro-Developmental State: Making Oil Work in Angola, Nigeria and the Gulf of Guinea*. London: Hurst, 2016.
Palley, Thomas I. "The Economic Case for International Labour Standards." *Cambridge Journal of Economics* 28, no. 1 (January 2004): 21–36.
Razmi, Arslan, and Robert A. Blecker. "Developing Country Exports of Manufactures: Moving up the Ladder to Escape the Fallacy of Composition?" *Journal of Development Studies* 44, no. 1 (January 2008): 21–48.
Rosenstein-Rodan, P. N. 'Problems of Industrialisation of Eastern and South-Eastern Europe'. *The Economic Journal* 53, no. 210/211 (1943): 202–211.
Shafaeddin, Mehdi. "Industrial Policy Relevant in the 21st Century?" *Journal of Development and Economic Policies* 14, no. 1 (2012): 5–55.
Stake, Robert E. "The Case Study Method in Social Inquiry." In *Case Study Method*, edited by Roger Gomm, Martyn Hammersley, and Peter Foster, 19–26. London: Sage, 2000.
Steel, William F., and Jonathan W. Evans. *Industrialization in Sub-Saharan Africa: Strategies and Performance*. World Bank Technical Paper. Washington, DC: World Bank, 1984.
Sutton, John, and Donath Olomi. *An Enterprise Map of Tanzania*. International Growth Centre, 2012.
Taylor, Ian. "Dependency Redux: Why Africa is Not Rising." *Review of African Political Economy* 23 (October 2015): 1–18. doi:10.1080/03056244.2015.1084911.
The Business Year. "Construction - Hammer Time." *The Business Year Tanzania*, 2015, sec. Real Estate and Construction. http://www.thebusinessyear.com/tanzania-2015/hammer-time/review.
Thirlwall, Anthony P. "A General Model of Growth and Development on Kaldorian Lines." *Oxford Economic Papers* 38, no. 2 (1986): 199–219.
Thirlwall, Anthony P. "Reflections on the Concept of Balance-of-Payments–Constrained Growth." *Journal of Post Keynesian Economics* 19, no. 3 (1997): 377–385.
URT. *The Tanzania Five Year Development Plan 2011/2012-2015/16*. Daressalam: United Republic of Tanzania - Ministry of Finance and Planning, 2011.
URT-ERB. *15 Years of Implementation of Tanzania Development Vision 2025*. United Republic of Tanzania: Engineering Registration Board, 2015.
URT-MOW. *Construction Industry Policy*. Daressalam: United Republic of Tanzania - Ministry of Works, 2003. http://www.tanzania.go.tz/egov_uploads/documents/Construction_Industry_Policy_sw.pdf.
Wade, Robert. "Choking the South." *New Left Review* 38 (2006): 115–127.
Wallis, William. "Aliko Dangote – Africa's Richest Man." *Financial times*, October 11, 2013.

Wangwe, Samuel, D. Mmari, J. Aikaeli, N. Rutatina, T. Mboghoina, and A. Kinyondo. *The Performance of the Manufacturing Sector in Tanzania: Challenges and the Way Forward*. Helsinki: United Nations University World Institute for Development Economics Research, 2014.

White, Lyal. "The Case of Cement." In *Africans Investing in Africa - Understanding Business and Trade, Sector by Sector*, edited by Terence McNamee, Mark Pearson, and Wiebe Boer, 124–146. Houndmills: Palgrave Macmillan, 2015.

White, Simon. "Regulating for Local Content: Limitations of Legal and Regulatory Instruments in Promoting Small Scale Suppliers in Extractive Industries in Developing Economies." *The Extractive Industries and Society*, 4 no. 2 (2017): 260–266.

Whitfield, Lindsay, Ole Therkildsen, Lars Buur, and Anne Mette KjÆr. *The Politics of African Industrial Policy: A Comparative Perspective*. Cambridge, UK: Cambridge University Press, 2015.

Williams, Michelle, ed. *The End of the Developmental State?* Routledge Studies in Development and Society. London: Routledge, 2015.

World Bank. *Accelerated Development in Sub-Saharan Africa - an Agenda for Action*. Washington, DC: World Bank, 1981.

World Bank. *Leveraging a Large Capital Investment to Develop Local Value Chains: "Local Content" in the Construction of Tanzania LNG Facility'*. Washington, DC: World Bank, 2016.

Zhu, Tianbiao. *Rethinking Import-Substituting Industrialization: Development Strategies and Institutions in Taiwan and China*. Working Paper. Helsinki: UNU-WIDER, 2006. http://www.wider.unu.edu/sites/default/files/rp2006-76.pdf.

Annex 1.

Table 5. Tanzania: manufacturing output by sector and selected commodities for selected years.

	Sector	Unit	1985	2004	2006	2008	2010	2012
3	Total manufacturing	Index	100	185	226	260	290	328
31	Food, beverages and tobacco	Index	100	240	314	351	386	458
311	*Rice, polished*	M.T	4,102	365	771	173	22	78
311	*Canned fruits and vegetables*	M.T	1,850	6,558	6,642	6,303	7,961	4,133
311	*Vegetable oils and fats*	M.T	6,516	76,681	106,393	131,301	162,657	151,586
313	*Bottled beer*	Ltr 000	75,760	202,628	299,036	293,543	242,327	338,650
313	*Soft drinks*	Ltr 000	48,230	264,145	367,675	318,277	444,245	585,567
314	*Tobacco, cured*	M.T	10,240	28,407	85,641	56,351	51,548	94,420
32	Textiles and leather	Index	100	277	271	286	244	186
321	*Woven fabrics*	Sq.m 000	54,200	115,524	107,884	134,717	103,605	83,592
321	*Textile bags*	Num 000	2,252	1,739	1,473	1,590	1,673	1,962
33	Wood and wood products	Index	100	211	256	263	244	374
331	*Plywood*	Cu.m	1,589	0	0	0	988	1,031
34	Paper and paper products	Index	100	78	74	310	317	360
341	*Paper*	M.T	7,553	0	0	37,971	38,733	45,286
35	Chemical, petroleum and plastic products		100	78	96	107	137	129
352	*Paints*	Ltr 000	1,364	13,338	18,384	24,857	28,201	34,868
352	*Soap and laundry / toilet detergents*	M.T	13,870	88,783	114,012	127,884	147,700	131,260
356	*Plastic articles*	M.T	1,940	6,470	6,552	5,627	11,138	15,383
36	Pottery, china, glass and non-metallic products	Index	100	288	320	415	526	576
362	*Glassware*	M.T	10,260	12,581	25,291	34,781	23,831	11,836
369	*Cement*	M.T	376,000	1,280,851	1,369,926	1,755,862	2,312,055	2,581,398
37	Basic metal industries	Index	100	115	135	177	235	298
371	*Corrugated iron sheets*	M.T	21,670	26,182	29,801	35,868	57,656	81,427
371	*Rolled steel*	M.T	11,300	32,255	44,543	125,484	134,145	133,229
38	Fabricated metal products, machinery and equip.	Index	100	55	56	74	76	91
381	*Metal containers*	Num 000	50,010	48	736	915	1,177	880
382	*Industrial machines*	Num	940	41	9	37	46	46
383	*Transformers*	Num	456	919	653	1,688	1,110	2,730

Compiled based on Tanzania National Bureau of Statistics (2013): Quarterly Production of Industrial Commodities 2004–2012.

Annex 2.

Table 6. Tanzania: output, employment and wages by manufacturing activity.

Manufacturing activity	Gross output all	Gross output 10+	Gross output < 10	Total person engaged all	Total person engaged 10+	Total person engaged < 10	Wages/ worker 10+	Wages/ worker < 10	Output per worker 10+	Output per worker < 10
Manufacturing	10,936,795,293	10,319,944,823	616,850,470	231,098	107,732	123,366	6,316	899	95,793	5,000
Food products	4,231,128,967	3,953,075,295	278,053,672	85,330	40,031	45,299	4,323	761	98,750	6,138
Beverages	1,744,910,475	1,743,088,863	1,821,612	7,004	6,859	145	24,241	1,440	254,132	12,563
Other non-metallic mineral products	807,924,053	759,227,505	48,696,548	9,384	4,548	4,836	11,990	1,556	166,937	10,070
Tobacco products	655,706,655	655,602,895	103,760	5,110	5,061	49	11,871	846	129,540	2,118
Rubber and plastics products	632,721,970	631,541,522	1,180,448	4,342	4,243	99	4,647	1,579	148,843	11,924
Chemicals and chemical products	555,780,538	554,110,816	1,669,722	6,645	6,380	265	5,397	1,155	86,851	6,301
Manufacture of furniture	452,616,950	369,045,542	83,571,408	23,739	2,977	20,762	5,475	989	123,966	4,025
Textiles	410,673,843	404,589,917	6,083,926	17,715	16,067	1,648	3,809	1,107	25,181	3,692
Printing and reproduction of recorded media	184,340,112	177,532,344	6,807,768	3,339	2,849	490	7,005	2,047	62,314	13,893
Fabricated metal products, except machinery	179,447,160	115,916,704	63,530,456	14,889	2,189	12,700	3,609	1,089	52,954	5,002
Manufacture of basic metals	170,916,202	170,807,241	108,961	2,194	2,174	20	2,620	1,869	78,568	5,448
Products of wood and cork, except furniture	155,563,390	124,421,255	31,142,135	9,418	3,769	5,649	2,602	1,115	33,012	5,513
Electrical equipment	106,975,511	102,967,334	4,008,177	1,740	949	791	5,259	1,124	108,501	5,067
Wearing apparel	101,343,980	24,619,377	76,724,603	30,538	1,743	28,795	3,733	731	14,125	2,665
Paper and paper products	96,887,918	96,702,739	185,179	2,253	2,228	25	4,501	1,017	43,403	7,407
Other manufacturing	74,793,473	70,300,894	4,492,579	1,709	1,166	543	2,762	1,548	60,292	8,274
Coke and refined petroleum products	70,051,898	70,051,898		243	243	0	5,886	n.a.	288,279	n.a.
Other transport equipment	61,066,394	60,480,031	586,363	330	199	131	12,661	847	303,920	4,476
Pharmaceutical products	60,192,711	60,170,009	22,702	790	778	12	6,606	413	77,339	1,892
Leather and related products	57,467,406	55,042,111	2,425,295	1,725	1,215	510	2,153	1,259	45,302	4,755
Motor vehicles, trailers	40,102,422	38,856,196	1,246,226	1,391	1,272	119	4,580	2,296	30,547	10,472
PC, electronic and optical products	36,552,771	36,455,945	96,826	124	115	9	29,965	2,995	317,008	10,758
Repair + installation of machinery + equipment	35,584,254	34,945,531	638,723	418	317	101	8,208	1,597	110,238	6,324
Machinery and equipment not elsewhere classified	14,046,240	10,392,859	3,653,381	725	358	367	8,860	1,675	29,030	9,955

Calculations based on 2013 Census of Manufacturing Production.

State-owned enterprises and the political economy of state–state relations in the developing world

Jewellord Nem Singh and Geoffrey C. Chen

ABSTRACT

The literature on developmental states has built theories of growth-enhancing strategies through a mutually constitutive state–business relationship and institutionalised expertise through a professional bureaucracy. Whilst most evidence bears on the East Asian context, recent empirical work has focussed on state agency and new industrial policies in response to global market integration. Our paper contributes to this debate by exploring multiple patterns of state enterprise reforms that have enabled governments to generate competitive domestic firms. These reforms, then, lead to new theoretical insights as regards the diverse institutional arrangements co-constituting state–state relationships across countries and sectors. Overall, the paper views state-owned enterprises (SOEs) as complex organisations that bear new developmental capacities rather than vessels of rent-seeking interests.

Introduction

In the era of global market integration, to what extent can state-owned enterprises (SOEs) serve as instruments of national industrial development? As neoliberal reforms advanced worldwide, privatisation and market competition became the dominant trend in economic reforms. Yet the growing number of reports on how to manage SOEs in advanced and industrialising countries point to a quite contrasting reality: that there remains a substantial number of countries which have publicly listed companies in their national economies, and where a non-trivial share of listed (former) state-owned companies worldwide operate and thrive despite powerful discourses of privatisation and market competition.[1] In Organisation for Economic Cooperation and Development (OECD) countries, there are 58 listed and 1617 non-listed SOEs, whose market value reaches US$ 632 billion, and the share of the total SOE sector value amounts to 32% of gross domestic product (GDP).[2] Remarkably, in China, the second largest economy in the world, the country's listed SOE assets have reached almost 67% of the market value of all domestic listed enterprises.[3] What is more difficult is that the scale of the industrial SOEs has 'increased from 134 million RMB in 1999 to 923 million in 2008, expanding by 589 percent in 9 years'.[4] In Latin America, notwithstanding the initial

Jewellord Nem Singh http://orcid.org/0000-0002-5216-4408 ;
Geoff rey C. Chen http://orcid.org/0000-0002-0868-3745

wave of privatisation, governments maintained state control of strategic industries[5] through SOEs.[6] As a consequence, SOE output by country is estimated at 15% of GDP – a figure that is close to the pre-privatisation levels.[7]

The proliferation of SOEs in the post-privatisation era should therefore not come as a surprise. The importance of national ownership in the upgrading process is widely acknowledged, especially when governments promote mid-tech and high-tech sectors.[8] Given that SOEs are unlikely to disappear in the coming decades, we consider the political and institutional conditions upon which SOEs can become efficient and internationally competitive. This paper revisits the developmental state model and extends its core assumptions to explore SOEs as developmental actors. Firstly, we provide an addendum to the traditional theoretical view of the developmental state which implies that successful developmental states can only emerge through mutually reinforcing state–business relations or political settlement.[9] Instead, 'embedded autonomy'[10] can emerge in the context of state–state relations given that state managers and policy elites are distinct political entities. In some cases, SOEs may well replace private capital as a means of developing new sectors if and when state managers can undertake comprehensive corporate governance reforms, solving some of the principal-agency problems associated with public ownership.

Secondly, while we confirm the centrality of institutionalised expertise through a professional bureaucracy in implementing developmental policy, effective SOEs can emerge by way of improving the quality of institutional channels and policy coordination between state managers and policy elites. In other words, state–state relations, as opposed to state–business relations, matter in successfully crafting development policies through SOEs. We then capture this relationship by investigating an array of corporate governance reforms in the public enterprise sector. Specifically, our paper creates a typology of SOE reforms: *centralised* vs *decentralised* state control and *majority* vs *minority* shareholder stake in the ownership of SOEs. By examining control and ownership structures of state companies, we observe that developmental states appear to show diverse institutional arrangements co-constituting state–state relations across countries and sectors. The paper extends the East Asian developmental state model by focussing on public management reforms in ways that strengthen – rather than weaken – state enterprises.

The paper is structured as follows. The next section offers a state capacity framework that explores the relationship between SOEs and developmental states. The third section discusses state–state relations and industrial policy in the context of China. The fourth section analyses the role of SOEs in resource-rich countries, which includes maximising natural resource rents to finance development policy. The fifth section examines the political and institutional challenges in designing effective state intervention through SOEs. We also note that our analysis is informed by five years of extensive fieldwork conducted in Brazil, China and Chile on the economic performance and political economy of state companies in emerging markets.

Making a case for SOEs and the developmental state model

The industrial success of East Asian tigers was widely noted in the 1980s and 1990s, but new fields of inquiry emerged in the post-2000 period, partly as a result of emerging forms of resource nationalism and state capitalism. These studies examine various themes related to new developmental states: (1) the origins of the developmental state model and its wider application to socialist and democratic states;[11] (2) the role of coalitional politics or political settlements in crafting successful industrial policies in Africa and Latin America;[12] and (3) regulatory and public management reforms that enhance state intervention in response to a changing world economy.[13] These studies build upon the traditional and widely known literature on developmental states, which focusses on the role of purposeful state intervention as a way to 'get the prices wrong' and pursue export-oriented industrialisation.[14] Without belabouring the point any further, the classic studies on developmental states coalesce around the significance of state–business relations and institutionalised expertise through a professional bureaucracy as basic preconditions for the emergence of developmentally oriented states.

Yet, as Figure 1(a–b) shows, the proliferation of SOEs worldwide appears to have been missed out by the resurgent literature on developmental states. Instead of SOEs, developmental state scholars have focused on top-down catalytic process of state intervention in the local network, ranging from the provision of government subsidies, the standardised enterprise performance assessment, to the subsequent reward and punishment.[15] These studies emphasise the state as a facilitator in the process of economic globalisation through its ability to maintain discipline over domestic business and to promote competitive local industries. However, after 2000, another variant of state-led networks in newly industrialised countries began to emerge – competitive SOEs that can foster efficient allocation of state resources to achieve developmental objectives. In the post-Washington Consensus era, convergence between market competition and re-incorporation of SOEs concretely offered a new developmental approach for emerging markets. Importantly, new developmentalism shifts the analytical focus from state–social alliances towards the remoulding of state–state relations.

It is also worth noting that while SOEs were not initially part of the core theorisation of the East Asian developmental state, public investment through taxation and public provision

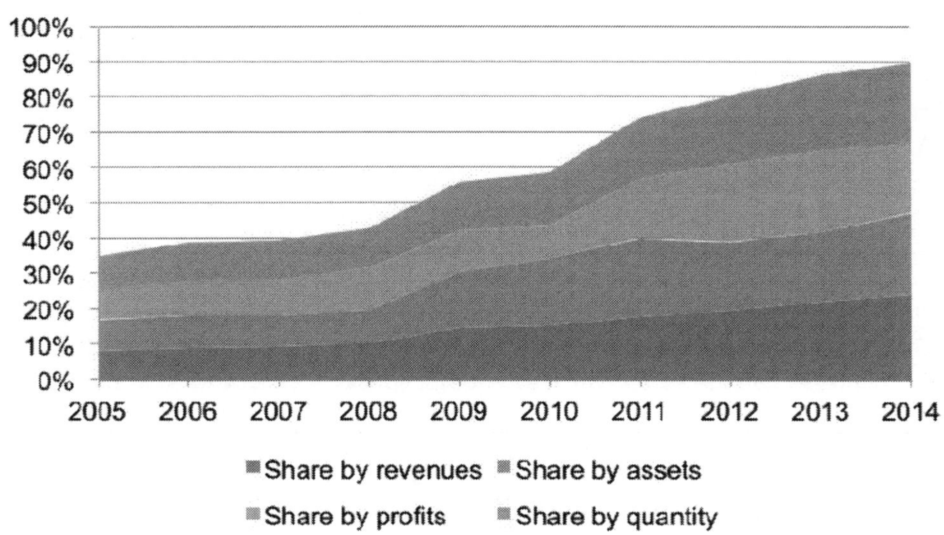

Figure 1(a). Shares of SOEs on Fortune Global 500 list.
Adapted from Kwiatkowski and Augustynowicz, "State-Owned Enterprises in the Global Economy," 1742.

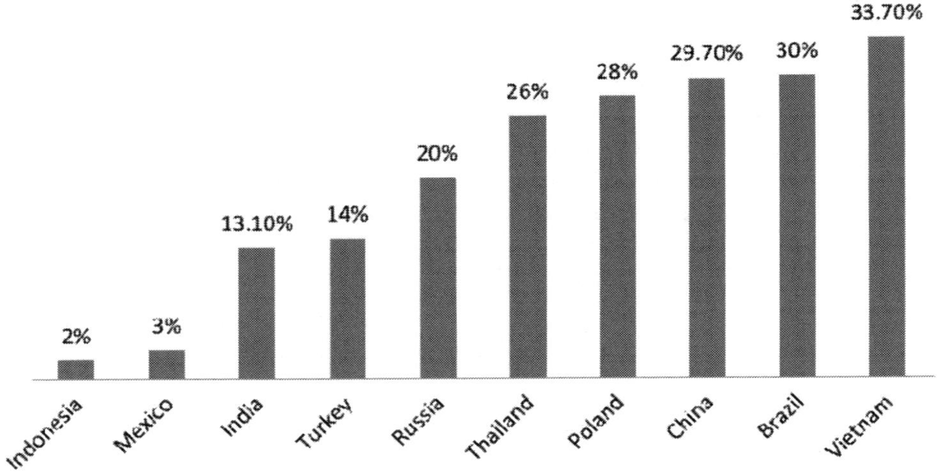

Figure 1 (b). State-owned Enterprise (SOE) output to Gross Domestic Product (GDP) in emerging economies.
Adapted from Musacchio and Lazzarini, "Leviathan in Business," 7.

has historically played a central role in the expansion of physical and human capabilities in Asia. It is a critical instrument to enhance private sector activities though the 'crowding in' effect, especially if made in areas that complement private investment. If SOEs are understood as instruments of public investment, we should be able to integrate the political economy of SOEs with an analysis of new developmentalism in emerging markets. A case needs to be made, therefore, regarding whether SOEs can be efficient and well run.

In arguing for a developmental state approach that incorporates SOEs, we begin with Ha-Joon Chang's intervention, wherein he notes that successful SOEs, such as Singapore Airlines, Korean steelmaker POSCO, and Brazilian regional jet manufacturer EMRAER, are all managed through a public trade holding company, according the government significant state control over the sector.[16] Crucially, many countries achieved economic success with a *large* SOE sector. The Singaporean government controls not only the usual industries like telecommunications, power, transport and ports, but also semiconductors, ship-building, and banking.[17] Similarly, Brazil underwent significant reforms in its SOE sector, and through its state-owned development bank BNDES, retains control over steel, mining, banking, airplane manufacturing, petrochemicals, and the oil and gas industry.[18] Historically, SOEs in OECD countries were at the forefront of industrial modernisation, for example in France, and throughout the post-WWII years, Austria, Germany, and Norway possessed large SOE sectors. Conversely, public ownership failed in Argentina and the Philippines – two widely cited examples of bad public management – and these countries had registered small SOE sectors. Between 1978 and 1991, Argentina's SOE sector only accounted for 4.7% of its GDP, which is rather miniscule compared to its neighbour Brazil whose SOE sector historically bears 30% of its GDP. While the SOE sector in Korea was at 9.9% of its GDP, that of the Philippines represented 1.9% of its GDP.[19]

Recent research shows that in emerging markets, especially Brazil, Russia, China, and India, an industrial policy focused on cultivating SOEs through monopoly and then scaling up the process of production of strategic industries seems to be becoming increasingly mainstream. There are many SOEs operating across sectors worldwide, which reflects the unrelenting presence of state participation in strategic industries in developed and developing countries. But, as our paper details later, the changing geographies of investment and shifting patterns of financial investment also mean that strategic industries in the Global South are increasingly concentrated in the field of natural resource extraction.[20] By 2014, more than three-fourths of the world's crude oil stocks were held in SOEs.[21] One explanation lies in the recent internationalisation of SOEs in emerging economies, which involve the combined strategies of outward foreign direct investment (FDI), mergers and acquisitions (M&As), and an activist state role in moulding the investment plans of state assets across the world.[22] The growing number of international operations of large SOEs from emerging countries has become a key strategy to rapidly achieve the economic scale required in pursuing large-scale developmental imperatives that are envisaged by countries like Brazil and China.

Domestically, the dominance of state ownership was justified by the principles of national security and economic autonomy from multinational capital. In many cases, military leaders were sceptical of the willingness of foreign capital in transferring knowledge, developing technological know-how, and training the local workforce to eventually transfer the management of strategic industries into domestic capitalist hands. The rationale for state companies was to ensure sufficient control over strategic industries and natural resources, which can subsequently provide policy latitude for industrial policy. Historically, it was clear for national governments that promoting SOEs was the only option to develop winning sectors given the lack of capital, unwillingness of foreign firms to invest, and the relative backwardness of domestic capitalists.[23]

In the context of economic globalisation, Chang writes about the main justifications why governments have established state companies instead of relying on private capital in generating long-term growth.[24] Firstly, state ownership offers a potential solution in situations of natural monopolies, in which the technical requirements of an industry can only be provided by one supplier who can extract high monopoly rents through pricing. As part of an industrial strategy, the monopolist can negotiate prices, especially if goods being sold are part of inputs for further production of high-capital goods. Conversely, SOEs can be set up if the state wants to counter monopoly pricing and to evenly distribute economic surpluses. Secondly, the state may set up an SOE to develop local capital markets, especially in cases of private investors refusing to finance projects that might generate high profits in the long term but bear significant risks in the short and medium term.[25] Thirdly, private investors typically bear no incentive to invest in industries that would create spillover effects to other industries without being paid for the service. For example, inputs into industrial goods production such as steel, mining, and petrochemicals are often too expensive for private sector undertaking. The state is then motivated to establish SOEs to operate in these sectors as a means to subsidise and promote cheaper inputs to industrialisation. Finally, public service provision that would not be profitable when extended to remote areas or to less profitable costumers, but is considered a 'social good', can oftentimes proffer a good reason to set up SOEs even if it runs the risk of being inefficient and costly.[26]

However, as logics of privatisation and market competition have advanced in economic governance, SOEs have often been judged in comparison with private sector performance.[27] The weakness of SOEs compared to private companies stems from fiscal and corporate governance problems. In terms of fiscal problems, the relative proximity of state companies to policy elites means that profits can be easily extracted from the SOE without going through appropriate channels of financial reporting. Unless SOEs are listed in stock markets, state managers are not legally obligated to report their financial activities, reinforcing traditional rent-seeking behaviour of politicians and state managers.[28] Conversely, the asymmetry of information between managers and politicians makes it harder for regulatory agencies to monitor SOE behaviour. When state companies are not listed in the stock markets, SOEs can become vessels of rent-seeking because there is no formal monitoring system to establish transparency in financial reporting, acquisitions, and transfer of assets. Public enterprises, in other words, must work with state agencies to enable their managers to make decisions that can compete with private firms.

Rethinking state–state relations: towards a typology of SOE reforms

The emergence of competitive SOEs amidst globalisation raises an important question: how do national governments build effective SOEs and utilise them for industrial policy? Many SOEs had to be transformed – undergoing public enterprise reforms – in OECD countries and elsewhere, and such institutional changes have focussed on state control and ownership.[29] This section outlines how to understand such changes. In Table 1, we map out corporate governance reforms in terms of (1) *centralised and decentralised* state control and (2) *majority and minority* shareholder ownership. In the first set of reforms, states can opt to create a centralised agency to monitor, regulate, and even privatise state companies. This can be undertaken either through a public holding company or a new regulatory agency to centralise information gathering and aid decision-making processes. This can partially resolve information asymmetry problems. In Brazil, the state exercises centralised control through the State-owned Enterprises Coordination and Control Department (DEST) and BNDES Participações S/A (BNDESPAR) to buy minority shares of privatised companies. In China, the State-owned Assets Supervision and Administration Commission of the State Council (SASAC) is a central government agency actively involved in the supervision of asset management for Chinese SOEs. By contrast, a decentralised approach enables specialisation of knowledge and a closer working relationship between specific agencies and state companies. Historically, this was justified as an effective way to pursue industrial policy given that policy coordination and sectoral learning can take place through the local networks of experts, entrepreneurs and local state managers.[30]

In terms of ownership structure, state companies can be partially privatised or corporatised, leading to majority or minority shareholder ownership of public firms. In a majority shareholder structure, the state through its holding company exercises control over asset management and keeps decision-making powers in the hands of governments. In a minority shareholder structure, corporate decisions are left in the hands of the market by giving private investors more leeway to influence the management of the firm. Because private actors are motivated by profit-seeking, they are likely to seek greater freedom from state control. To maintain state authority, governments oftentimes issue 'golden shares', which refer to special capital shares that accord states the right to outvote or block specific decisions as outlined in company charters. But unlike majority ownership, it does not grant any right to influence the management and decision-making processes of the firm. Using the 2 ×2 matrix, we can therefore establish four types of SOE reforms: (1) *centralised state control with majority ownership*, (2) *decentralised state control with majority ownership*, (3) *centralised state control with minority ownership*, and (4) *decentralised state control with minority ownership*.

Table 1. Typology of state-owned enterprise (SOE) reforms.

		Form of state control	
		Centralised	Decentralised
Degree of State Ownership	Majority	Government centrlises the monitoring of SOEs under one government agency or holding company – usually requires the creation of a central SOE agency or a department of SOEs to undertake monitoring, evaluation, and sometimes privatisation of state assets.+	Government leaves the monitoring, evaluation, and supervision of the SOEs to its professional managers and CEOs, offering managers very wide latitude over reporting and pursuit of multiple objectives.++
		SOE controlled by state through 50% ownership or more of shareholder capital.	SOE controlled by state through 50% ownership or more of shareholder capital.
		Examples: Brazil's Petrobras, Russia's Aeroflot, China's Chery Automobil	Examples: New Zealand's Solid Energy, Singapore's STATS ChipPAC Ltd, US' Alaska Railroad Corporation
	Minority	Government centralises the monitoring of SOEs under one government agency or holding company – usually requires the creation of a central SOE agency or a department of SOEs to undertake monitoring, evaluation, and sometimes privatisation of state assets.	Government leaves the monitoring, evaluation, and supervision of the SOE, offering managers very wide latitude over reporting and pursuit of multiple objectives.
		SOE is a mixed enterprise with a predominantly private shareholder; usually state ownership is diversified but 'golden shares' are retained by the government to ensure control over the SOE. This is oftentimes synonymous with *corporatisation* or *partial privatisation* of state assets.	SOE is a mixed enterprise with a predominantly private shareholder; usually state ownership is diversified but 'golden shares' are retained by the government to ensure control over the SOE. This is oftentimes synonymous with *corporatisation* or *partial privatisation* of state assets.
		Examples: Brazil's Vale and Embraer, China's Dazhong Transport, Russia's Rosgosstrakh	Examples: Portugal's Galp Energia, Kuwait's United Arab Shipping Company, South Korea's Hanna Financial Group

Notes: +The OECD and World Bank recommend a centralised model of management and control as a way of reducing the multiple-principals problem, enabling government to introduce ex-ante procedures to monitor state managers' behaviour, and helping to standardise financial reporting, procurement rules, etc.

++The decentralised approach was used in the 1960s and 1980s because it allowed states to pursue industrial policy through local networks of experts and firms. However, it is also the main reason for the proliferation of the multiple-principals problem and non-standardised procedures over financial reporting and auditing.

Overall, the typology offers a heuristic framework to understand public management reforms that have changed the character of SOEs. These reforms partially address principal-agency dilemmas and rent-seeking problems. However, institutional and political conditions still determine whether SOEs are able to perform their function as developmental actors. There is no conclusive evidence whether public enterprise reforms will always deliver more effective SOEs, but through these reforms, SOEs are better able to function as developmental actors.

The typology makes two important corrections in the literature as regards existing understandings of state–state relations. Firstly, institutional change that delineates state control and ownership can partially address the principal-agency problem. Consequently, public enterprise reforms (see Table 1) enable SOEs to transform themselves into vehicles of economic development, in particular, by playing a central role in new industrial policies. Our framework highlights the continuity in the role of SOEs as development actors, although the variety of different forms of state ownership is a critical factor in promoting this development strategy. We highlight in the empirical sections below that the distinctive types of state ownership that emerged around the world are based on several factors – for example, the salient features of a country's model of development, as the case of China details; the existence of a resource boom that enabled radical change in ownership policies among resource-rich states; and the enduring features of a strategic sector, notably mining, oil and gas sectors, in Brazil, Chile and elsewhere. All in all, despite the 'inefficiencies' of state ownership, our framework explains how SOEs have survived market competition and why sectors deemed strategic have remained under tight control of the state albeit with varying degrees of state participation. Secondly, while we recognise the multiple types of ownership structures in the SOE sector, it should not come as a surprise that state involvement is still associated with waste and inefficiency. Indeed, as Amsden points out, to develop and create competitive advantage in a fiercely competitive world economy requires a state that has the institutional capabilities and political will to waste resources in creating new sectors.[31] To analyse this argument, we provide real-world examples based on China and resource-rich countries, exploring the prospects and challenges of SOE-driven state-crafting.[32]

Chinese SOE and the developmental state: from insolvency to outward operations

The question of how to sustain public enterprises has been a vexing problem throughout the industrialisation process after 1978 in China. The transformation of the public sector is marked by a notable shift from the near-bankruptcy stage of SOEs in the 1980s to a remarkable marketisation and internationalisation of SOEs in the 2000s. China's market capacity has been opened up by eliminating certain characteristics of state socialism and moving towards long-term planning of distributive market economy.[33] Policy elites, in particular, have incorporated a profit-oriented motive in the SOEs, thus increasing the corporate autonomy of SOEs in China.[34] This, then, became a credible strategy as policy elites and intellectuals sought to promise economic benefits to the public in exchange of market reforms. The gradualist approach to SOE reforms was only possible if the ruling party maintained its dominance in the political system, which enabled the Communist Party to selectively open non-strategic industries for competition, to deliberately reinforce the key industries through state support, and to adopt new regulatory institutions to effectively manage the response of the Chinese state to economic changes brought forth by globalisation.[35]

However, while many commentators foretell the demise of the state-owned economy, there is a conspicuous resurgence of China's SOEs in the context of globalisation. After the painful restructuring during the 1990s and with the help of a specific industrial policy, Chinese SOEs seem to carry a more competitive organisation of assets, thanks to active state support under the 'bigger, stronger and superior' campaign ('*zuoda, zuoqiang, zuoyou*'). This, then, deliberately transformed the SOEs *without* privatisation to enhance their performance, such that a new development strategy distinctive from standard neoliberal practices elsewhere has been deployed by the Chinese state. In hindsight, the strategy was to keep *central enterprises* as the mainstay development actor in the economy. Based on Table 1, the majority of Chinese SOEs consist of majority shareholder ownership structures with high levels of political and institutional controls through a centralised regulatory agency. Through these reforms, state managers were able to seek technology upgrading and to invite private entrepreneurs to participate in the sectors.

The top and most centrally governed entities are those situated in the core strategic industries – oil, electricity, banks, aircraft – which are then often referred to as central SOEs, located at the commanding heights of the economy. These 53 central SOEs are owned by SASAC majority share and their organisational structure is typically very centralised, with senior executives appointed by the Central Organization Department and systematically rotated regularly.[36] In addition, even in the Party's *nomenklatura* system, there is a set of mechanisms increasingly implemented for the central party apparatus to grasp more control over its business sector, through which cadre rotation has increasingly occurred between SOE executives and provincial leaders.[37] This approach prevents the potential slippage of sensitive information while at the same time narrowing the gap of interests between the Communist Party and the state managers. During the reorganisation of the company, the party-state has sought to strengthen its monitoring capabilities and reduced information asymmetry (as a way to resolve the principal-agency dilemma) by institutionalising *ex ante* mechanisms within the SOEs. Such mechanisms include attempts at establishing a single supervision agency and reforms aimed at improving the *nonmenklatura* system[38] to mitigate divergent interests between SOEs and the party-state.

The second category, or the middle tier of the industry, includes companies which the central government considers important but which are intent on loosening regulations such as pharmaceuticals and new energy equipment manufacturing sectors.[39] In this tier, there is a mixture of central and local industries, but the common denominator is that they are both supervised under a relatively decentralised form of regulatory mechanisms. The final category, or the last tier of the industry, includes the services, retail and small- and medium-sized manufacturing sectors.[40] These industries are perceived by the Chinese state as non-strategic and small scale, with the vast majority belonging to state-owned township enterprises in the rural areas. They are highly decentralised and are controlled by minority state-linked institutional holders.

Unlike the emphasis on state–business alliances in East Asian developmental state models, the Chinese developmental state can be best described as a complex network of public and private entities. Since the introduction of the Company Law in 1994 and within the three-tier economic structure explained above, a network of central, local public enterprises and private entrepreneurs has been formed through which foreign managerial experience has been learnt and adopted in the Chinese environment. State support to acquire technological learning is particularly salient at the top and middle levels of SOEs. Key measures aimed at more efficient industrialisation have been implemented to ensure the survival and subsequent thriving of public enterprises in China. One of these strategies includes the renationalisation of private competitive assets, which in recent times has become a priority for the Communist Party.[41] The new policy campaign promotes mixed ownership, which led to a series of reforms that offer SOEs with corporate practices on how to form diversified ownership structures and how to restructure private and state assets to enhance sectoral competitiveness. In practice, the state emphasises the flow of capital between public and private sectors, seeking to boost specific industries by injecting or merging state and private shares, depending on their comparative advantages and whether such companies offer public services. These measures have been deployed through several parallel mechanisms: investment shares, public and private joint investments, and the establishment of co-sponsored funds of industrial 'private–public partnership' management. In many high-tech sectors, for instance, the main innovation capacity is driven by private enterprises.[42] But where capital facilities remain relatively scarce, state-owned capital is considered one of the resources for enterprise development. In the process, private shareholders transfer their shares to state-owned capital, and the private sector has also been able to obtain equity in SOEs through capital increase.[43]

In strategic areas of science and technology, China seems to have followed moderate East Asian success with a particular focus on the optimisation of state-owned assets. Examining Taiwan's industrial upgrading strategy, Chu and Amsden show that latecomers to technological innovation involves a learning phase and capacity-building for firms.[44] In the first phase, economic actors must learn specific knowledge for new products over a period of time until firms reach a critical point where scale of mass production is possible. The second phase involves strengthening firm capacity for execution and production aimed at lowering costs and rapidly obtaining excess of market share. The role of industrial policy, then, is to support firms through publicly financed research and to create development institutes and state-led industrial clusters that would be able to stimulate local employment opportunities. It is noteworthy that such a local system has been inherited from the early administrative decentralisation through which the local government has received economic policy latitude from the central government in the 1950s. Instead of production units, the discretionary power was transferred to the hands of provincial government officials.[45] In Schurmann's term, this pattern of decentralisation in China should be considered 'the second type of decentralisation' (Decentralisation 2), and such decentralisation has facilitated local governments' autonomy, which is different from the first type of decentralisation (Decentralisation 1) which occurred under the Soviet regime where effective economic decisions making processes have been impeded by multiple organisational decision makers. After China's political transition, the provincial party committee was able to enjoy more economic autonomy,[46] and the provision of such institutional changes built a system basis for China's economic rise after 1978.[47] In this context, SOEs have obtained rapid access to funding for carrying on research and development and for securing capital to generate economic output.

The Chinese example demonstrates the need to coordinate SOE reforms and risky industrial policy. The Chinese state has thus far implemented 'price-wrong' instruments[48] and created policy networks similar to traditional developmental states that have supported domestic firms in finding their niche in science and technology sectors. Policy instruments such as tariff protection for specific industries and local content requirements are adopted from abroad,[49] relying on state-owned development banks for the ventures of new industries and cooperating with foreign companies to construct industrial parks.[50] In terms of fiscal measures, a variety of tax deductions are designed for selected enterprises and/or sectors[51] to rapidly transform the labour-intensive export economic structure into a model that has the potential to create added value and local high-salary opportunities. In developing the appropriate technological expertise, Chinese enterprises, whether in key strategic industries (especially SOEs) or in the competitive private sector, have sought overseas acquisitions as a means to acquire the technical capacity and international management experience.[52] In 2001, after joining the World Trade Organization, China lifted tight control measures to further promote and encourage the global expansion of large SOEs. Although the approach of early expansion strategies was based on resource exploitation, this expansion has opened up a new pathway for rapid capital accumulation. In addition to targeted support through the state-owned banks,[53] SOEs have attempted to obtain funds from international capital markets. Since the late 1990, SOEs have been listed on the Hong Kong and New York stock exchanges. In other words, state managers are undertaking new commercial strategies similar to private investors by way of market expansion through domestic and international mergers, particularly with companies in other emerging market economies, such as the Indonesian Energy Corporation.[54] Overall, China's SOEs, through non-neoliberal reforms, have been listing their assets without privatisation, seeking technological upgrading through overseas expansion, and consolidating their political control to a considerable extent through the restructuring of property rights. It has not only adjusted the state–state relationships for development purposes, but has equally strengthened the firm capacity of SOEs in conjunction with a carefully formulated industrial policy. This, then, allows the state to design a development-oriented national strategy focusing on state-owned economy. Although some scholars have suggested that lifting government intervention from the market would be the necessary prescription for sustainable economic growth,[55] our argument is that there is an alternative for the developing world. The Chinese state has attempted to draw lessons from the successful private sector and strategically incorporate such experience into the state economic structure, seeking to upgrade SOEs as the main actors of developmental capacity in the context of post-neoliberalism.

The potential for SOE-based resource growth

An important turn of events in the developing world since the 2000s has been the renationalisation of privatised assets in the mining sector and the reorganisation of the oil and gas industry in favour of direct state participation. However, prior to these reforms, the neoliberal revolution in the early 1980s combined with a commodity price downturn compelled economic restructuring in the global extractive industry. Apart from increasing problems with ineffectiveness and poor management of SOEs, resulting poor profits and industry decline were exacerbated by low commodity prices throughout the 1990s. By the early 2000s, metal mining was almost completely privatised, and what remains are a few exclusive or well-performing companies like Chile's Codelco, Sweden's LKAB, Polish Copper, and NDMC in India while others like Venezuelan iron ore and other parts of India are kept under state hands for its long-term potential.[56] Many governments implemented market opening reforms that removed discriminatory barriers against transnational mining capital, the establishment of a contracts-based regime that supports private property rights for mineral exploration and development, and, crucially, a fiscal strategy that attracts corporations through low taxation and minimal royalties.[57]

Despite the wave of privatisation and market competition in extractive industries, the market power of SOEs differs between the mining and the oil and gas industries. This is largely an outcome of the market structure of the sectors. Since most mining companies in the developing world have been successfully privatised, the big players in the global mining industry are either Western transnational companies or SOEs from BRIC countries. As Figure 2 demonstrates, metal mining has experienced a steady decline in state control although some countries have managed to retain their SOEs (notably Chile's Codelco, Brazil's Vale and CSN, and Korea's Posco) through the aforementioned reforms in state ownership and control. Importantly, as Figure 2 shows, state control was maintained in the sector largely as a result of China's aggressive acquisition of new mines through its state-controlled enterprises. By contrast, Figure 3 shows the persistence of dominant state control through national oil companies (NOCs) in the oil industry, where they control 58% of world oil supply and where 100 companies produce 82% of crude oil. Among the top oil exporters, SOEs have experienced dramatic reforms in order to retain their market share in the sector.[58] The oil and gas industry remains subject to direct state participation, which became possible through SOE reforms on ownership structure and control. Since oil and gas is often associated with industrialisation and energy security, policy elites resisted the privatisation of national oil companies.

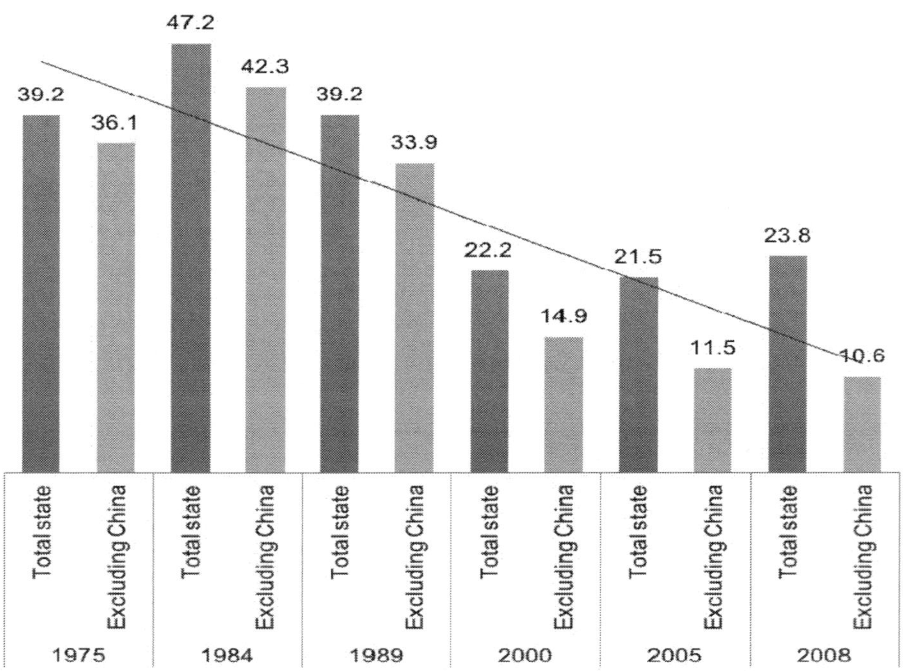

Figure 2. State shares of global metal mine production value (% of total value).
Raw materials data for 2010 cited and adapted from World Bank, *Overview of State Ownership*. The metal minerals include the following: bauxite, copper, gold, iron ore, lead, manganese, nickel, tin and zinc.

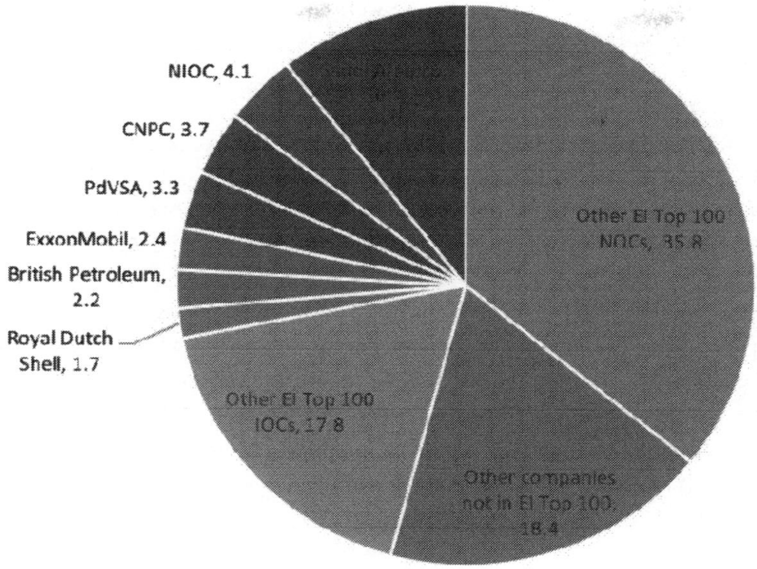

Figure 3. Share of world oil production by type of company, 2014.
Note: EI – Extractive Industry.

While controversial in the political economy literature, it is plausible to argue that SOEs can play a vital role in economic development through natural resources. Firstly, SOEs provide a direct mechanism for national governments to maximise rent capture especially during a price boom. Given that imposing a royalty or increasing mining taxes often involves complex legislative processes, state companies are relatively easier channels through which the state can extract mineral rents without significant changes in institutional configuration. While the political decision over how mineral rents are allocated and invested are undoubtedly salient in realising industrialisation objectives, developing-country governments oftentimes face a more basic challenge, namely how to establish a political bargain with transnational companies over taxation and rent extraction. Mining states often suffer from low tax capture and a fragile political relationship with global capital. At subnational levels, mining provinces experience a 'local resource curse' as communities suffer from lack of social mobility, limited employment opportunities, and disproportionate environmental impacts. To remedy this problem, some countries like Brazil and Chile have utilised their SOEs as a *buffer* between the state and private sector, leading to greater fiscal resource capture and more leverage over investment decisions.

Secondly, extractive state companies can function as a catalyst for effective industrial policy. The recent experience of oil and gas exporters is instructive, in situations where governments explicitly linked their oil policy with national industrialisation. Unlike mining, crude oil serves as an input or intermediate product for transportation, capital goods formation, and technological development in various fields of engineering and science. Through a well-crafted industrial strategy, the oil and gas sector can become instrumental in adding value to crude oil, creating a high-quality labour force, and producing intermediate goods through vertical or horizontal integration. As an example, Brazil's Petrobras has historically played a role in creating the oil industry despite the absence of proven oil reserves between the 1950s and the 1970s. The company began by importing crude oil from overseas, and then investing in its refining capacity to create gasoline, diesel, and other petrochemicals. In the process, Petrobras expanded its operations from exploration to transport, petrochemicals, and even renewable energy. Thanks to its culture of innovation, Petrobras was also able to train engineers and geologists, to establish research activities with universities and institutes, and to enhance technological learning that eventually led Petrobras to become a leading firm with deep-sea engineering technology. The history of Brazil's oil enterprise is a reminder that when state companies are run efficiently, there is potential for future industries to be built through the natural resource sector.

The possibilities for economic development through natural resource SOEs are, however, based on a premise that state companies can be managed well. Hence, our typology provides a roadmap in order to understand varying patterns of state control and ownership in the natural resources sector. As Table 1 notes, state control over the industry directly influences the balance of power between the state, SOE, and global mining capital. In many countries, mining is often managed through a *decentralised* approach. There are very few examples where a single agency or public holding company is created to manage the SOE. Even in a highly centralised country like Brazil, competition in the mining industry is managed very loosely. The previously state-owned firm Vale was partially privatised from 100% to minority ownership.[59] Since a decentralised approach requires an institutional overhaul, it is more difficult to rely on mining SOEs to promote industrial policy. In this context, developing-country governments have relied on partial renationalisation (ie acquiring majority shareholding assets of SOEs) and taxation reform packages as a means to promote economic growth through mining. African and Latin American governments sought for the partial renationalisation of their previously privatised state enterprises, which effectively forced transnational mining capital to sell these assets below market prices, as observed in Bolivia and Argentina. Based on our typology, renationalisation exhibits a change from minority/private shareholder to majority state ownership.[60]

The policy dynamics in the oil and gas industry is quite different from that of the mining sector. Unlike in the minerals sector, resource nationalism has historically offered a coherent framework through which regulatory reforms in the oil industry were embraced. The historical weight of SOEs is a reflection of the oligopolistic market structure of the oil industry; it is also the manifestation of state power through which national security is protected. Hence, the sector is managed through a *centralised* approach, meaning that a single agency and/or public trading company is in charge with the governance of state companies. Brazil, for example, created a regulatory agency called ANP to manage the sales of oil reservoirs and to facilitate joint ventures between Petrobras and foreign companies. In poorer countries with weaker institutional capacity (eg Angola), the government has made a conscious decision to centralise decision-making through the state enterprise rather than creating a separate regulatory agency. This, then, concentrates institutionalised expertise into one institution as a way to overcome the notable absence of human capital in the country.

Having said this, the extent to which NOCs are developmental has been subject to intense academic debates, and even extensive comparative studies such as Victor et al.'s *Oil and Governance* could only make context-specific conclusions. While the propensity for rent-seeking and principal-agency dilemmas is recognised in the literature, there is comparative evidence that some SOEs can perform at par with private firms. Highly efficient state companies in the oil industry do exist, although we should recognise that SOE reforms are politically costly, and therefore there are many examples of poorly managed SOEs. Notable exceptions include Brazil's Petrobras (which was arguably well managed until the Workers' Party came to power), Norway's Statoil, and Malaysia's Petronas, whereby a culture of innovation and successful investment in R&D catapulted positive changes in SOE performance. These firms undertook corporate governance reforms that improved financial reporting, increased the number of professionals in the Board of Directors, and ultimately, separated the structures of ownership and control.[61]

None of the discussion above means that we can completely eliminate the problem of rent-seeking that is often the principal motivation for SOE privatisation. As the corruption scandal in Brazil demonstrates, one can have a highly efficient, technologically advanced SOE like Petrobras while simultaneously operating in a political system entrenched in corruption and rent-seeking. These are quite distinctive problems, and it is vital that policy elites are able to distinguish policy solutions that will promote corporate autonomy of SOEs and reduce clientelism and rent-seeking within the state system.

Conclusions

The comparative analysis of China and resource-based SOEs as well as our theoretical framework leads us to make three conclusions. Firstly, despite privatisation and market competition, state enterprises have remained important actors in development. If developmental state theory is to remain relevant, it needs to consider not only state–business relations but also state–state relations as the foundation of innovative development policymaking. Secondly, there are many factors that influence the decision to retain SOEs and support their developmental roles – a country's model of development based on state capitalism, the strategic relevance of a sector to government policy, and the particular features of an industry. Finally, after establishing the rationale to maintain SOEs, we analysed contemporary economic reforms in the public enterprise sector that provided states with greater capacity to overcome traditional problems associated with state companies. Across the cases, we argue that corporate governance reforms, especially on state ownership and control, have been the most significant strategies to strengthen firm capabilities of SOEs, enabling them to meet both commercial and non-commercial objectives.

To conclude, we highlight the implications for developing countries if a new developmental strategy requires a more robust SOE sector. The first implication is that the political contexts of SOE reforms are embedded in highly contentious policymaking arenas. For late innovators such as Brazil and China, there are multiple governance dilemmas ranging from fragmentation of decision-making especially between central and regional/local SOEs, the extent to which SOEs can 'crowd out' private firms, and the necessity for a coherent approach in policy coordination between state managers and government bureaucrats. The East Asian model has relied on targeted support and a clear punitive mechanism for maintaining fairness over the performance of economic actors. However, state companies are still embedded in party politics, especially in the case of China, and this means that its capability for resource allocation may be compromised depending on the degree of autonomy from politicians. This change in political–business relations has become increasingly evident in recent days. For instance, in their 2015 policy document, the Chinese Communist Party Central Committee and the State Council introduced the 'Guidelines on Deepening the Reform of State-Owned Enterprises', in which Article 7 clearly stipulates that the party secretary should 'diligently fulfil the first responsibilities of party building work'. In practice, the party-state has explicitly required state managers to incorporate the party secretary into the corporate governance structure, thereby giving the party secretary genuine authority in the business sector. At the same time, the party organisations are encouraged to be involved in the future central SOE economic decision-making, as there are pre-procedures requiring the board members and top executives to report major issues to the party organisation for investigation prior to decisions being concluded.[62] While policy creativity and institutionalised expertise are crucial for any SOE reform, diverse political contexts in the developing world mean that no quick fix exists to address rent-seeking, inefficiency, and corruption.

Secondly, we note that SOE reforms focussed on ownership and control may not always lead to the 'right sort' of institutional change needed for industrialisation. While centralised regulatory interventions were implemented in Brazil, China, and other countries to mitigate the principal-agency problem, SOEs can still lead to local capture and rent-seeking, thereby making the SOE an obstacle rather than a solution to the implementation of national industrial policies. Local protection of strategic assets can sometimes obstruct the implementation of a performance-based industrial policy. A case-by-case analysis should be considered when policymakers are making political decisions over what routes of reforms to pursue. In this context, privatisation might be a better option given that the corporate governance reforms are unlikely to address the problems. In addition, the problems of SOEs might also be rooted in other areas, such as the practice of hiring personnel and building a professionalised bureaucracy. The practice of hiring professional civil servants may not always be addressed by corporate governance reforms; instead, public administrative reforms involving merit-based qualifications may well have greater impacts in improving the overall quality of the SOE rank and file. Overall, SOE reforms should be widely understood as an attempt to improve the efficiency and day-to-day operations of the company. As such, context-specific analysis of SOE reforms is the best way to achieve the developmental potential of state companies.

The task of this paper was to identify the role of SOEs in economic development and the ways in which reforms can enhance the overall capacity of public enterprises. We have shown that SOEs have been largely ignored by the developmental state literature, and in light of the post-2000 changes in the global political economy, we should reconsider SOEs as part of a new developmental strategy. We then used examples from China and resource-based SOEs to illustrate the linkages between state ownership and economic development. We hope that the paper has shed light on a very complex and controversial topic. Our main contribution is to provide theoretical basis and empirical nuance as regards the possibility for state companies to become a developmental actor.

Disclosure statement

No potential conflict of interest was reported by the authors.

Acknowledgements

We would like to acknowledge Pablo Heidrich, Isamu Okada, and Jesse Ovadia as well as the anonymous reviewers for their comments.

Notes

1. Chang, *State-Owned Enterprise Reform*; Mussachio et al., "New Varieties of State Capitalism"; OECD, *Size and Sectoral Distribution of SOEs*; OECD, *Broadening the Ownership*.
2. OECD, *Broadening the Ownership*, 15.
3. OECD, *Broadening the Ownership*, 52.
4. Li and Cui, *Impact of Capital Structure on Agency Costs*, 94; see also Xu, *State-Owned Enterprises in China*.
5. Strategic SOEs are either those firms in charge of exploring and exploiting non-renewable natural resources like oil, gas and mining enterprises, or firms providing basic public services such as electricity, water and sewage, and waste management.
6. Mussachio et al., "Leviathan in Business"; Nem Singh and Massi, "Resource Nationalism."
7. Sheshinski and Lopez-Calva, "Privatization and Its Benefits."
8. Amsden, *Escape from Empire*, 142–7.
9. Hickey et al., *Politics of Inclusive Development*; Whitfield et al., *Politics of African Industrial Policy*.
10. Evans, *Embedded Autonomy*.
11. Doner et al., "Systemic Vulnerability."
12. Saylor, *State Building in Boom Times*; Whitfield et al., *Politics of African Industrial Policy*.
13. Hsueh, *China's Regulatory State*; Breslin, "The 'China Model' and the Global Crisis."
14. Amsden, *Asia's Next Giant*; Johnson, *Miti and the Japanese Miracle*; Wade, *Governing the Market*.
15. Amsden, *Asia's Next Giant*.
16. Chang, *State-Owned Enterprise Reform*, 8.
17. Chang, *State-Owned Enterprise Reform*.
18. Massi, this volume.
19. Chang, *State-Owned Enterprise Reform*, 11.
20. Nem Singh and Bourgouin, *Resource Governance and Developmental States*.
21. UNCTAD. *World Investment Report 2014*, 21.

22. SOEs in emerging economies such as China and Russia have been simultaneously acquiring assets from other countries. CNOOC's acquisition of Nexen in Canada and Rosneft acquisition of BP's 50% of assets, making it the world's largest oil and gas company.
23. Massi, *Political Economy of Development Finance*.
24. Chang, *State-Owned Enterprise Reform*, 12–3.
25. OECD, *State-Owned Enterprises in the Development Process*.
26. Mann, "Autonomous Power of the State."
27. Shirley, "Bureaucrats in Business."
28. OECD, *Size and Sectoral Distribution of SOEs*.
29. Bruton et al., "Entrepreneurship and Strategy in Emerging Economies."
30. Amsden, *Escape from Empire*.
31. Amsden, *Escape from Empire*.
32. Bruton et al., "Entrepreneurship and Strategy in Emerging Economies," 101; Musacchio, Lazzarini, and Aguilera, "New Varieties of State Capitalism"; Wade, *Governing the Market*; Mussachio and Lazzarinni, *Reinventing State Capitalism*; Nem Singh, *Building Developmental Capacity*.
33. Walder, "China's Bureaucratic Capitalism."
34. McNally, "Sino-Capitalism," 753–4.
35. Hsueh, *China's Regulatory State*.
36. Pearson, "State-Owned Business and Party-State Regulation."
37. Brødsgaard , "Cadre and Personnel Management in the CPC," 77.
38. Brødsgaard, "Politics and Business Group Formation."
39. Pearson, "State-Owned Business and Party-State Regulation."
40. Ibid.
41. NDRC, *State-Owned Enterprise Mixed Ownership Reform*; People's Daily, "Report of State-Owned Assets Management."
42. For instance, Huawei has been outperformed by SOEs in patent application and Research and Development (R&D) spending, which, as a solely owned private telecommunication enterprise, was not funded by the central government's capital.
43. NDRC, *State-Owned Enterprise Mixed Ownership Reform*, 83–97.
44. Amsden, *Beyond Late Development*.
45. Schurmann, *Ideology and Organization in Communist China*, 175.
46. Ibid, 176.
47. Such autonomy also paves the way for the divergence of institutional adaptability and the attributes of state–economic actors' relationships in local development. See Shen and Tsai, "Institutional Adaptability in China"; Goodman, *China's Regional Development*.
48. Chen and Lees, "Growing China's Renewables Sector," 578.
49. Lewis, "Rise of Renewable Energy Protectionism."
50. Yeung, "Local Politics and Foreign Ventures"; Yeung, "Regional Development and the Competitive Dynamics."
51. Amsden and Chu, *Beyond Late Development*.
52. Haft, *Unmade in China*, 70; Nolan, *Is China Buying the World?*
53. Wang, "China's Dualist Model," 390.
54. However, such a successful listing was usually based on the separation between productive and nonproductive assets. Nonproductive assets such as social security and education allowances are classified as the duties of unlisted parent companies, which are no longer bearded by listed corporations.
55. Naughton, "China's Economic Policy Today"; Lardy, *Markets over Mao*.
56. World Bank, *Overview of State Ownership*, 4, 31.
57. World Bank, *Overview of State Ownership*.
58. Victor, Hults and Thurber, *Oil and Governance*.
59. Nem Singh and Massi, "Resource Nationalism."
60. However, state control is harder to execute because institutional change requires the creation of a new public holding company or a regulatory agency that has substantial powers to reorganise state–market relations in the industry.

61. Jones Luong and Weinthal, *Oil is not a Curse*; Pargendler et al., "In Strange Company."
62. Yang and Lin, "Fostering the Implementation of the Party."

Bibliography

Amsden, Alice H. *Asia's Next Giant: South Korea and Late Industrialization*. Oxford: Oxford University Press, 1992.

Amsden, Alice H. *Escape from Empire: The Developing World's Journey through Heaven and Hell*. Cambridge, MA: MIT Press, 2007.

Amsden, Alice H, and Wan-wen Chu. *Beyond Late Development: Taiwan's Upgrading Policies*. Cambridge, MA: MIT Press, 2003.

Breslin, S. "The 'China Model' and the Global Crisis: From Friedrich List to a Chinese Mode of Governance?" *International Affaires* 87, no. 6 (2011): 1323–1343.

Brødsgaard, Kjeld Erik ."Politics and Business Group Formation in China: The Party In Control?." *The China Quarterly* 211 (2012): 624 –648.

Brødsgaard, Kjeld Erik. "Cadre and the Personal Management in the CPC." *China: An International Journal* 10, no. 2, August (2012): 69–83.

Bruton, Garry D., Igor Filatotchev, Steven Si, and Mike Wright. "Entrepreneurship and Strategy in Emerging Economies." *Strategic Entrepreneurship Journal* 7, no. 3 (September 1, 2013): 169–180.

Chang, H.-J. *State-Owned Enterprise Reform*. National Development Strategies. New York: United Nations, 2007.

Chen, G. C., and C. Lees. "Growing China's Renewables Sector: A Developmental State Approach." *New Political Economy* 21, no. 6, (2016): 574–586.

Doner, Richard F., Bryan K. Ritchie, and Dan Slater. "Systemic Vulnerability and the Origins of Developmental States: Northeast and Southeast Asia in Comparative Perspective." *International Organization* 59, no. 2 (2005): 327–361.

Evans, Peter B., and Embedded Autonomy. *States and Industrial Transformation*. Princeton, N.J.: Princeton University Press, 1995.

Goodman, S. G. D., ed. *China's Regional Development*. London: Routledge, 2013.

Haft, Jeremy. *Unmade in China: The Hidden Truth about China's Economic Miracle*. Cambridge: Polity Press, 2015.

Hickey, Sam, Kunal Sen, and Badru Bukenya. *The Politics of Inclusive Development: Interrogating the Evidence*. Oxford: Oxford University Press, 2014.

Hong, Eunsuk, and Laixiang Sun. "Dynamics of Internationalization and Outward Investment: Chinese Corporations' Strategies." *China Quarterly* 187 (2006): 610–634.

Hsueh, Roselyn. *China's Regulatory State: A New Strategy for Globalization*. Ithaca: Cornell University Press, 2011.

Johnson, Chalmers. *Miti and the Japanese Miracle: The Growth of Industrial Policy, 1925–1975*. Stanford: Stanford University Press, 1982.

Jones Luong, Pauline, and Erika Weinthal. *Oil is Not a Curse: Ownership Structure and Institutions in Soviet Successor States*. Cambridge: Cambridge University Press, 2010.

Kennedy, Andrew B. "Slouching Tiger, Roaring Dragon: Comparing India and China as Late Innovators." *Review of International Political Economy* 23, no. 1 (January 2, 2016): 65–92.

Kernen, Antoine, and Katy N. Lam. "Workforce Localization among Chinese State-Owned Enterprises (SOEs) in Ghana." *Journal of Contemporary China* 23, no. 90 (November 2, 2014): 1053–1072.

Kwiatkowski, Grzegorz, and Paweł Augustynowicz. "State-Owned Enterprises in the Global Economy – Analysis Based on Fortune Global 500 List." paper presented at Managing Intellectual Capital and Innovation for Sustainable and Inclusive Society, Bari, Italy, May 27–29, 2016.

Lardy, N. R. *Markets over Mao: The Rise of Private Business in China*. New York: Columbia University Press, 2014.

Lewis, Joanna I. "The Rise of Renewable Energy Protectionism: Emerging Trade Conflicts and Implications for Low Carbon Development." *Global Environmental Politics* 14, no. 4 (November 2014): 10–35.

Li, H., and L. Cui. "Impact of Capital Structure on Agency Costs in Chinese Liked Firms." In *Globalisation, Competition and Growth in China*, edited by J. Chen and S. Yao, 94–110. Abingdon: Routledge, 2006.

Lu, Xiaobo. "Booty Socialism, Bureau-Preneurs, and the State in Transition: Organizational Corruption in China." *Comparative Politics* 32, no. 3 (April 1, 2000): 273–294.

Mann, Michael. "The Autonomous Power of the State: Its Origins, Mechanisms and Results." *Archives Europeénes De Sociologie* 25 (1984): 185–213.

Massi, Eliza. *The Political Economy of Development Finance: The BNDES and Brazilian Industrialisation.* PhD diss., School for Oriental and African Studies, University of London, 2014.

McNally, Christopher A. "Sino-Capitalism: China's Reemergence and the International Political Economy." *World Politics* 64, no. 4 (October 2012): 741–776.

Musacchio, Aldo, and Sérgio G. Lazzarini. *Reinventing State Capitalism: Leviathan in Business, Brazil and Beyond*. Cambridge, MA: Harvard University Press, 2014.

Musacchio, Aldo, and Sérgio G. Lazzarini. "Leviathan in Business: Varieties of State Capitalism and Their Implications for Economic Performance." SSRN Scholarly Paper. Rochester, NY: Social Science Research Network. Accessed May 30, 2012. https://papers.ssrn.com/abstract=2070942

Musacchio, Aldo, Sérgio G. Lazzarini, and Ruth V. Aguilera. "New Varieties of State Capitalism: Strategic and Governance Implications." *The Academy of Management Perspectives* 29, no. 1 (February 1, 2015): 115–131.

Musacchio, Aldo, Pineda Emilio, and García, Gustavo. *State-Owned Enterprise Reform in Latin America. Issues and Possible Solutions*. IDB Discussion Paper 401. Washington, DC: Inter-American Development Bank, 2015.

Naughton, B. "China's Economic Policy Today: The New State Activism." *Eurasian Geography and Economics* 52, no. 3 (2011): 313–329.

NDRC. *State-Owned Enterprise Mixed Ownership Reform – Interpretation of the Development of Mixed Ownership Economic Policy* (In Chinese). Beijing: People'sPress, 2015.

Nee, Victor, and Sonja Opper. *Capitalism from Below: Markets and Institutional Change in China*. Cambridge, MA: Harvard University Press, 2012.

Nem Singh, Jewellord. *Building Developmental Capacity: State-Owned Enterprises and Natural Resources in Latin America*. forthcoming.

Nem Singh, Jewellord, and France Bourgouin. *Resource Governance and Developmental States in the Global South: Critical International Political Economy Perspectives*. Basingstoke: Palgrave Macmillan, 2013.

Nem Singh, Jewellord, and Eliza Massi. "Resource Nationalism and Brazil's Post- Neoliberal Strategy." In *The Political Economy of Natural Resources and Development: From Neoliberalism to Resource Nationalism*, edited by Paul Haslam and Pablo Heidrich, 158–173. London: Routledge, 2016.

Nolan, Peter. *Is China Buying the World?* Cambridge: Polity, 2012.

OECD. *The Size and Sectoral Distribution of SOEs in OECD and Partner Countries*. Paris: OECD Publishing, 2014.

OECD. *State-Owned Enteprises in the Development Process*. Paris: OECD Publishing, 2015.

OECD. *Broadening the Ownership of State-Owned Enterprises: A Comparison of Governance Practices.* Paris: OECD Publishing, 2016.

Pargendler, Mariana, Aldo Musacchio, and Sergio Lazzarini. "In Strange Company: The Puzzle of Private Investment in State-Controlled Firms." *Cornell International Law Journal* 46, no. 3 (2013): 569–610.

People's Daily. 2016. "The Report of State-Owned Assets Management and System Reform Shows Nearly 70% of the Central SOEs Are of Mixed Ownership Structure (in Chinese)." July 1. Accessed November 1, 2016, http://paper.people.com.cn/rmrb/html/2016-07/01/nw.D110000renmrb_20160701_3-03.htm

Priest, Tyler. "Petrobras in the History of Offshore Oil." In *Ben Ross Schneider, Editor, New Order and Progress: Development and Democracy in Brazil*. Oxford: Oxford University Press, 2016, 53–77.

PwC. *State-Owned Enterprises: Catalysts for Public Value Creation?*. Accessed December 3, 2016, http://www.pwc.com/gx/en/industries/government-public-services/public-sector-research-centre/publications/state-owned-enterprises.html

Saylor, Ryan. *State Building in Boom times: Commodities and Coalitions in Latin America and Africa*. Oxford: Oxford University Press, 2014.

Schurmann, F. *Ideology and Organization in Communist China*. Berkeley, CA: University of California Press, 1966.

Shen, X., and K. S. Tsai. "Institutional Adaptability in China: Local Developmental Models under Changing Economic Conditions." *World Development* 87 (2016): 107–127.

Sheshinski, E. "And Luis Felipe Lopez-Calva "Privatization and Its Benefits: Theory and Evidence."" *CESifo Economic Studies* 49 (2003): 429–459.

Shirley, M. "Bureaucrats in Business: The Roles of Privatization versus Corporatization in State-Owned Enterprise Reform." *World Development* 27, no. 1 (1999): 115–136.

The Chinese Communist Party Central Committee and the State Council. "Guidelines on Deepening the Reform of State-Owned Enterprises (In Chinese)." August 24, 2015. Accessed April 26, 2017. http://www.gov.cn/zhengce/2015-09/13/content_2930440.htm

Tordo, S., and Y. Anouti. *Local Content in the Oil and Gas Sector: Case Studies*. Washington, DC: The World Bank, 2013.

Tordo, S., M. Warner, O. E. Manzano, and Y. Anouti. *Local Content Policies in the Oil and Gas Sector*. Washington, DC: The World Bank, 2013.

UNCTAD. *World Investment Report 2014*. Geneva: UNCTAD, 2014.

Victor, David, David Hults, and Mark Thurber, eds. *Oil and Governance: State-Owned Enterprises and the World Energy Supply*. Cambridge: Cambridge University Press, 2012.

Wade, R. *Governing the Market: Economic Theory and the Role of Government in East Asian Industrialization*. Princeton: Princeton University Press, 1990.

Walder, Andrew G. "China's Bureaucratic Capitalism: Creating the Corporate Steel Sector." In *Globalization and Public Sector Reform in China*, edited by Kjeld Erik Brødsgaard, 159–176. London: Routlede, 2014.

Wang, Jenn-hwan. "China's Dualist Model on Technological Catching up: A Comparative Perspective." *The Pacific Review* 19, no. 3 (September 1, 2006): 385–403.

Whitfield, Lindsay, Ole Therkildsen, Lars Buur, and Anne Mette Kjar. *The Politics of African Industrial Policy. a Comparative Perspective*. Cambridge: Cambridge University Press, 2015.

World Bank. *Overview of State Ownership in the Global Minerals Industry*. Washington, D.C.: World Bank, 2011.

Xu, G. 2010. "State-Owned Enterprises in China: How Big Are They?" World Bank, January 19. http://blogs.worldbank.org/eastasiapacific/state-owned-enterprises-in-china-how-big-are-they.

Yang, Y., and Y. Lin. 2017. "Fostering the Implementation of the Party Building Responsibility in Central SOEs." *Economic Information Daily*, February 23. http://dz.jjckb.cn/www/pages/webpage2009/html/2017-02/23/content_28824.htm

Yeung, Henry Wai-chung. "Local Politics and Foreign Ventures in China's Transitional Economy: The Political Economy of Singaporean Investments in China." *Political Geography* 19, no. 7 (September 2000): 809–840.

Yeung, Henry Wai-chung. "Regional Development and the Competitive Dynamics of Global Production Networks: An East Asian Perspective." *Regional Studies* 43, no. 3 (April 2009): 325–351.

Yeung, Henry Wai-chung, and Weidong Liu. "Globalizing China: The Rise of Mainland Firms in the Global Economy." *Eurasian Geography and Economics* 49, no. 1 (January 1, 2008): 57–86.

Yip, George S, and Bruce McKern. *China's Next Strategic Advantage: From Imitation to Innovation*. Cambridge, MA: MIT Press, 2016.

The developmental state of the twenty-first century: accounting for state and society

Jennifer Hsu

ABSTRACT
As development is no longer simply conceived of as economic growth, but also as encapsulating human development, the role of the developmental state must be rethought. Focusing on the state's ability to deliver collective goods such as welfare has become an important task for developing and developed nations alike, and nowhere is this more important than in China. Consequently, intimate connections between the political and industrial elites are no longer sufficient and may actually be counterproductive to the success of the developmental state. Diverging from traditional developmental states, China shows that incorporation of new stakeholders is not premised on principles of human development. The novelty that China brings to re-thinking and re-articulating a new developmental state framework is that the development state of the twenty-first century can create new alliances such as with non-governmental organisations to meet human development objectives, but substantive change with regards to how the state is organised is not a precondition.

The debate over whether China fits the East Asian developmental state (DS) model has been the subject of scholarly discussion over the last decade or so. My point of departure is to assess China's DS within a broader theory of what outcomes represent 'development' and what factors are most crucial to generate these results, a challenge set forth by Evans and Heller.[1] While the technocracy, industrial policies and subsequent industrial transformation are still important elements to a DS, the empirical realities of the concept have moved beyond these components. As development is no longer simply conceived of as economic growth or industrialisation, but also as encapsulating human development, the role of the DS must be rethought. Focusing on the state's ability to deliver collective goods such as welfare has become an important task for developing and developed nations alike, and nowhere is this more important than in China. With a rapidly ageing population, inadequate social safety nets for marginalised groups such as internal migrants and a spectrum of health issues, the success of the Chinese DS requires new dynamics between state and society to deliver services to various segments of society. Consequently, intimate connections between the political and industrial elites are no longer sufficient and may actually be counterproductive to the success of the DS. I will advocate for a DS framework that accounts for an emphasis on human development, using China as a case study to contemplate new articulations of a new DS framework by looking at new state–society alliances. As noted in this special issue's introductory essay, for the DS concept to be useful in a new era of economic globalisation, we need to move beyond the narrow confines of 'East Asian' developmental states – that is, beyond the state as a regulator of market competition. Sing and Ovadia's essay observes the need to see the state as an activist and entrepreneur through innovation, in order to comprehend how the state has responded to the global economic dynamics of the twenty-first century.

The first section briefly considers the DS framework and provides context for China's own experience. The second section outlines the human development approach (HDA) and its relevance to contemporary development thinking and practice. The third section sketches Japanese and South Korean development states' realignment of developmental priorities to focus on human development as a way to think through the factors impacting on developmental states in responding to the economic challenges of the twenty-first century. The fourth section charts the role of non-governmental organisations (NGOs) in development for the purpose of comprehending the linkages between the DS and non-state stakeholders in the production of welfare. The fifth section brings together the traditional development state framework and that of the human development with reference to China, to argue that this fusion is particularly useful and necessary to maintain the relevancy of the DS approach to comprehending development in the twenty-first century. I frame my argument by considering the relationship between state and NGOs in the delivery of social services. China is an apt case to re-examine and update the framework because it demonstrates the necessity of both state and society in addressing a range of social issues, many a result of rampant and at times unchecked economic growth. Both central and local states are increasing their engagement with NGOs within the context of welfare delivery. I argue that this greater awareness of both NGOs and welfare needs of society can be viewed as leading to a new articulation of the DS. However, if we consider the motives behind these engagements from the perspective of the human development framework, it becomes clear that the primary motivation is to ensure socio-political stability[2] and not to increase human capabilities. The final section discusses this state–society re-centring of the DS beyond the Chinese case.

This paper, like others in this volume, seeks to re-examine the DS, particularly as the global economic conditions have changed since the East Asian newly industrialised countries (NICs) developed. As such, states like China have initially sought to enhance their global economic competitiveness through the use of cheap labour, but social consequences of such strategies are visible across China. Addressing these social issues has been pushed down from the central level to the individual, and it is here where NGOs – and, more broadly, civil society stakeholders – have become increasingly needed and critical to state-led development. My aim is therefore to draw upon such realities, the emergence of new social stakeholders, to understand how the DS is redefined under new socio-economic circumstances. The DS framework is one of many to explain the state–society alliance, along with corporatism and civil society, but it is the aspect of socio-economic development that makes the DS apt for understanding China's heterogeneous development experience, and that of other nations.

The developmental state and China

The Chinese state's involvement in economic development is regarded by some observers as following in the tradition of the East Asian DS. The concept of the DS was initially seen as a way to note and interpret different paths to capitalist development.[3] Economists such as Westphal[4] argued that East Asia's economic success can be largely attributed to the realms of free market forces, despite state intervention in certain areas. Amsden[5] and others believe it was more due to coordinated state action in the industrialisation and modernisation processes that caused the region's high growth rates. East Asia's economic success is often tied to the developmental state's post-World War II pursuit of industrialisation. As Haggard notes, when we talk about industrial policy vis-à-vis East Asia, it is 'selective intervention designed to influence the allocation of resources among different activities'.[6]

The state interventionist perspective of the DS is further reinforced when it is compared to and contrasted with countries like India. Chibber[7] sees India's failure to achieve the same level of results as South Korea – even though both set out on the development path at the same time and were at similar levels of manufacturing in the 1950s and 1960s – to be largely a result of the Indian state failing to negotiate relationships with societal groups, particularly its capitalists. The lack of state intervention to consolidate the disparate voices, paralleled by the 'excessively bureaucratic style [of the Indian state], lack of coherence in policy, and utter inability to discipline domestic business',[8] inhibited India's ability to achieve a level of growth comparable to that of South Korea. Evans'[9] notion of embedded autonomy speaks to this need to have political elites closely linked with various societal actors to achieve development goals, as clearly the state alone has its limitations. Leftwich's[10] argument brings greater nuance by emphasising the agency of the stakeholders where the co-ordination of leaders, elites and coalitions and the exercise of their agency in achieving development aims are key to overcoming institutional constraints. While industrialisation is often equated with development, as in the case of East Asia, the shift to focus on social policies by the East Asian states suggest that development is not confined to the realms of the economy. Consequently, in articulating a new DS framework, I consider the social aspects of developmental states and how they affect the delivery of social services and welfare to its citizens.

What is the developmental state's application to China and how does it explain the change in state–society relations? The Chinese state has indeed pursued a rapid course of industrialisation leading to greater labour mobility between rural and urban areas, and this has put the state in a position of greater responsibility. However, as we have seen with the DS, there is little room to account for the influence of local forces, as it assumes that all stakeholders are beholden to the central state's goals. From a financial and regulatory perspective, Hsueh[11] argues that China has developed by greatly liberalising foreign direct investment, departing from the experiences of its East Asian neighbours. Howell similarly emphasises the variations within the Chinese state, thus diverging from the DS model.[12] First, political and policy elites are not committed to a united plan of economic growth and transformation. Second, the state administration demonstrates a level of incompetency in the economic sphere. The divisions that are emerging across China, and also what Howell[13] terms a 'polymorphous' state, clearly affect the state's ability for direct development. She writes: 'A polymorphous state displays both contradictory features and processes such as autonomy and clientelism, developmentalism and predation, control and chaos, as well as contradictory outcomes such as rapid economic growth'.[14] The interests of the multiple layers of the Chinese state indicate that unity under the central state is not immediately observable. Despite this, it would be premature to announce the collapse of the Party-state because of divergent interests. Each level of the state will pursue its own strategy of engagement with new social stakeholders, thereby strengthening and reshaping the state.[15] Meanwhile, its credibility may be enhanced for collaborating with social stakeholders, such as NGOs, thereby renewing its position within society. Consequently, local authorities' strategies will have implications for state–society relations: what is evident is the tendency for local authorities to adopt various engagement strategies with NGOs, at times involving co-optation. And, similarly, this extends to the central state in its policies directed at NGOs. Thus, the DS framework seen from the Chinese case ought to better capture the involvement of the local state, social stakeholders and, more importantly, human development objectives, particularly in an era of great social change and adaptation. The co-ordination of the state in addressing the myriad of issues affecting China from a rapidly ageing population to incorporation of rural migrants into urban communities is a task that requires significant state–society collaboration. The intensification of globalisation and democratisation challenges the utility of the DS[16] – and similarly the ability for states to deliver sustainable development – but China demonstrates that there is a case to be made for re-articulating a DS framework, whereby we see engagement between state and social stakeholders in producing social development. Next, I outline the main principles of the HDA with the view of articulating a new understanding of the DS given the empirical realities that affect developing nations, such as China.

The human development approach

'Successful' development is no longer solely confined to the realms of achieving and sustaining high rates of economic growth. If the unit of analysis is the economy, social problems emerging as a result of rapid growth such as environmental damage and protection of the vulnerable are left to the market to resolve. However, an HDA redirects our priorities to enable individuals and communities to achieve their goals and at the same time contribute to the overall economy. A focus on human development is not exclusive of economic growth; income is an important instrument that enables individuals to achieve their full potential. Sen's work on the 'capability approach' underpins the philosophy behind the HDA.[17] There is broad consensus on the following aspects of the human development paradigm[18]:

- development must be people-centred;
- the purpose of development is to widen individual choices, and the human development approach is focused on enhancing human capabilities and to utilise those capabilities more fully;
- the four essential pillars of human development are: equity, sustainability, productivity and empowerment;
- the quality of economic growth and its distribution is critical to facilitating human development.

The creation of enabling environments in which individuals can exercise agency to make choices is a key objective to the human development paradigm. When individuals and groups are recognised as agents of change, they will then begin to articulate their priorities and determine how best to achieve them. However, the emphasis on human agency must be paired with fostering an environment of freedom of expression and association. As Sen writes: 'human development incorporates the need to remove the hindrances that people face through the efforts and initiatives of people themselves'.[19]

In short, Sen's theory of development starts from the idea that its purpose is to improve the quality of human lives by broadening the range of human experience, from being healthy and nourished to being knowledgeable and participatory in society. From this perspective, development is therefore about providing opportunities to enable individuals to participate in society; these opportunities would include education, access to health care, resources, and civil and political freedoms. Haq outlines four procedural principles to operationalise the HDA: equity, productivity, empowerment and sustainability. Drawing on the notions of justice and fairness, equity incorporates contemplation for distributive justice between groups. Thus, equity in human development is about eliminating barriers, and this may take the form of affirmative action to help various marginalised groups, to enable them to have the same level of capabilities as the rest of the population. Productivity is about achieving goals through the most efficient use of resources. Individuals and groups have to be involved and empowered to participate in every stage of development, not only as beneficiaries but as agents of change. Sustainability can be considered across a number of realms, including environmental, social and financial, where decisions made about development do not penalise future generations. With more than 25 years of history – if we take the first Human Development Report as a possible starting point – the HDA is not new, making it even more pressing for nations to prioritise developing human capabilities in conjunction with economic development. Japan and South Korea, as outlined below, demonstrate that DSs can reprioritise development goals, whether through internal and/or external pressures.

The DS of the twenty-first century thus requires a new outlook and a set of priorities to successfully deliver the goods of development, beyond economic growth, because it alone is insufficient to sustain individuals and communities through the recent economic crisis. Moreover, the state alone can no longer guarantee the delivery of development and, thus, as seen across the developed and developing world, the emergence of non-state stakeholders, such as NGOs. Yet Japan and South Korea demonstrate the possibility of reorienting developmental goals along the lines of welfare and the development of human capacity, but paired with economic objectives.

Japan and South Korea: changing developmental priorities

The literature on the DS is centred on economic development and/or growth. However, growth alone does not automatically lead to inclusiveness.[20] If the DS's capacity is ultimately about setting development goals and mobilising resources to achieve them, then it is not inconceivable to suggest that the mobilisation of resources should include human capital. Nonetheless, Japan and South Korea, for example, are instructive as to why a focus on inclusive growth and expansion of human capabilities is necessary. Until the 1990s, Japan and South Korea's social policies traditionally focused on supporting the productive sectors of society – male industrial workers, public sector employees, government civil servants, military personnel and teachers – and leaving others to rely on families.[21] The shift since the 1990s to focus on social investment policies directed towards the non-productive sectors of the populations, including, women, children and the elderly, was in line with the Japanese and South Korean governments' attempts to re-think social investment as a solution to adapt to the new economy,[22] following the Asian Financial Crisis (AFC) of 1997–1998 – that is, investing in human capital, and reducing income inequality. Equally important were changing domestic attitudes and family structures – families still being major providers of welfare – such as increased labour participation rates of women, higher divorce rates and declining birth rates, all of which meant a greater need for the DS to assume welfare responsibilities.

A focus on welfare priorities dovetailed with the two economies seeking to tap into new areas of productivity to regain and retain international competitiveness post AFC.

The impact of the 1970s oil crisis on the Japanese economy indicates external factors can reshape the DS's priorities. The passing of Japan's Employment Insurance Act in 1974 was a response to rising unemployment due to the oil crisis. Rather than emphasising unemployment assistance, government support focused on unemployment prevention and employment integration. Until the mid-1980s, Japan's Employment Insurance was provided to employers in the form of subsidies to re-train and re-skill male industrial workers who were at risk of redundancy, which can be characterised as a traditional DS approach,[23] where the state intervenes. More recently, deregulation of Japan's labour market exemplified in laws such as the 1999 Worker Dispatching Law, altered the traditional hiring practices by deregulating dispatch work; and the 2003 Labour Standard Law was reformed by relaxing the regulations on worker dismissals. To compensate the restructured labour market, the government broadened its social insurance coverage, social welfare and employment assistance programmes with a significant proportion of expenditure directed at younger and older workers, helping them adjust to the new labour market.[24] Between 1991 and 2000, government expenditure on unemployment insurance more than doubled from 1.18 trillion yen to 2.67 trillion yen, or 2.3% of the total social security budget to 3.4%.[25] Such a focus on human development and welfare need not be seen as at odds with the DS objectives. As Peng[26] notes: 'there has been an increasing enmeshment of labour and social welfare policies, as economic and social policies are being regarded as having synergies with each other, and the welfare state is seen as a potential driver of [the] economic growth engine'.

There are parallels between the South Korean and the Japanese case. As South Korea's international competitiveness declined throughout the 1990s, further exacerbated by the AFC – during the 1990s, average wage increase was 14.3%, while labour productivity increased by 10.4%[27] – the need for a more flexible workforce was met with the introduction of the Employment Insurance Programme in 1995, where the responsibility for the welfare and retraining of workers shifted from companies to the state. While such programmes continued to demonstrate the South Korean state's effort 'to utilize social policy as an instrument of economic policy',[28] what was emerging to be a significant factor in the support and implementation of these policies, and ultimately tacit public acceptance of the new economy, was the South Korean government's ability to forge social consensus. President Kim Dae-jung established a tripartite committee in 1998 with participation of the Korean Federation of Trade Unions – with unions suppressed until South Korea's democratisation – in the Employees–Employers–Government Committee, thus creating a social consensus for labour market reform. The new democratic politics enabled the implementation of socio-economic reforms leading to greater social inclusion.[29]

As East Asia's developmental states adapt to the changing global economic environment, new priorities emerge. Japan's and South Korea's focus on human development and greater social inclusion complemented national economic objectives. For example, employment insurance programmes were implemented to enable the participation of old and young workers in a new economy and regain international competitiveness. Japan and South Korea present apt examples of the convergence of domestic and external pressures of the global economy in reshaping the DS's objectives towards welfare and social inclusion, with the need to incorporate social stakeholders in giving the state the legitimacy and credibility to undertake such reforms. These two cases are instructive to see how DSs can and do evolve, but I am by no means arguing that China is following in the footsteps of its East Asian neighbours; the context in which South Korea and Japan implemented their welfare policies is steeped in the internal and external political and economic conditions of the time. Nonetheless, what we do need to take note of is the emergence of new developmental state coalitions, as seen in the Chinese NGO case.

The role of NGOs in development

Taking Evans and Heller's observation of the role of civil society as a key component in policy innovation, I argue that NGOs are essential stakeholders in the development process. NGOs are particularly important in the Chinese context, where the state has offloaded much of that responsibility onto the local state, and with budgetary constraints often at play, communities, families and individuals are frequently left to deal with the social and economic consequences of reform. Consequently, an understanding of the DS and how it can promote and expand the capabilities of the population in the twenty-first century requires a consideration of how and with whom the state engages to achieve such ends. An exploration of state–NGO engagements in the co-production of welfare allows us to think through the emerging social, political and economic strategies to foster new forms of comparative advantage[30] of the DS as it responds not only to the pressures of economic globalisation but also to the impacts of such processes on society.

Careful analysis of the activities of NGOs provides insight into the claims of the progressive transformative potential of NGOs. Adopting a broad perspective on the points of connection (and disconnection) in state–NGO relations illuminates the process by which social and political stakeholders utilise NGOs as an arena to produce, articulate and reconstruct ideas (and ideologies) of progress and development. NGOs possess material, symbolic, interpretive and geographical power[31] and, thus, have been pushed forth as agents of socio-political change by NGOs themselves and international organisations such as the United Nations and World Bank, and to a lesser extent national governments through their respective development agencies.[32] Scholars have cast NGOs in many ways, including as alternate service providers to the state[33] and as facilitators of citizen participation and democratic change.[34] Recent NGO literature does provide an alternative to re-orient our focus on and understanding of NGOs as potential partners with the state. It is in this context that we may derive new scholarship, through an investigation of the intricacies of state–NGO relations.

When state and NGOs interact with one another, the process is likely to impact and transform both actors. Before further conceptualising their interactions, it is appropriate to first define 'NGO'. The heterogeneity of the sector means that as an analytical category, 'NGO' remains imprecise and complex.[35] The difficulty of pinpointing a precise definition of 'NGO' is reflective of the diversity of organisations with varying sizes, organisational structures and goals. Moreover, a nation's legal and cultural contexts will inevitably have an effect on the definition of the term. A tangible definition of NGOs is provided by the World Bank, which outlines the following common characteristics of NGOs:

> NGOs comprise a wide variety of associations, societies, foundations, and charitable entities that are (i) entirely or largely independent of government; (ii) not operated for profit; and (iii) exist to serve humanitarian, social or cultural interests, either of their memberships or of society as a whole.[36]

Furthermore, the United Nations (UN) observes that the institutional structure of NGOs enables them to be accountable to their members and donors.[37]

Although NGOs can engage in a wide array of activities, the nature of their interaction with the state has been succinctly categorised by Lewis[38] into three primary roles: implementer, catalyst and partner. As implementers, NGOs are responsible for mobilising resources for the delivery of social services to those in need. This role is becoming increasingly common (and in China too), since governments and donors are contracting out the delivery of goods and services to NGOs as part of government reforms and privatisation plans. As catalysts, NGOs can act as facilitators of social transformation through their 'ability to inspire, facilitate or contribute to improved thinking and action'.[39] As partners, NGOs may work with the government, donors, private sector or communities to achieve specific goals in mutually beneficial relationships.[40] Through engaging and partnering with one another, the process is likely to transform both state and NGO.

I have considered the role of NGOs in development and their engagement with the state. It is clear that the embeddedness of political elites, in the DS framework, needs to occur within a social context where the state still plays a central co-ordinating role. Inclusion of NGOs into the DS framework in co-producing social development demonstrates that new coalitions can be formed for the purpose of development. The following section considers the Chinese case, locates the analysis of the DS within a human development paradigm and considers what inputs are most crucial to producing those outcomes.

Re-thinking the developmental state in the twenty-first century: a case study of China

China is a suitable case study to inform new articulations of a DS framework. China is at the crossroads of its development: a decline in economic growth paired with an increasing number of social problems challenges both state and society. The empirical realities of China's development demonstrate that the state has evolved over time, where the heterogeneity of the Chinese state has involved not just the central state in development but also that of the local state, where regional development saw the active participation of local authorities.[41] China therefore shows that states evolve, adapt and reorganise their priorities. However, it is also a case to demonstrate that failures to take into account human development priorities can have severe consequences in terms of socio-political stability. Thus, this section considers how DSs can meet the challenges of the twenty-first century through enhancing state–society connections, specifically seen from the perspective of state–NGO relations in social service delivery. I show that the Chinese state is making headway in collaborating with social stakeholders to 'co-produce' things like health and welfare,[42] thereby highlighting a new interpretation of the DS framework. Co-production is taken to mean the involvement of NGOs – along with the state – in the delivery of public services. Furthermore, the relationship between NGOs and the production process is a dynamic one, where they are transformed and 'incorporated into the institutionalized system of provision'.[43] State incorporation of NGOs suggests that new coalitions can occur,[44] leading to a more hybrid approach to development, thus informing a new DS model. The case shows that the adoption of new strategies by the Chinese state, incorporating NGOs and involving local states in the delivery of social services, departs from the traditional models of DS, not only in terms of the new stakeholders involved but also in terms of the state's focus. Yet, when we look deeper into the motivations and priorities of the state in this shift, it becomes clear that incorporating social stakeholders is not necessarily matched with an emphasis on human development priorities. Consequently, a new DS is visible from the Chinese case but its motivations are misaligned vis-à-vis HDA.

State and society in the delivery of social services

If policy innovation is key to a successful DS, as noted in Vu's analysis of Singapore in this issue, then success in today's terms requires a much more holistic way of thinking: incorporating human development objectives and addressing social challenges. Evans and Heller[45] highlight the importance of the DS in organising the relationship between a capitalist economy and capability-enhancing development measures. To promote capabilities, the state needs to be broadly embedded in society via linkages with diverse set of groups; create multiple contact points between state and society; create ways to reduce transaction costs; and facilitate co-production and co-ordination, instead of domination, coercion or dependency.[46] Given this premise as a way to articulate new priorities for a DS of the twenty-first century, we see China exhibiting characteristics of a more socially embedded DS, particularly in the area of social and welfare delivery.

Diversifying welfare provision first appeared in the 1980s and 1990s when the state passed these responsibilities to markets and individuals. A residual approach characterised the state's attempt at welfare provision during this period,[47] while simultaneously finding new ways of financing existing welfare commitments, and engaging with multiple suppliers in order to have minimal government expenditures on welfare. The state's retreat from the health sector has had one of the most pronounced effects in exacerbating the growing regional inequalities. The marketisation of health services, rather than continuing collective healthcare, impacted on the affordability of healthcare.[48] Impoverishment as a result of rising healthcare costs and lack of insurance coverage for rural residents has been a marked consequence of the health system reform.[49] The introduction of the New Co-operative Medical Scheme (NCMS) in 2003 helped subsidise voluntary health insurance programme for rural residents, and improved access to and utilisation of health facilities by rural residents. While the central state has introduced the market as a key player in health provision, thereby co-producing health delivery, current indicators suggest the mixed approach is insufficient to meet the needs of the population, particularly as rural patients' out-of-pocket expenses have increased.[50]

Given the vast problems associated with welfare provision and the impacts on individuals and families, the gradual acceptance of and opening up of space for the participation of social organisations in welfare delivery have produced new options and challenges for all stakeholders. The Government Procurement Law of 2003 now permits local governments to purchase services from various for- and non-profit organisations (NPOs). The 12th Five Year Plan (FYP; 2011–2015) articulated goals to increase the amount and to expand the range of outsourced services. Social services outsourcing (SSO) refers to the provision of public funds by the government to an NPO or a business to deliver public goods and services. At its simplest, SSO is premised on a relationship between the government and the implementing organisation. This contractual relationship, where the government purchases services from the organisation, requires the two parties to be independent of each other.[51] The government assumes the role of regulator, where a legal framework is established for the delivery of services; and the service provider assumes the responsibility of the task and is able to make decisions independently of the government. Savas[52] delineates four primary forms of 'collaborative service delivery', where non-state stakeholders are involved: contract, franchise, grant and voucher. Beyond these four forms, private financing and public–private partnerships have also come to the fore.[53] This model of welfare provision redefines the role of state and society, where the state becomes the 'purchaser of outcomes supplied by public and private sector organisations'.[54] Unlike Australia, Canada, New Zealand, the UK and other Western welfare states, China's move towards general welfare reform, which SSO is part of, was not born out of a social democratic renewal,[55] where emphasis is on reciprocity with individuals having a stake in their own well-being. While the move into welfare reform, with emphasis on SSO, is a result of various pilot projects that have informed this shift[56] and is articulated in the 12th FYP, scholars such as Shih[57] argue that the trend is reflective of the social management principles of the Party-state. The Chinese state is putting more emphasis on meeting the needs of society, but given the top-down nature of such actions,[58] social actors are still subordinates rather than equal partners in the co-production of social services. SSO in the Chinese context is attuned more to management of social stakeholders, rather than as noted above, an adherence to political ideals.

The 12th FYP sets out a number of principles for the participation of social stakeholders in service delivery under the leadership of the Party-state. These principles include abiding by a multi-stakeholder governance mechanism with regards to welfare provision, strengthening the capacity and autonomy of local communities to provide services, and emphasising the development of social organisations, amongst others. Government procurement of social services started in 1996, punctuated by four main stages.[59] During the first stage (1991–1996), pilot projects and research into procurement of services were placed on the national agenda, and at the same time, the Shanghai Civil Affairs Bureau began its own experimentation with SSO. Shanghai in 2001 allocated 10% of its service expenditures to competitive bidding process.[60] In phase two (1998–2000), we see more local experimentation and scaling up of projects. In particular, Shenzhen Municipal People's Congress was the first local government to promulgate regulations on procurement via the Regulations of Shenzhen Special Economic Zone on the Procedure of Government Procurement. Local pilot projects across the nation informed the first national policy, Provisional Regulation on the Procedure of Government Procurement, advanced in April 1999 by the Ministry of Finance. The third stage (2000–2002) saw the intensification of procurement and was noted as an important mechanism for social service delivery. The National People's Congress in June 2002 approved the Government Procurement Law of the PRC. In phase four (2003 to present), we see greater standardisation of SSO and making provisions for the likes of NGOs to participate in this work. Each phase highlights the importance of local experiments in advising national policy. Guangdong, a province that had already had widespread usage of SSO prior to the 2012 Government Procurement of Services from Social Organisations, provides an outline for the practice of SSO. Such experiments and subsequent local policies have considerable impact on policy-making. As I argued previously, a new articulation of the DS needs to account for the fact that the state is comprised of various levels and that it is the local level that is tasked with the implementation of social policies, as is the case in China. Consequently, in thinking about co-production, we must broaden our understanding of the state.

In the 12th FYP we see significant shifts at the central level with regards to the participation of NGOs in SSO, mirroring some of the local trends. Undoubtedly, the central state is seeking to improve ways to incorporate NGOs into the fold. For example, in 2012 the Ministry of Civil Affairs, in partnership with the China Association of Non-Profit Organisations, established a centrally managed procurement fund for financing social services delivered by NGOs – an unprecedented move, particularly as this was the first time funding was made available to NGOs via an institutionalised mechanism at the national level, where NGOs would be assessed via a set of procedures.[61] While the 12th FYP has subsequently encouraged various forms of government financing of NGOs, these actions can be seen as couched within the broader framework of boosting NGOs' participation in SSO, and not necessarily the expansion of civil society or space for NGOs. NGOs have come under increasing scrutiny, including the sources of their funding. Notably, in January 2017 the Overseas NGO Law curtailed not only the role of overseas NGOs in China but also how they fund domestic NGOs. Such juxtapositions suggest that the contribution of NGOs to SSO will be constrained by the political and institutional environment, despite the Party-state rhetoric. While this may be a justification to refocus our attention on the state, this would be at the expense of seeing the transformative potential of NGOs, even when operating in a strict regulatory environment like China.

The Chinese case suggests that the DS is capable of re-orienting development focus to matters of social welfare by bringing in a variety of different stakeholders. However, the Chinese state has not embedded itself into social networks to facilitate the delivery of social services. Political elites are not embedded in the NGOs' social networks; rather, they are tasked by the state to manage and regulate the NGO sector as they conduct social service delivery. Thus, the central state continues to play a key co-ordinating role in the social realm but without feedback mechanisms in place to ascertain the successes and failures of NGOs as service providers[62] to inform future programmes; the central state is missing out on a crucial component of policy innovation that is at the core of a successful DS. As a result, NGOs are not fully involved in the co-production because they are constrained in the exercising of their agency given the regulatory environment; therefore, their full potential as providers of welfare and as innovators cannot be captured by the state. NGOs may experience significant constraints on their work; however, organisations with close ties to the authorities, namely government-organised NGOs (GONGOs) need not be burdened with such regulations due to their government affiliation.[63] In the area of HIV/AIDS in Yunnan, GONGOs offer more extensive coverage and are the vehicles in which funding is channelled through from both international and government sources.[64] Despite GONGOs' lack of autonomy, they benefit from higher trust levels with the government[65] and they are able to quickly mobilise resources from local governments to achieve their goals, but as a result they 'follow rather than lead in social service innovations'.[66] The Chinese case shows us even an authoritarian state can adapt to change and orient priorities in line with the dynamics of its population. Yet a consideration of social services delivery indicates that the Chinese state is still firmly in control, whether it is via the inclusion of NGOs or GONGOs.

What are the implications of such control? It is clear that a focus on the welfare needs of the population has not extended to the expansion of capabilities. The way SSO is organised shows that equity, sustainability, productivity and empowerment are not factors that are part of the equation for the Chinese state, as important as they are for the future success of the DS. However, these arrangements do not discount the utility of the DS framework in understanding China and its developmental complexities, nor do they prevent us from considering non-state stakeholders because it is these factors that demonstrate that from a social policy standpoint, the Chinese state is exploring and innovating. Nonetheless, the top-down nature of welfare reforms and delivery does not project notions of equity. NGOs are strictly monitored and lack collaborative dialogue as to how services are delivered. Such reorientation of the state, while praiseworthy, will not be sustainable. Much of the service outsourcing lies at the discretion of the local state, and thus the lack of standards to ensure quality delivery can lead to misuse of power on the part of the local state. Chinese NGOs face a number of institutional constraints in their day-to-day operations, and as such the state misses out on tapping into the full potential of NGOs because their concern is about socio-political stability and not about maximising NGOs' productivity. Therefore, NGOs are not empowered, nor are their constituents empowered to make decisions that affect their daily lives, a key aspect of co-production. China demonstrates that local conditions matter and thus the local state matters. Nevertheless, the Chinese case suggests that establishing new coalitions to achieve the DS's goals of a new development era is hollow and potentially counterproductive without subscription to the guiding principles of HDA.

Conclusion

Using China as a case study to inform a new understanding of the DS in the twenty-first century suggests that states are capable of adapting to the challenges brought on by economic globalisation. If the success of the DS is defined by its ability to focus on human development objectives and expanding capabilities by integrating social stakeholders into the development project, then the Chinese experience suggests that there is movement on that front. Yet the DS framework must also capture the variation in the state – that is, the local levels of the state matter to the overall national goals. And, thus, their role in this new conceptualisation of the DS is critical to its future success. This conceptualisation, one that accounts for various levels of the state involvement in development outcomes and their engagement with civil society, including NGOs, shows us that there is still analytical purchase in the DS, but taking into consideration contemporary empirical realities.

The heterogeneity of China's development, and across different jurisdictions, certainly does not preclude the use or utility of the DS framework, as demonstrated in this special issue, where we see cases ranging from Singapore's technological innovation strategies as outlined by Vu to Saunders' and Caramento's examination of resource industrialisation strategies of Zambia and Zimbabwe. Consequently, the diverse development experiences and the role of the state vis-à-vis new economic dynamics and new stakeholders in various sectors of the economy, NGOs in the case of this paper, allow us the opportunity to explore new configurations of the DS of the twenty-first century.

Diverging from traditional DSs, China shows that incorporation of new stakeholders is not premised on principles of human development to dovetail with economic objectives. The Chinese state's control of the NGO sector reveals that the threat of socio-political instability undermines policy innovation. Thus, China is caught in a bind: to maintain stability, the state exercises its strength, but this can suffocate successful outcomes in the social realm – NGOs are prevented from maximising their potential – and thus lead to further social dissatisfaction. Therefore, the novelty that China brings to re-thinking and re-articulating a DS framework – along with state strategies of establishing new coalitions – is that the DS of the twenty-first century can create new alliances with NGOs to meet human development objectives, but substantive change with regards to how the state is organised is not a precondition. While it is not the aim of this paper to contemplate political change, Evans and

Heller[67] may be right in their assessment: 'Technocratic and organizational capacities are still fundamental to the success of the developmental state, but absent a complementary politics of encompassing engagement with a broad cross-section of society, technocratic capacity is sterile and ineffectual'. The success of the Chinese DS perhaps lies somewhere in between authoritarianism and more meaningful participation of social organisations in co-producing welfare and social services.

Disclosure statement

No potential conflict of interest was reported by the author.

Acknowledgements

I am grateful for the valuable feedback received at the *Developmental States Beyond East Asia* Workshop, 5 June 2015, at Newcastle University, UK. During the different stages of writing the paper, Jesse Ovadia and Jewellord Nem Singh offered insightful comments and suggestions; my sincere thanks for their time and careful reading. I am also thankful for the constructive feedback offered by the anonymous reviewers.

Notes

1. Evans and Heller, "Human Development, State Transformation."
2. See Huang, "Politics of Social Welfare Reform."
3. White, "Developmental States and Socialist Industrialisation."
4. Westphal, "Republic of Korea's Experience."
5. Amsden, *Asia's Next Giant.*
6. Haggard, "Institutions and Growth in East Asia," 64.
7. Chibber, *Locked in Place.*
8. Ibid., 7.
9. Evans, *Embedded Autonomy.*
10. Leftwich, "Beyond Institutions."
11. Hsueh, *China's Regulatory State.*
12. Howell, "Reflections on the Chinese State."
13. Ibid.
14. Ibid., 292.
15. Hsu, *State of Exchange.*
16. Stubbs, "What Ever Happened"; Wu, "Taiwan's Developmental State."

17. I thank an anonymous reviewer for noting the utility of the inclusive growth paradigm. Ideas of inclusive growth are embodied in that of human development, as the United Nations Development Programme (UNDP) *Human Development Report 2016* notes: 'Investing in human priorities is intended to reach those who lack basic social services such as education and health care that are essential for enhancing human capital so that these people can not only be part of inclusive growth, but also enhance their capabilities, which are intrinsically valuable' (108).
18. Haq, *Reflections on Human Development*.
19. Sen, "Foreword," vii.
20. Leftwich, "Developmental States, Effective States," 4.
21. Peng, "'New' Social Investment Policies."
22. Ibid.
23. Ibid.
24. Peng, "Social and Political Economy of Care."
25. Ibid., 642.
26. Peng, "'New' Social Investment Policies," 158.
27. Park, "Labor Regulation and Economic Change."
28. Kwon, "Transforming the Developmental Welfare States," 10.
29. Ibid.
30. Singh and Ovadia, this issue.
31. Hasmath and Hsu, "Isomorphic Pressures, Epistemic Communities."
32. For example, the US Agency for International Development (USAID) in 2011 dedicated US$17 billion to the programme areas under its Strategic Goal of Governing Justly and Democratically: promoting human rights, democratic governance, civil societies and broad-based economic growth, amongst others. See USAID, *Foreign Operations FY 2011*.
33. See Green and Matthias, "NGOs – A Policy Panacea"; Henderson, "Alternative Service Delivery"; and Leonard, "When Both States and Markets Fail."
34. See Bratton, "Politics of NGO Relations in Africa"; and Diamond, "Rethinking Civil Society." See also Mercer's review and critique of the NGO literature that equates and/or associates NGOs with democratisation: Mercer, "NGOs, Civil Society and Democratization."
35. Najam, "Understanding the Third Sector," has identified at least 47 different acronyms in reference to NGOs. Lewis and Kanji have made modifications: Lewis and Kanji, *Non-Governmental Organizations and Development*. For a concise treatment of the term NGO and its history, see Lewis, "Nongovernmental Organizations and History."
36. World Bank, "Bank's Relations with NGOs," 2.
37. UN Economic and Social Council, *Resolution and Decision*.
38. Lewis, "Nongovernmental Organizations and History."
39. Lewis and Kanji, *Non-Governmental Organizations and Development*, 13.
40. Ibid.
41. See Oi, "Role of the Local State."
42. Evans and Heller, "Human Development, State Transformation."
43. Brandsen and Pestoff, "Co-production, the Third Sector," 496.
44. See Stubbs, "The East Asian Developmental State."
45. Evans and Heller, "Human Development, State Transformation."
46. Ibid.
47. Shang and Wu, "Changing Approaches of Social Protection."
48. Duckett, *Chinese State's Retreat from Health*.
49. Liu, Rao, and Hsiao, "Medical Expenditure and Rural Impoverishment."
50. Wagstaff et al., "Extending Health Insurance"; You and Kobayashi, "New Cooperative Medical Scheme."
51. Jia and Su, *Final Report on Government Procurement*.
52. Savas, *Priviatization*.
53. Jing and Savas, "Managing Collaborative Service Delivery."
54. Strathdee, "Outsourcing and the Provision," 63.
55. Giddens, *Third Way*.

56. Jagusztyn, "Social Services Outsourcing."
57. Shih, "New Mode of Public–Private Welfare."
58. Hsu, "China's Development."
59. Jia and Su, *Final Report on Government Procurement.*
60. Pu, "Reform and Innovations."
61. Wu, He and Simon, "Capacity Development," 18.
62. Teets and Jagusztyn, "Evolution of a Collaborative Governance Model."
63. My thanks to the anonymous reviewer for noting the importance of GONGOs as another stakeholder in SSO.
64. Jagusztyn, "Social Services Outsourcing."
65. Ibid., 8.
66. Jing, "From Stewards to Agents?"
67. Evans and Heller, "Human Development, State Transformation," 28.

Bibliography

Amsden, A. *Asia's Next Giant: South Korea and Late Industrialization*. New York: Oxford University Press, 1989.

Brandsen, T., and V. Pestoff. "Co-production, the Third Sector and the Delivery of Public Services: An Introduction." *Public Management Review* 8, no. 4 (2006): 493–501.

Bratton, M. "The Politics of NGO Relations in Africa." *World Development* 17, no. 4 (1989): 569–587.

Chibber, V. *Locked in Place: State-Building and Late Industrialization in India*. Princeton: Princeton University Press, 2003.

Diamond, L. "Rethinking Civil Society: Toward Democratic Consolidation." *Journal of Democracy* 5, no. 3 (1994): 4–17.

Duckett, J. *The Chinese State's Retreat from Health: Policy and the Politics of Retrenchment*. London: Routledge, 2011.

Evans, P. *Embedded Autonomy: States and Industrial Transformation*. Princeton: Princeton University Press 1995.

Evans, P., and P. Heller. "Human Development, State Transformation and the Politics of the Developmental State." In *The Oxford Handbook of Transformations of the State*, edited by S. Leibfried, E. Huber, M. Lange, J. D. Levy, and J. D. Stephens, 691–713. New York: Oxford University Press, 2014.

Giddens, A. *The Third Way*. Cambridge: Polity Press, 1998.

Green, A., and A. Matthias. "NGOS – a Policy Panacea for the Next Millennium?" *Journal of International Development* 7, no. 3 (1995): 565–573.

Haggard, S. "Institutions and Growth in East Asia." *Studies in Comparative International Development* 38, no. 4 (2004): 53–81.

Hasmath, R., and J. Y. J. Hsu. "Isomorphic Pressures, Epistemic Communities and State-NGO Collaboration in China." *The China Quarterly* 220 (2014): 936–954.

Haq Mahbub ul. *Reflections on Human Development*. Oxford: Oxford University Press, 1995.

Henderson, Keith. "Alternative Service Delivery in Developing Countries: NGOs and Other Non-Profits in Urban Areas." *Public Organization Review: A Global Journal* 2, no. 2 (2002): 99–116.

Howell, J. "Reflections on the Chinese State." *Development and Change* 37, no. 2 (2006): 273–297.

Hsu, J. Y. J. "China's Development: A New Development Paradigm?" *Third World Quarterly* 36, no. 9 (2015): 1754–1769.

Hsu, J. Y. J. *State of Exchange: Migrant NGOs and the Chinese Government*. Vancouver, BC: University of British Columbia Press, 2017.

Hsueh, R. *China's Regulatory State: A New Strategy for Globalization*. Ithaca: Cornell University Press, 2011.

Huang, X. "The Politics of Social Welfare Reform in Urban China: Social Welfare Preferences and Reform Policies." *Journal of Chinese Political Science* 18, no. 1 (2013): 61–85.

Jagusztyn, M. *Social Services Outsourcing to Social Organizations in the HIV Sector in Yunnan Province Unleashing Social Innovation or Business as Usual? Exploratory Study*. Research Triangle Park, NC: RTI International, 2012.

Jia, X., and M. Su. *Final Report on Government Procurement of Public Services People's Republic of China*. Manila: Asian Development Bank, 2009.

Jing, Y. "From Stewards to Agents? Competitive Contracting for Social Services in China." Paper presented at the Public Management Research Conference, Hong Kong, October 14–16, 2010.

Jing, Y., and E. S. Savas. "Managing Collaborative Service Delivery: Comparing China and the United States." *Public Administration Review* 69, no. 3 (2009): S101–S107.

Kwon, H. J. "Transforming the Developmental Welfare States of East Asia." Economic & Social Affairs DESA Working Paper No. 40, 2007. https://www.un.org/esa/desa/papers/2007/wp40_2007.pdf?TB_iframe=true

Leftwich, A. *Developmental States, Effective States and Poverty Reduction: The Primacy of Politics*. Geneva: UNRISD Project on Poverty Reduction and Policy Regimes, 2008. https://www.unrisd.org/80256B3C005BCCF9/httpNetITFramePDF?ReadForm&parentunid=EE2D4DF653F6077BC1257A5D004C7E5E&parentdoctype=paper&netitpath=80256B3C005BCCF9/(httpAuxPages)/EE2D4DF653F6077BC1257A5D004C7E5E/$file/Leftwichweb.pdf

Leftwich, A. "Beyond Institutions: Rethinking the Role of Leaders, Elites and Coalitions in the Institutional Formation of Developmental States and Strategies." *Forum for Development Studies* 37, no. 1 (2010): 93–111.

Leonard, K. L. "When Both States and Markets Fail: Asymmetric Information and the Role of NGOs in African Health Care." *International Review of Law and Economics* 22, no. 1 (2002): 61–80.

Lewis, D. "Nongovernmental Organizations and History." In *International Encyclopedia of Civil Society*, edited by H. K Anheier, S. Toepler and R. A. List, 1056–1062. New York: Springer, 2010.

Lewis, D., and N. Kanji. *Non-Governmental Organizations and Development*. London: Routledge, 2009.

Liu, Y., K. Rao, and W. C. Hsiao. "Medical Expenditure and Rural Impoverishment in China." *Journal of Health, Population and Nutrition* 21, no. 3 (2003): 216–222.

Mercer, C. "NGOs, Civil Society and Democratization: A Critical Review of the Literature." *Progress in Development Studies* 2, no. 1 (2002): 5–22.

Najam, A. "Understanding the Third Sector: Revisiting the Prince, the Merchant, and the Citizen." *Nonprofit Management and Leadership* 7, no. 2 (1996): 203–219.

Oi, J. "The Role of the Local State in China's Transitional Economy." *China Quarterly* 144 (1995): 1132–1149.

Park, B.-G. 2001. "Labor Regulation and Economic Change: A View on the Korean Economic Crisis." *Geoforum* 32, no. 1 (2001): 61–75.

Peng, I. "Social and Political Economy of Care in Japan and South Korea." *International Journal of Sociology and Social Policy* 32, no. 11/12 (2012): 636–649.

Peng, I. "The 'New' Social Investment Policies in Japan and South Korea." In *Inclusive Growth, Development and Welfare Policy: A Critical Assessment*, edited by R. Hasmath, 142–160. London: Routledge, 2015.

Pu, Z. "Reform and Innovations in Governmental Procurement in Pudong District." *Shanghai Finance and Economics* 21, no. 8 (2002): 14–17.

Savas, E. S. *Privatization: The Key to Better Government*. Chatham, NJ: Chatham House, 1987.

Sen, A. "Foreword." In *Readings in Human Development: Concepts, Measures and Policies for a Development Paradigm*. 2nd ed., edited by S. Fukuda-Parr, and A. K. Shiva Kumar, vii–viii. New Delhi: Oxford UP, 2004.

Shang, X., and X. Wu. "Changing Approaches of Social Protection: Social Assistance Reform in Urban China." *Journal of Social Policy and Society* 3, no. 3 (2004): 259–271.

Shih, J. S. "A New Mode of Public–Private Welfare Mix? Promoting Partnership by Social Management in China." Paper presented at the American Association for Chinese Studies, Rutgers, State University of New Jersey, New Brunswick, October 11–13, 2013.

Strathdee, R. "Outsourcing and the Provision of Welfare-Related Services to Unemployed Youth in New Zealand." *Cambridge Journal of Economics* 28, no. 1 (2004): 59–72.

Stubbs, R. "What Ever Happened to the East Asian Developmental State? The Unfolding Debate." *The Pacific Review* 22, no. 1 (2009): 1–22.

Stubbs, R. "The East Asian Developmental State and the Great Recession: Evolving Contesting Coalitions." *Contemporary Politics* 17, no. 2 (2011): 151–166.

Teets, J., and M. Jagusztyn. "Evolution of a Collaborative Governance Model: Social Service Outsourcing to Civil Society Organizations in China." In *NGO Governance and Management in China*, edited by R. Hasmath and J. Y. J Hsu, 69–87. London: Routledge, 2016.

UNDP. *Human Development Report 2016*. New York: UNDP, 2016.

UN Economic and Social Council. *Resolution and Decision of the Economic and Social Council E1996/96*, 1996. https://csonet.org/content/documents/199631.pdf

USAID. *Foreign Operations FY 2011 Performance Report, FY 2013 Performance Plan*. Washington DC: USAID, 2012.

Wagstaff, A., M. Lindelow, J. Gao, L. Xu, and J. Qian. "Extending Health Insurance to the Rural Population: An Impact Evaluation of China's New Cooperative Medical Scheme." *Journal of Health Economics* 28, no. 1 (2009): 1–19.

Westphal, L. E. "The Republic of Korea's Experience with Export-Led Industrial Development." *World Development* 6, no. 3 (1978): 347–382.

White, G. "Developmental States and Socialist Industrialisation in the Third World." *Journal of Development Studies* 21, no. 1 (1984): 97–120.

World Bank. "The Bank's Relations with NGOs." Social Development Papers No. 28. Washington DC: World Bank, 1998.

Wu, F., J. He and K. Simon. "Capacity Development of Civil Society Organizations Towards Inclusive Social Management in China." *Research Paper for EU-China and UNDP Governance for Equitable Development Project*, n.d.

Wu, Yu-Shan. "Taiwan's Developmental State: After the Economic and Political Turmoil." *Asian Survey* 47, no. 6 (2007): 977–1001.

You, X., and Y. Kobayashi. "The New Cooperative Medical Scheme in China." *Health Policy* 91, no. 1 (2009): 1–9.

Twenty-first century developmental states? Argentina under the Kirchners

Christopher Wylde

ABSTRACT
Can the policies pursued by successful examples of developmental states be transferred to other countries under current global conditions? This question has represented one of the key concerns of the academic community in the wake of this reinterpretation of East Asian developmental success. This article will contribute to both the Latin American literature and the developmental state literature simultaneously and symbiotically, through arguing that Argentina in the period 2003–2015 represents an excellent empirical opportunity to revisit key debates associated with the concern of transferable lessons from the original East Asian developmental state experience.

There has never been a greater need for development. The political, social, and environmental challenges faced by the world in the early twenty-first century insist upon the need for solutions to underdevelopment and associated state failure, immiseration, mass migration, and ecological degradation. However, examples of successful catch-up development since the end of World War II are few and far between; none has transitioned towards any kind of sustainable development model. Of those successful cases, at least in terms of a human development approach,[1] most are clustered in the East Asia region. Japan, South Korea, and Taiwan – in their respective periods – all achieved significant gross domestic product (GDP) growth combined with sustained increases in standards of living across sufficiently lengthy periods of time so as to fundamentally transform their societies.

Academic explorations of these cases generated sophisticated accounts of their development experiences that led to a new emphasis on the role of the state in achieving economic growth and poverty reduction. From these endeavours the term 'developmental state' was coined,[2] defined as a state that has 'sufficient state capacity to be effective in its targeted areas and has a developmental vision such that it chooses to use this capacity to work towards economic development'.[3] State capacity here refers to the ability to implement goals, especially over the actual or potential opposition of powerful social groups or in the face of recalcitrant socio-economic circumstances.[4] Interpretations of East Asian development success grounded in the developmental state concept conflicted with neo-classical focused accounts of their success; accounts fitting the contemporary global development consensus commensurate with policies that minimised state interventions in the market, understood as the 'Washington Consensus'.[5]

Can the policies pursued by successful examples of developmental states be transferred to other countries under current global conditions? This question has represented one of the key concerns of the academic community in the wake of this reinterpretation of East Asian developmental success. This article will contribute to both the Latin American literature and the developmental state literature simultaneously and symbiotically, through arguing that Argentina in the period 2003–2015 represents an excellent empirical opportunity to revisit key debates associated with the concern of transferable lessons from the original East Asian developmental state experience. The developmental state needs to be brought into the twenty-first century. There are many challenges to achieving this goal. Through drawing on the case of Argentina in the period 2003–2015, this article will contribute to two core facets of the transferability debate within the developmental state literature. This will help revive the possibilities for refreshing our understanding of developmental states and associated development success, and the lessons they may offer to the rest of the Global South.

The first contribution concerns Vu's[6] distinction between 'developmental structures' and 'developmental roles'. Institutional analysis has dominated the debate on developmental structures, or state capacity; debates on developmental roles, or hegemonic ideologies/projects,[7] have been less researched. This article will suggest that the forging of hegemonic ideologies is a complex process of social interaction that requires an understanding of structure as well as agency, of social relations as well as ideas. Argentina demonstrates this through its articulation of a *neodesarrollismo* model of development[8] in the wake of its 2001 crisis of neoliberalism, leading to an increasingly interventionist role for the state in the development process. This represents one variant of a broader interventionist trend across Latin America that some scholars have termed 'post-neoliberalism'.[9] The second contribution to the transferability debate will be to begin the process of refreshing our understandings of how international pressures and global forces interact with developmental states. The clear majority of the developmental states literature has focused on the 'national' level,[10] although now with several attempts to refine the model.[11] Through an analysis of how globalisation and associated social forces helped shape both Argentine state structures and state roles during the Kirchner period, an empirical foundation can be used to induce associated theoretical confrontations.

This analysis of transferability and the developmental state will proceed in three parts. The first will develop the theoretical contributions outlined above, exploring the nature of developmental structures and developmental roles, and integrating globalisation. The second section will outline the empirical analysis, offering an account of the administrations of Nestor Kirchner (2003–2007) and Cristina Fernandez de Kirchner (hereafter CFK; 2008–2015). This will show how post-crisis social forces aligned with ideas to generate *neodesarrollismo*: creating a virtuous cycle of state-driven (but market-friendly) economic growth accompanied with reductions in poverty and inequality. However, after a period this project began to fall apart through tensions and fractures in Argentine social forces, as well as more international forces associated with global capital. A closing section will suggest that with further refinement and empirical study the developmental state concept continues to have value in the twenty-first century global political economy.

Overcoming theoretical restrictions in the transferability debates

Key to a virtuous pattern of global development, and one of the central debates in developmental state theory since its inception, is the question of transferability. Are there any transferrable lessons from the East Asian development experience for the rest of the Global South? Whilst interventions from Vu[12] suggest that 'the experience of developmental states may not be worth emulating', attempts by Wade[13] and Evans[14] sought to determine what can be learned from the East Asian experience. The intended target of these lessons in the literature has often been sub-Saharan Africa,[15] although Latin America has recently come to offer a fertile ground for comparative political economy within the developmental state tradition. An important but nascent literature comparing the 'East Asian Miracle' with contemporary Latin American experiences has been built upon in the context of the rise of the 'Pink Tide', or left and left-of-centre states, across Latin America from 1998 onwards.[16]

This literature has always recognised the dangers of dogmatic pursuit of models or blueprints, rather proposing the 'fabricat[ion of] the institutions of their own developmental states from local materials'.[17] Evans[18] articulates this as an 'invitation to indigenous innovation'. This is certainly no less true today than it was then. Not only have potentially important geo-strategic considerations such as the Cold War[19] and 'systemic vulnerability' through national security threats[20] associated with the original developmental states passed, but changing relationships between local and global capital – or certain aspects associated with globalisation – have fundamentally changed the nature of current global political economy and accompanying possibilities for rapid, catch-up development.[21]

In the twenty-first century, successful developmental states must depart fundamentally from existing models.[22] A Global South in which manufacturing employs a shrinking minority of the population while most depend on the service sector undercuts the twentieth-century story of increased general well-being built on Fordist production.[23] To be effectively developmental, the twenty-first-century state must take more responsibility, achieve greater autonomy in relation to private elites, and construct more complex and demanding forms of embeddedness.[24] In turn, academics must refresh their understandings of developmental processes to stay relevant in the context of deep structural change in societies and their relationships with different fractions of capital, both domestic and international. Such a refresh requires embracing recent scholarship in the political economy of development – as well as the social sciences more broadly – to reinvigorate some of the developmental state's core assertions. In the context of the transferability debate: the usefulness in analytically separating the capacity to develop from the autonomy to develop and the role of twenty-first century global political economy, and avoiding the deductive tautology. Each of these will now be taken in turn, with simultaneous exploration of their inter-relationships.

The capacity to develop, or state capacity, involves 'the administrative and coercive abilities of the state apparatus to implement official goals'.[25] Institutions thus become of central concern, not only because their quality has implications for policy success, but also because they can influence the nature of a state's policy mix. Research on developmental states has subsequently been dominated by studies that seek to understand the 'organisational features' of a state,[26] understood as a set of organisations through which collectives of officials may be able to formulate and implement distinctive strategies or policies. One example of this approach is Sikkink,[27] who emphasises bureaucratic competence as the chief independent variable that explains the different degrees of success in the Argentine and Brazilian developmentalist experiences under Frondizi and Kubitschek, respectively.

Perhaps the most enduring example of this is Evan's concept of 'embedded autonomy'.[28] His argument suggests that a Weberian-style bureaucracy in the sense of selective, meritocratic entrance requirements and independent long-term career rewards gave the South Korean state the necessary capacity for success. However, here he departs from Weber and suggests that far from being insulated from society, 'they are embedded in a concrete set of social ties that binds the state to society and provides institutionalised channels for the continual negotiation and renegotiation of goals and policies'.[29] These ties are predominantly with captains of industry – or domestic bourgeoisie – and it is this embedded autonomy that best facilitates the state's role in industrial transformation.

This analysis was subsequently critiqued for having an inadequate or incomplete understanding of state–society relationships; it was not a sufficient explanation of successful development experience as *both* strong states and strong economic groups in society are needed to create 'governed interdependence'.[30] Pempel's[31] analysis captured this well when he critiqued the developmental state literature for privileging the political and economic role played by state bureaucrats. This is because they are treated as totally depoliticised, socially disembodied, and in rational pursuit of a self-evident national interest.[32] In the words of Chalmers Johnson[33] 'politicians merely reign, whereas the bureaucrats actually rule'. This led Bruce Cumings[34] to suggest that the state then emerges as a 'web without a spider'. This critique sees that 'if not from the politicians from whom do bureaucrats get their sense of direction?'[35] Bureaucracies may well be rational, but in whose interests are they rational?

Understanding the motivations of developmental states is something relatively under-researched in the existing developmental state literature.[36] Sikkink places great weight on the role of agency and ideas.[37] Using the term 'state purpose', she outlines a co-constitutive relationship between ideas or orientations and institutions, and thus fuses this concept into that of state capacity. In other words, the administrative and coercive abilities of the state apparatus shape the nature of the official goals that it implements, as well as being shaped by them through the orientations and ideas of key officials and decision-makers. Whilst noting that ideas do 'not operate unfettered of material constraints',[38] they remain the key independent variable that explains the rise of a particular state purpose – that of developmentalism in Argentina and Brazil in her analysis. The failure of this project in Frondizi's Argentina compared with relative success in Kubitschek's Brazil is put down to the strength of its institutions and the strength of its ideas and leadership.[39] The problem with this analysis is that it fails to resolve the issue of why developmentalist ideas were adopted by the Argentine and Brazilian regimes. It offers a convincing account of how ideas help shape state capacities through institutions and institutionalisation, but is unable to answer in any systematic way the question of why certain ideas were adopted in preference to others. In placing agency at the core of the analysis Sikkink is driven to the conclusion that change in the leadership of Argentina – the rise of Frondizi – was not sufficient as his developmentalist plan ultimately failed.

One way the literature has framed this problem is through Vu's[40] distinction between 'developmental structures' and 'developmental roles'. Developmental structures are synonymous with state capacity, whilst developmental roles concern the political will to use that capacity for developmental ends. This analytical distinction is useful because developmental structures may exist within a state, but it requires their active use to achieve developmental ends. A state may have the capacity to be developmental, but not the autonomy. The motivation and political will to do so requires what Pempel termed a 'hegemonic project'.[41] This draws attention not only to the role of ideology, but also to how ideas and material interests interact in very complex and mutually re-constitutive ways.

Johnson[42] suggests that the key advantage of an authoritarian regime is its ability to mobilise the population towards developmental ends. The growth and development that could subsequently emerge become the source of the regime's legitimacy, with the effect of side-lining civil society.[43] However, this emergence of a suitable developmental ideology can come from several sources within civil society itself. Nationalism has been a dominant theme in the literature,[44] as has the existence of broader systemic threats that drive populations together in the face of common enemies.[45] What is certainly true is that the existence of a common, hegemonic, developmental vision emerges from a series of political settlements.[46] For these political settlements to be of a developmental type, specific constellations of social relations must be present that engender a common national interest in favour of rapid, catch-up development. Following Gramsci, those social relations are grounded not just in ideas but also material interests, and the complex mutually reconstitutive relationship between them.

The second substantive section of this article will show how such a hegemonic project emerged in Argentina. Dubbed '*neodesarrollismo*'[47] this led to not only changing relationships between the state and the market with attendant impacts on developmental structures, but also an attempt to forge a new contract between the state and the people with a distinctive developmental role. This emergence of a hegemonic project was key as it gave Argentina the autonomy to pursue key breaks with neoliberal policy prescriptions (in the wake of the neoliberal crisis of 2001) and instead forge an alternative social contract that sought an inclusive, state-led growth model. Beginning with an outline of the economic characteristics of the period, the paper will highlight how appropriate understanding of contemporary political economy can only be appreciated through analysing both ideas and material interests, and how they interact. In so doing it will draw invaluable insight from the developmental state literature. The analytical separation of developmental structures and developmental roles reveals in Argentina the changing social relations that facilitate the stalling of *neodesarrollismo* under CFK. Because of changing ideas and material interests, the hegemonic vision of contemporary Argentina becomes rearticulated and subsequently reshapes Argentine developmental structures and roles away from a successful twenty-first-century developmental state.

Hegemonic projects are formed domestically, but are also subject to international forces. Sharpening our understandings of how international pressures and global forces interact with developmental states becomes imperative. However, the clear majority of the developmental states literature has focused on the 'national' level.[48] Global forces clearly shape the contours of state autonomy, and place restrictions upon it. However, those global forces present today – in the form of a globalisation dominated by the ideas and institutions of neoliberalism – possess significant differences from those present in the twentieth century. As Fine and Kyung-Sup[49] suggest: 'neoliberally driven globalisation, coordinated by the Washington-centred league of advanced capitalist states and radicalised by global financial capital, has ironically undermined – if not eliminated – the global framework of development'.

They suggest that the bi-polar nature of international relations during the Cold War led to the respective hegemonies of the USA and USSR being expressed and exercised through developmental support, supervision, and control of developing countries. This was important, indeed arguably essential, in understanding the emergence of East Asian developmental states.[50] Taiwan, South Korea, and Japan were all strategically important to the USA during the Cold War, receiving financial and military aid, as well as preferential access to US markets for their products.

The decline of this global dynamic in the wake of the collapse of the Berlin Wall has led to claims that the developmental state experiences of the twentieth century cannot be repeated:

> In the neoliberal era, particularly after the demise of the communist bloc, this global or interstate framework of national development has been replaced by a global economic disciplinary regime that purports to control developing countries as individually responsible debtors rather than deal with them as collective developmental dependents.[51]

It is true that the rise of transnational economic actors such as transnational corporations (TNCs), fund managers, migrant workers, and transnational employees have fundamentally changed the Fordist nature of production that dominated most of the twentieth century. Furthermore, the ideology of neoliberalism has clearly permeated key sites of global governance, sites that could shape the autonomy of any state, particularly developing ones. However, this represents a call to refresh and reinvigorate our understandings of the developmental state, rather than call for its retirement as a useful concept in the twenty-first century.

The analysis in the next section will suggest that an interpretation of the contemporary global political economy as an absolutely constraining influence on states' developmental prospects is a false one. Contemporary forces of neoliberal globalisation will be shown to shape a 'political economy of the possible'[52] where global imperatives are refracted through the lens of the state,[53] which is able to bend and mould those forces to shape both materially and ideologically its autonomy – or hegemonic project – towards, in the case of Argentina, a national developmentalist vision. Furthermore, these same dynamics can contribute to an understanding of the breakdown of that model under CFK – a breakdown that occurred because of both changing domestic social relations and wider patterns of global political economy.

In summary, developmental roles emerge through a complex relationship between material relations and structures, combined with ideas and ideologies. The analytical separation of roles from structures reveals the role of material interests, previously obscured through an integration of state purpose and institutions when analysing state capacity. These are present at distinct levels of spatial analysis – national, regional, and global – and interact in complex ways to shape and limit any given state's (developmental) autonomy, although not to the extent of being absolutely constraining. When understood in these terms, the developmental state can move away from the lionising of narrow bureaucratic embeddedness and authoritarianism. Instead, broader suites of socio-economic relationships can be examined, which are the product of complex, mutually reconstititive relationships between material interests and ideas at multiple spatial sites of analysis.

Argentina under the Kirchners

The Argentine state and development

Post-2001 crisis Argentina underwent notable change regarding its development trajectory. This change can be summarised as a redefinition, and associated strengthening, of the state in two core aspects. First is the role of the state as an agent of redistribution for social justice; second is the state as regulator of markets. The redefinition of the role of government was in the context of the neoliberalism of Carlos Menem in the 1990s, where the government was an 'absent state'.[54] Public expenditures were focused on poverty reduction and social deprivation through a variety of *Planes*. Whilst the first – *Plan Jefes y Jefas de Hogar* – was initiated under Duhalde, under Nestor Kirchner this programme was run down by preventing new entrants and instead placing them on his own *Planes*: *Planes Trabajar* and *Plan Familias*.[55] These were expanded under CFK in terms of the number as well as the scope. One particularly important flagship policy was the AUH (*Asignacion Universal por Hijo*). Initiated in 2010, this programme provides approximately 200 Argentine pesos a month for nearly 4 million children and families.[56] Collectively, these policies facilitated a reduction in the poverty rate (USD $2/day at Purchasing Power Parity [PPP]) from 16.4% in 2003 to 2.9% by 2011 (see Table 1), although this must be treated with caution given the government manipulation of Instituto Nacional de Estadistica y Censos de la Republica Argentina (INDEC) – the official statistical agency of the state – after 2007. However, even if alternative data is used – such as the Catholic University data set – whilst the figures are higher, they still display the same general downward trend (see Table 1). Increases in per-capita public spending (in USD at 2010 prices) from $1301 in 2003 to $2002 by 2007[57] reflected this emphasis on social welfare programmes in the form of the various *Planes* as detailed above.

In addition to redistributive policies, Argentine political economy shifted its public policy profile in terms of the state as an agent of redistribution for social justice came through its policies towards the labour market. Precipitous drops in unemployment from 16.1% in 2003 at the start of Nestor Kirchner's administration to 7.5% in 2013, steadily increasing real wages (in spite of significant inflation post 2007), several increases in the minimum wage throughout the period, a reduction in the informal labour sector, and a new form of 'segmented neocorporatism'[58] to manage relations between the state, labour, and business all facilitated a state that was active and interventionist in the labour market in order to help facilitate redistribution of wealth for social justice reasons.

The second core aspect of the post-crisis Argentine public policy profile came in the form of market regulation. Under Néstor Kirchner Argentina experienced substantial economic growth, with GDP exceeding pre-crisis levels within a year of the start of his administration. The policies that achieved this growth can be grouped under the two main themes of macroeconomic policy and industrial policy. In terms of macroeconomics, the administration adopted an exchange rate policy that Frenkel and Rapetti[59] have termed a 'stable and competitive real exchange rate' (SCRER). This was one of a suite of policies that led to a significant boost in exports, manifesting in a sustained surplus in the current account. Furthermore, given the presence of export taxes, this policy also helped to provide sustained fiscal surpluses, as well as expansions of state spending in areas such as welfare (see above), reduction of national debt, and industrial policy. Whilst the role of record international commodity prices cannot be ignored, Kirchner was still able to harness these forces to maximum benefit, as well as the fact that a sizable proportion of the economic growth seen during the period

Table 1. Key economic indicators in Argentina, 2003–2014.

	2003	2004	2005	2006	2007	2008	2009	2010	2011	2012	2013	2014
Gross Domestic Product (GDP) growth (%) (World Bank)	8.8	9.0	9.1	8.3	8.0	3.1	0.05	9.1	8.5	0.9	2.9	2.8
Inflation (%) Instituto Nacional de Estadistica y Censos de la Republica Argentina (INDEC)	4.9	6.1	12.3	9.8	8.5	7.2	7.7	10.9	9.5	10.2	10.6	
Inflation (%) (Congreso Nacional)*	–	–	–	–	–	–	–	–	22.64	25.25	28.27	38.53
Primary Balance (% GDP) Comisión Económica para América Latina y el Caribe (CEPAL)	2.1	3.2	2.3	2.7	2.7	2.8	1.4	1.5	−0.1	−0.1	−1.4	−2.0
REER (2005 = 100) (CEPAL)	96.9	100.2	100	101.9	101.4	97.2	99.3	98.5	99.5	94.8		
Poverty at $2/day Purchasing Power Parity (PPP) (%) (World Bank)	16.4	12.3	9.8	7.4	6.4	5.7	5.4	3.9	2.9	–	–	–
Poverty (%)**	–	–	–	–	–	–	–	17.6	14.3	15.5	16.5	
Indigence at $1.25/day (PPP) (World Bank)	9	6.3	4.6	3.8	3.0	2.7	2.7	1.7	1.4	–	–	–
Indigence**	–	–	–	–	–	–	–	7.3	6.2	5.8	5.5	
Unemployment (%) International Labour Organisation (ILO)	16.1	12.6	10.6	10.1	8.5	7.8	8.6	7.7	7.2	7.2	7.5	
Current account balance (% GDP) (World Bank)	6.2	2.1	2.3	2.9	2.2	1.6	2.2	0.3	−0.4	−0.2	−0.7	
Central government gross public debt (% GDP) (CEPAL)			60.2	51.7	44.2	39.0	39.6	36.1	33.3	35.4	37.9	39.6
Gini index (World Bank)	53.54	50.18	49.27	48.26	47.37	46.27	45.27	44.5	43.57			
Commodity prices (eg oil and precious metals) (2000 = 100) Economist Intelligence Unit (EIU)	99.7	103.6	106.9	110.7	116.1	123.1	117.4	123.1	133.0	133.5	133.0	132.3

*Since 2011, opposition members of the National Congress have published inflation data that is an aggregate from eight different independent consultants.
**Data produced by Universidad Católica Argentina *Observatorio de la Deuda Social Argentina*. Figures are individual urban poverty and indigence based on ability to buy a basic basket of goods.

2003–2007 was in the manufacturing sector[60] and therefore independent of the reversal in terms of trade during this time.

There was also a shift in emphasis in the management of the Argentine economy since 2003. This was to encourage production, more specifically the industrial sectors of the economy, at the expense of the financial sector, especially the banking and capital markets.[61] There were dozens of mechanisms and promotion programmes that offered tax breaks, subsidies, sponsored credit, and technical assistance which formed the core of Kirchner's industrial policy, and thus facilitated this change in the structure of the Argentine economy.[62] In addition, there were many public works programmes such as road building, bridge construction, etc. to promote private levels of economic activity.[63] This represented a key source of change in the structure of the post-crisis Argentine economy in comparison to the Menem period. Banking and capital markets that took centre stage during the 1990s, whilst not actively discouraged, were relegated to low importance in comparison to industry and the 'real' economy broadly defined.

This was all part of an attempt by the Argentine state under the Kirchners to forge a new social contract. The first important development was regarding the poor and working classes, who benefited from expanding welfare combined with expanding employment opportunities. In addition, substantial increases in the minimum wage complemented these trends. Second, trade union groups have formed part of the alliance, although not in as central a role as under former models of capital accumulation such as *Peronismo*. This is since welfare provision moved beyond formal unionised sectors of society and into family life, thus reducing the influence of clientelistic links present between the state and the trade union movement present under *Peronismo*.[64] Third, middle-class elements were brought into the regime. The stabilisation of the macroeconomic environment from 2003 onwards combined an exchange rate policy that favoured domestic bourgeoisie elements (and especially exporters) brought these elements into the *Kirchnerismo* model. Furthermore, the consumer boom that such policies facilitated fed into underlying middle-class support, ensuring that the state brought widespread benefits across different class fractions rather than simply representing any one discrete class or class fraction. Finally, stimulation of exports also favoured agro-industrialists. Given that the agro-industry in Argentina is dominated by TNCs (especially soy), this policy also brought these interests of international capital into the model.

During the presidency of CFK from 2008 onwards, several underlying issues manifested themselves into several strain points that facilitated shifts in this broad class alliance and Argentina's public policy profile. The first area of tension was concerning relations with domestic rural oligarchs, agricultural TNCs, and the state. In 2008 there was widespread social unrest as farmers all over the country blocked major routes and roads to ports and cities, preventing the passing of trucks transporting agricultural commodities. This was in response to the government's announcement of an extension of export taxes (*retenciones*) on soyabean products from 35 to 45%, greatly affecting soy, maize, wheat, and sunflower seed producers' interests. Due to the flat nature of the tax it produced an unlikely coalition of interests between rural oligarchs, TNCs, and medium- and small-scale producers.[65] Second, there were those creditors who did not agree to the debt swap and haircut in 2005 (and in 2010 after a second deal was struck by CFK with 93% of the holdouts from 2005), or at least the vulture funds (such as Elliott Management) who bought the outstanding debt on secondary markets. These firms used legal systems in friendly countries to try to force Argentina to repay on defaulted debt in full, including accrued interest. This led to a 'technical default' in August 2014, and the protracted locking out of Argentina from international capital markets – facilitating a shortage of foreign currency domestically. Third, there was widespread unrest from September 2012 across the country, including rioting and looting in December 2012.[66] The rioters were a mix, involving middle classes protesting foreign exchange restrictions, curbs on imported goods, and high inflation making it impossible to save. Also present were organised labour movements protesting lower real wages because of high inflation, demanding further extensions in welfare provision, and wanting greater involvement in the creation of state policy like they had had under previous regimes such as those of Péron.[67]

The collapse of international demand that followed the global financial crisis hit Argentine exports hard. A key cornerstone of Argentine political economy post 2001 has been the rise in exports. As well as the direct impact on exports of a manufacturing origin, this dynamic also served to restrict the revenues gained from agricultural exports due to associated declining terms of trade. This was exacerbated in 2012 by severe drought which affected yields. In turn, this impacted on Argentina's public finances. After *retenciones* were reintroduced in 2002 they became an important source of state income, representing an average of 12% of budget revenues by 2010.[68] The attempt by CFK to increase *retenciones* in 2008 was a direct response to these changing international dynamics, coupled with a desire to maintain fiscal surpluses in the face of declining revenues.

The drop in international demand for Argentina's exports facilitated downward pressure on its nominal exchange rate. This trend was further exacerbated by the need to import increasing amounts of energy to fuel Argentina's rapid (although by now the rate of GDP growth was declining) economic expansion in the absence of domestic investment in energy production. In turn, this eroded Argentina's current account surplus. A drop in the nominal exchange rate combined with increasing inflation to increase Argentina's Real Exchange Rate (see Table 1), further eroding export competitiveness and thus causing a further drop in the current account surplus. This fall in the current account surplus (to a small deficit by 2011) threatened to undermine one of the key cornerstones of *Kirchnerismo*. Persistent current account deficits in the 1990s during neoliberal restructuring led to excessive foreign debt accumulation, mounting on top of an already significant debt accrued during the bureaucratic–authoritarian period. Ultimately, this helped precipitate economic meltdown in 2001–2002. and the associated dislocation of Argentine politics and society.[69]

Many of CFK's policies can be interpreted as attempts to correct these pressures on the current account balance. A series of foreign exchange restrictions to prevent domestic US dollar hoarding caused tensions with middle-class elements of Argentine society as foreign travel and holidays become more expensive. In addition, several import restrictions, as well as measures to require businesses that import to also export goods, widened these tensions to domestic bourgeois elements of the middle classes. The re-nationalisation of Yacimientos Petroliferos Fiscales (YPF) to reignite energy investment and thus reduce the levels of imported energy (which in turn would help relieve pressure on the current account balance) also created tensions with elements of international capital.

High inflation after 2007 was a persistent trend (see Table 1), causing further tensions amongst different socio-economic groups in Argentine society. The middle classes, once again, were hit through difficulties in saving given the level of inflation in the economy, especially when combined with the foreign exchange restrictions that made it difficult to use the US dollar as a more inflation-proof store of value. The working classes and trade unions were hit because of the erosion of real wages that this began to facilitate. Whilst there was some redistribution to these elements of Argentine society because of the state taking responsibility for economic growth, this began to be undermined by 2012 as growth stalled but the inflationary trend persisted. Many of the poorest in Argentina were protected from this trend through a persistently expansionary fiscal stance that saw the extension of welfare benefits beyond the more traditional clientelist links with trade union organisations.[70] Therefore, whilst important in the political context of increasing tensions between the Argentine state and organised labour, the impact of inflation on real income levels of the poor should not be exaggerated.

In summary, the policies of CFK represented departures from her husband's more cautious and pragmatic approach. They were the result of twin forces at play in contemporary Argentina: first, the deteriorating international economic conditions, in contrast to the relatively benign international economic environment that prevailed in the 2003–2009 period; second, the collapse of international demand in the wake of the global financial crisis which severely impacted on Argentina's export-driven growth model. This was also exacerbated by a fall in international commodity prices in 2009 (see Table 1) as agricultural commodities still represented by far the largest share of Argentine exports. However, this should not be overemphasised as Table 1 also shows that international commodity prices soon bounced back after 2009, and many other countries in the region were not as affected by the same changes in prices (Bolivia, for example). The second factor that has played a significant role in the deterioration of GDP growth (see Table 1) was Cristina's policies intended to 'deepen the model'. This came in the form of extending welfare – through, for example, the AUH – and extension of the minimum wage to non-unionised workers, counter-cyclical fiscal spending in the wake of the global financial crisis, and maintaining (or even increasing) subsidies and price controls in a few areas – especially transport, energy, and fuel. Cristina's heterodox policies prevented outright recession, and maintained reductions in poverty and reductions in the Gini index (see Table 1), but at the expense of rampant inflation, and the key loss of the twin surpluses in the current and fiscal accounts.

The evolution of Neodesarrollismo

Neodesarrollismo was the defining concept of this distinct political economy, and was based on a set of national and international relationships that fused populism with neoliberalism. This was different from both traditional *Peronismo* and the associated *desarrollista* political economy of the 1940s and 1950s, and from the neoliberal *Menemismo* of the 1990s.[71] This is something that can only be understood through analysis of material interests and their interaction with ideas to generate social relations inclined towards developmentalism. This evolution was detailed in the previous section; unlike the case of *Peronismo*, there was no clear link between citizenship and social welfare in *Kirchnerismo* and its associated *neodesarrollismo* model. Rather, it was closer to *Menemismo* and neoliberal-style social safety nets. Under Nestor Kirchner *neodesarrollismo* displayed constructive relations with both business and trade unions different to both *Peronismo* and *Menemismo*.[72] Developmental strategy was grounded in a pursuit of GDP growth based on selective protectionism and targeted state intervention to facilitate macroeconomic stability. This contrasted with *Peronism*'s developmentalist policies of state intervention through import substituting industrialisation and citizenship defined in terms of economic rights. Furthermore, this contrasted with *Menemismo*, which stressed stability through controlling inflation via its fixed exchange rate mechanism, *Convertibilidad*, as well as reducing the role of the state in the economy through neoliberal-inspired policies such as privatisation.[73]

The generation of successful developmental structures and a sufficiently powerful developmental role through *neodesarrollismo* concluded under CFK. Understanding the nature of that decline through the same framework further reveals the importance of the interaction of material interests and ideas, and the subsequent generation of distinct developmental structures and developmental roles. Analysing institutions and ideas alone[74] leads to the privileging of institutionalist and bureaucratic accounts as well as overly favouring the agency of leadership, rather than seeing institutions as a product of the interaction of ideas and material interests. It was not the undermining of key bureaucratic institutions such as the INDEC, or increasingly confrontational corporatist politics, or fractures with international capital markets that gives us the reason why Argentina's post-crisis developmentalist model spluttered under CFK. Whilst these are certainly symptoms of a disfunctional and rapidly disappearing developmentalism, they were the product of underlying changes in material interests, which interacted with changing ideas about 'deepening the model' from CFK. This change was not resisted institutionally due to the historically weak nature of the Argentine state, itself due to the consistent shifting of development cycles in the *longue durée*.[75] Instead, the role of social relations is highlighted, and in Argentina the always fragile class consensus that underpins state power, drawing attention away from a weak bureaucracy, or overly individualised accounts centring on the agency of CFK.

In the context of the transferability debates, focus should shift away from the organisational features of a state, such as its bureaucracy, and instead look to understanding empirically induced accounts of changing social relations and evolving ideologies. The coalescence of durable developmental visions or state roles with distinct developmental structures draws attention back to the politics and power relationships present in societies. In the case of Argentina this allows for an account of developmental decline under CFK not as the product of historically weak institutions,[76] but due to the fact that those weak institutions were the product of shifting social relations that did not coalesce for sufficiently long periods around principles of (neo)developmentalism.

In summary, Argentina's development trajectory underwent clear shifts away from previous forms of political economy in the form of both *Peronismo* and *Menemismo.* From a shift in the link between citizenship and welfare to the renegotiation of Argentina's relationship with international capital, *Kirchnerismo* represented a different model of capital accumulation. This renegotiation was not to hold, however. Many of the CFK administration's policies served to unravel core aspects of the socio-economic relations that underpinned *Kirchnerismo* in the immediate post-crisis period. By abandoning fiscal and current account surpluses, by allowing inflation to erode the previously favourable exchange rate, and by using export restrictions to limit the amount of foreign exchange in the domestic economy, CFK's extension of the post-neoliberal developmental regime in Argentina became incoherent and unsustainable. Changing ideas and social relations ended up resulting in policies designed to buy certain groups support in a clientelist manner, rather than foster long-term support for a distinctly neo-developmentalist model that could be institutionalised in an enduring way.

Conclusions: the developmental state in the twenty-first century

The case of Argentina has clear implications for the developmental state literature, with those concerning transferability being addressed in this article. The developmental state literature's highlighting of the difference between developmental structures and developmental roles represents a key access point into understanding the dynamics of Argentine development under the Kirchners. As a concept, it therefore remains useful in the twenty-first century. Such a separation allows focus upon both ideas and material interests in forming the necessary developmental political consensus and attendant institutions for successful catch-up development. In drawing attention to the nature of post-crisis social relations in the Argentine context, this article has suggested that interrogating the changing nature of state–society relations reveals new understandings of contemporary developmental states. Having the legitimacy and political will to pursue developmentalism is as important as possessing the capacities to do so. Finally, this article has drawn attention to the fact that the (re)forging of state power towards social contracts grounded in developmentalism also occurs under conditions of multi-level governance. Whilst the state acts as the key site of congruence of different governance imperatives, any understanding of developmental states today must trace the contours of power relations that reveal how a state's autonomy and capacity are shaped by forces in the global political economy. In the case of Argentina, this led to the shaping of key aspects of the state's capacities because of its terms of access to foreign capital markets, which, in turn, limited its autonomy and undermined underlying social relations.

Argentina offers a clear lesson to the transferability debates that a country can be a failed developmental state as well as a successful one. In the context of a changing global political economy, a developmental state is clearly not static, or necessarily robust. Indeed, Argentina offers an empirical insight into the potentially fragile nature of a developmental state. The constellation of social relations, institutions, and ideas that shape a state's developmental structures and developmental roles can be transitory, fleeting, and subject to change from both above and below the state. This draws attention to the need to further investigate and research the objective conditions under which developmental states can flourish: not only in terms of maintaining the necessary developmental structures in the face of sometimes contradictory political and economic pressures, but also in terms of maintaining developmental roles conducive to the creation and maintenance of a hegemonic ideology consistent with rapid, catch-up development.

Disclosure statement

No potential conflict of interest was reported by the author.

Acknowledgements

I would like to thank the Institute of Latin American Studies (ILAS) in the School of Advanced Study (SAS) at the University of London for their support in the form of a Visiting Research Fellowship, which offered invaluable resources during the drafting of this article.

Notes

1. Sen, *Development as Freedom*.
2. Johnson, *MITI and the Japanese Miracle*.
3. Routley, *Developmental States*, 8.
4. Evans et al., *Bringing the State Back In*, 9.
5. Little, *An Economic Reconnaissance*; and Rodrik, *Limits of Trade*.
6. Vu, *State Formation*, 38.
7. Woo-Cummings, *Developmental State*; Pempel, *Developmental Regime*, 171.
8. Katz, *Las Tendencias*; Wylde, *State, Society, and Markets*.
9. Grugel and Riggirozzi, *Post-neoliberalism in Latin America*; Wylde, *Post-neoliberal Developmental Regimes*; Ruckert, Macdonald, and Prouix, *Post-neoliberalism in Latin America*.
10. Routley, *Developmental* States, 13.
11. see Leftwich, *States of Development*; Evans, *21st Century Developmental State*; Wylde, *Developmental State is Dead*.
12. Vu, *State Formation*, 49.
13. Wade, *Governing the Market*.
14. Evans, *Transferrable Lessons?*
15. see Mkandawire, *Developmental States in Africa*; Musamba, *Developmental State Concept*.
16. see Panizza, *Contemporary Latin America*; Grugel and Riggirozzi, *Post-neoliberalism in Latin America*; Nem Singh, *Post-neoliberal Resource Politics*; Wylde, *Developmental State is Dead*.
17. Johnson, *MITI and the Japanese Miracle*, 323.
18. Evans, *Transferrable Lessons?*, 83.
19. Leftwich, *Developmental States, Effective States*, 16; Pempel, *Developmental Regime*, 146–7.
20. Doner, Ritchie, and Slater, *Systemic Vulnerability*.
21. Strange, *New Political Economy of Development*.
22. Williams, *End of the Developmental State?*
23. Evans, *21st Century Developmental State*, 10; Hayashi, *Developmental State*, 59.
24. Evans, *21st Century Developmental State*, 17.
25. Sikkink, *Ideas and Institutions*, 11.
26. Evans, Rueschemeyer, and Skocpol, *Bringing the State Back In*, 20–1.
27. Sikkink, *Ideas and Institutions*.
28. Evans, *Embedded Autonomy*.
29. Ibid., 12.
30. Weiss, *Myth of the Powerless State*, 38.
31. Pempel, *Developmental Regime*, 157.
32. Ibid., 144.
33. Johnson, *MITI and the Japanese Miracle*, 356.
34. Cumings, *Webs with no Spiders*, 61.
35. Ibid., 145.
36. Haggard, *Institutions and Growth*, 70.

37. Sikkink, *Ideas and Institutions*, 19–20.
38. Ibid., 19.
39. Ibid., 21.
40. Vu, *State Formation*, 38.
41. Pempel, *Developmental Regimes*, 171.
42. Johnson, *The Developmental State*, 42.
43. Leftwich, *Developmental States, Effective States*, 16.
44. Sikkink, *Ideas and Institutions*, 120–1; Pempel, *Developmental Regime*, 168.
45. Doner, Ritchie, and Slater, *Systemic Vulnerability*.
46. Haggard, *Institutions and Growth*, 71.
47. Katz, *Las Tendencias*; Wylde, *State, Society, and Markets*.
48. Routley, *Developmental States*, 13.
49. Fine and Kyung-Sup, *Devevlopmental Politics*, 300.
50. Pempel, *Developmental Regimes*, 177; Leftwich, *Developmental States, Effective States*, 16; Fritz and Menical, *Developmental States in the New Millennium*, 542.
51. Fine and Kyung-Sup, *Developmental Politics*, 301.
52. Santiso, *Political Economy of the Possible.*
53. Nem Singh, *Towards Post-neoliberal Resource Politics*, 331.
54. Kirchner, cited in Cohen, *Argentina's Economic Growth and Recovery*, 106.
55. Beccaria et al., *Crisis y recuperación*.
56. Grugel and Riggirozzi, *Post-neoliberalism in Latin America*, 9.
57. CEPAL, *Economic Survey*.
58. Etchemendy and Collier, *Down but Not Out*, 363.
59. Frenkel & Rapetti, *Five Years*, 217.
60. Bezchinsky et al., *Inversion extranjera directa en la Argentina*; Wylde, *States, Society, and Markets*, 439.
61. Ferrer, *La economia argentina*, 370–1.
62. Baruj and Porta, *Politicas de Competitividad*; see also Ortiz and Schorr, *Crisis Internacional*, 5.
63. Heidrich and Tussie, *Post-neoliberalism and the New Left*, 45.
64. Grugel and Riggirozzi, *Post-neoliberalism in Latin America*.
65. Cohen, *Argentina's Economic Growth and Recovery*, 133.
66. The Economist, *President and the Potbangers*, 47; The Economist, *Sarks in the Dark*, 32.
67. The Economist, *President and the Potbangers*, 48.
68. INDEC, *Anuario Estadístico*.
69. Svampa, *Revisiting Argentina*.
70. Grugel and Riggirozzi, *Post-neoliberalism in Latin America*, 9.
71. Wylde, *State, Society, and Markets*, 449.
72. Etchemendey and Collier, *Down But Not Out*.
73. Wylde, *State, Society, and Markets*, 450.
74. See Sikkink, *Ideas and Institutions*.
75. Chudnovsky, *Elusive Quest*.
76. For an argument centred on institutional weakness related to capacity in the *desarrollista* period see Sikkink, *Ideas and Institutions*.

Bibliography

Baruj, G., and F. Porta. *Politicas de Competitividad en la Argentina y su Impacto Sobre la Profundizacion del Mercosur* [Argentine Competitiveness Policy and its Impact on the Deepening of Mercosur]. Santiago de Chile: CEPAL, 2005.

Beccaria, L., V. Esquivel, and R. Maurizio. *Crisis y recuperación: Efectos sobre el mercado de trabajo y la distribución del ingreso* [Crisis and Recovery: Impacts on Employment and Income Distribution]. Argentina: Universidad Nacional de General Sarmiento, 2007.

Bezchinsky, G., M. Dinenzon, L. Guissani, and O. Caino. *Inversion extranjera directa en la Argentina. Crisis, reestructuracion y nuevas tendencias despues de la convertibilidad* [Foreign Direct Investment in Argentina: Crisis, Restructuring, and New Trends after Convertibility]. Documento de Proyecto. Santiago: CEPAL, 2007.

CEPAL *Economic Survey of Latin America and the Caribbean: 2010–2011*. Santiago de Chile: CEPAL, 2010.

Chang, D. "Labour and the 'Developmental State': A Critique of the Developmental State Theory of Labour." In *Beyond the Developmental State: Industrial Policy into the Twenty-First Century*, edited by B. Fine, J. Saraswati, and D. Tavasci, 85–109. London: Pluto Press, 2013.

Cohen, M. A. *Argentina's Economic Growth and Recovery: The Economy in a Time of Default*. London: Routledge, 2012.

Cumings, B. "Webs with No Spiders, Spiders with No Webs: The Genealogy of the Developmental State." In *The Developmental State*, edited by Woo-Cumings, 61–93. New York: Cornell University Press, 1999.

Chudnovsky, D. *The Elusive Quest for Growth in Argentina*. Palgrave: PalgraveMacmillan, 2007.

Doner, R. F., B. K. Ritchie, and D. Slater. "Systemic Vulnerability and the Origins of Developmental States: Northeast and Southeast Asia in Comparative Perspective." *International Organization* 59, no. 2 (2005): 327–361.

Etchemendy, S., and R. B. Collier. "Down but Not out: Union Resurgence and Segmented Neocorporatism in Argentina (2003–2007)." *Politics and Society* 35, no. 3 (2007): 363–401.

Evans, P. B., D. Rueschemeyer, and T. Skocpol. *Bringing the State Back in*. Cambridge: Cambridge University Press, 1985.

Evans, P. *Embedded Autonomy: States and Industrial Transformation*. Princeton: Princeton University Press, 1995.

Evans, P. "Transferrable Lessons? Re-Examining the Institutional Pre-Requisites of East Asian Economic Policies." *Journal of Development Studies* 34, no. 6 (2007): 66–86.

Evans, P. B. "In Search of the Twenty First Century Developmental State." *CGPE Working Paper Series*, No.4, December, 2008.

Ferrer, A. *La Economía Argentina* [The Argentine Economy]. Buenos Aires: Fondo, 2005.

Fine, B., and C. Kyung-Sup. "Developmental Politics beyond the Neoliberal Era." In *Beyond the Developmental State: Industrial Policy into the Twenty-First Century*, edited by B. Fine, J. Saraswati, and D. Tavasci, 299–318. London: Pluto Press, 2012.

Frenkel, R., and M. Rapetti. "Five Years of Competitive and State Real Exchange Rate in Argentina 2002–2007." *International Review of Applied Economics* 22, no. 2 (2008): 215–226.

Fritz, V., and A. R. Menical. "Developmental States in the New Millennium: Concepts and Challenges for a New Aid Agenda." *Development Policy Review* 25, no. 5 (2007): 531–552.

Grugel, J., and P. Riggirozzi. "Post-Neoliberalism in Latin America: Rebuilding and Reclaiming the State after Crisis." *Development and Change* 43, no. 1 (2012): 1–21.

Haggard, S. "Institutions and Growth in East Asia." *Studies in Comparative International Development* 138, no. 4 (2004): 53–81.

Hayashi, S. "The Developmental State in the Era of Globalization: Beyond the Northeast Asian Model of Political Economy." *The Pacific Review* 23, no. 1 (2010): 45–69.

Heidrich, P., and D. Tussie. "Post-Neoliberalism and the New Left in the Americas: The Pathways of Economic and Trade Policies." In *Post-Neoliberalism in the Americas*, edited by L. MacDonald and A. Ruckert, 37–53. PalgraveMacmillan: Basingstoke, 2009.

INDEC *Anuario Estadístico De La República* Argentina. Buenos Aires: INDEC, 2010.

Johnson, C. *MITI and the Japanese Miracle*. Stanford: Stanford University Press, 1982.

Johnson, C. "Political Institutions and Economic Performance|: The Government-Business Relationship in Japan, South Korea, and Taiwan." In *The Political Economy of New Asian Industrialism*, edited by F. C. Deyo, 165–179. Ithaca: Cornell University Press, 1987.

Johnson, C. "The Developmental State: Odyssey of a Concept." In *The Developmental State*, edited by M. Woo-Cumings, 32–60. Ithaca: Cornell University Press, 1999.

Katz, C. 2006. "Las Tendencias De La Economia Argentina." [Trends in the Argentine Economy.] *Argenpress*, 19 April. Accessed August 16, 2016. http://rebelion.org/docs/25473.pdf.

Leftwich, A. *States of Development: On the Primacy of Politics in Development*. Cambridge: Polity Press, 2000.

Leftwich, A. "Developmental States, Effective States and Poverty Reduction: The Primacy of Politics." *UNRISD Project on Poverty Reduction and Policy Regimes* (2008): 211–229.

Little, I. M. D. "An Economic Reconnaissance." In *Economic Growth and Structural Change in Taiwan: The Post-War Experience of the Republic of China*, edited by W. Galenson, 448–507. Ithaca: Cornell University Press, 1979.

Mkandawire, T. "Thinking about Developmental States in Africa." *Cambridge Journal of Economics* 25 (2001): 289–313.

Musamba, C. "The Developmental State Concept and Its Relevance for Africa." In *The Developmental State in Africa: Problems and Prospects*, edited by P. Meyns and C. Musamba. INEF: University of Suisburg-Essen, 2010.

Nem Singh, J. T. "Towards Post-Neoliberal Resource Politics? The International Political Economy (IPE) of Oil and Copper in Brazil and Chile." *New Political Economy* 19, no. 3 (2014): 329–358.

O'Donnell, G. *Modernisation and Bureaucratic Authoritarianism*. Berkeley: Institute of International Studies, 1973.

Ortiz, R., and M. Schorr. "Crisis internacional y alternativas de reindustrialización en la Argentina." [International Crisis and Alternatives for Reindustrialisation in Argentina.] Documentos de Investigación Social, IDAES, Número 7, 2009.

Önis, Z. "Review: The Logic of the Developmental State." Comparative Politics 24, no. 1 (1991): 109–126.

Panizza, F. *Contemporary Latin America: Development and Democracy beyond the Washington Consensus*. London: Zed Books, 2009.

Pempel, T. J. "The Developmental Regime in a Changing World Economy." In *The Developmental State*, edited by M. Woo-Cummings, 137–181. Ithaca: Cornell University Press, 1999.

Pirie, I. "Globalisation and the Decline of the Developmental State." In *Beyond the Developmental State: Industrial Policy into the Twenty-First Century*, edited by B. Fine, J. Saraswati, and D. Tavasci, 146–168. London: Pluto Press, 2013.

Radice, H. "The Developmental State under Global Neoliberalism." *Third World Quarterly* 29, no. 6 (2008): 1153–1174.

Rodrik, D. "The Limits of Trade Policy Reform in Developing Countries." *Journal of Economic Perspectives* 6, no. 1 (1992): 87–105.

Routley, L. "Developmental States: A Review of the Literature." *ESID Woking Paper No. 3*. www.effective-states.org, 2012.

Ruckert, A., L. Macdonald, and K. R. Proulx. "Post-Neoliberalism in Latin America: A Conceptual Review." *Third World Quarterly* (2016): 1–20. doi:10.1080/01436597.2016.1259558.

Santiso, J. *The Political Economy of the Possible: Beyond Good Revolutionaries and Free Marketeers*. Cambridge: MIT Press, 2006.

Sen, A. *Development as Freedom*. New York: Alfred A, 1999.

Strange, G. *Towards a New Political Economy of Development: States and Regions in the Post-Neoliberal World*. Basingstoke: PalgraveMacmillan, 2014.

Svampa, M. "Revisiting Argentina 2001-13: From *"¡Que Se Vayan Todos!"* to the Peronist Decade." In *Argentina since the 2001 Crisis: Recovering the past, Reclaiming the Future*, edited by C. Levey, D. Ozarow, and C. Wylde, 155–175. New York: PalgraveMacmillan, 2014.

The Economist. *The President and the Potbangers*, September 29, 2012.

The Economist. *Sparks in the Dark*, January 19, 2013.

Vu, T. "State Formation and the Origins of Developmental States in South Korea and Indonesia." *Studies in Comparative International Development* 41, no. 4 (2007): 27–56.

Wade, R. *Governing the Market: Economic Theory and the Role of Government in East Asian Industrialisation*. Princeton: Princeton University Press, 1990.

Weiss, L. *The Myth of the Powerless State*. Cambridge: Polity, 1998.

Williamson, J. "What Washington Means by Policy Reform." In *Latin American Adjustment: How Much Has Happened?*, edited by J. Williamson, 7–20. Washington: Institute for International Economics, 2011.

Williams, M., ed. *The End of the Developmental State?* London: Routledge, 2014.

Woo-Cummings, M., ed. *The Developmental State*. Ithaca: Cornell University Press, 1999.

Wylde, C. "State, Society, and Markets in Argentina: The Political Economy of *Neodesarrollismo* under Nestor Kirchner, 2003-2007." *Bulletin of Latin American Research* 30, no. 4 (2011): 436–452.

Wylde, C. "The Developmental State is Dead, Long Live the Developmental Regime! Interpreting Néstor Kirchner's Argentina 2003–2007." *Journal of International Relations and Development* 17, no. 2 (2014): 191–219.

Wylde, C. "Post-Neoliberal Developmental Regimes in Latin America: Argentina under Cristina Fernandez De Kirchner." *New Political Economy* 21, no. 3 (2016): 322–341.

OPEN ACCESS

Industrial policy and state-making: Brazil's attempt at oil-based industrial development

Eliza Massi[§] and Jewellord Nem Singh

ABSTRACT
This paper examines the changing strategies of developmental states using Brazil's oil-based industrial policy as a case study. We analyse the relationship between the state, Petrobras and industrial elites in the context of Brazil's renewed emphasis on sector-specific industrial development strategy. Taking stock and re-examining the developmental state model, we suggest that developmental states are inherently political, particularly their bureaucracy and state-owned enterprises (SOEs), and that money politics is intricately woven into state-guided high growth regimes. Given the difficulty of privatisation as a solution to SOE (mis)governance, the challenge for Brazil is to mediate extreme political interventions that have eroded Petrobras' autonomy in the past and to sustain institutional capacity to direct rents towards investment and innovation.

Introduction

> Petrobras was a victim of the [Lava Jato] criminal scheme – in not one moment was it a beneficiary.
>
> Pedro Parente, Petrobras CEO[1]

The *Lava Jato* (Car Wash) scandal that embroiled Petrobras, Brazil's state-controlled energy firm, into the centre of political corruption marked the gradual unravelling of state interventionist policies in Brazil. What became a crisis of Brazilian state capitalism has tentatively put an end to Lula da Silva and his Workers' Party (PT) deepening of state capitalism as a development strategy. As the crisis deepened, and more politicians, state bureaucrats and private companies become implicated by the investigation, questions have arisen whether Brazil's developmental state has turned into predatory capitalism. These moments of crises are interesting times, which compel scholars and policy-makers to partake their assessments over

Jewellord Nem Singh http://orcid.org/0000-0002-5216-4408

§ The views expressed in this paper are those of the author and do not refl ect the offi cial policy or position of the Brazilian government or any of its agencies.

the policies, politics and institutions that generate successful industrial policy, and the associated costs that have to be borne with as an outcome of these development strategies.

In this context, our paper takes a step back to assess what state capitalism entails from a sectoral perspective. In evaluating Brazil's developmental state model and its effectiveness in managing economic globalisation, we focus on the PT government's attempts at crafting sectoral linkages and reviving the capital goods industries through the oil and gas (O&G) sector – a strategy reflective of some familiar instruments characterising the state-led high growth regimes of East Asia. It is undoubtedly the case that Brazil's model of development centred on state intervention, achieving key features of Northeast Asian developmental states. However, in contrast to Northeast Asia, Brazil lacked the coherence and social cohesion found in classic developmental states and failed to promote an overall re-orientation of the economy towards high value-added manufacturing.[2] For these reasons, Schneider suggests that Brazil's economic performance as a developmental state is medium, at best, since the country's political elites are coherent in terms of ideology and political intent (or developmental role) as well as capacity to direct policies (or developmental structures), leading to several successes in creating competitive sectors, such as in aerospace and O&G. However, the state falls short in terms of sustaining industrial growth and in creating innovation systems.[3]

Our substantive contribution to this special issue rests on advancing a critical appraisal of the successes and shortcomings of Brazil's sectoral policies as a means to promote industrial growth. Our argument is as follows. Firstly, we claim that developmental states are motivated by political as opposed to economic rationale in pursuit of state-guided high growth regimes. Hence, the unravelling of Brazil's developmental strategy is partly a consequence of how state-owned enterprises (SOEs) are intrinsically embedded in political interventions by national elites, leading to constrained choices over an SOE's ability to make productive investments that would lead to innovation and competitiveness in the economy. Secondly, by focussing on the O&G sector as a case study, our paper argues that developmental states can design resource-intensive development strategies provided that a clear vision exists as regards how the national government will meet the high capital requirements and intensive technological innovation systems necessary to push for structural transformation through natural resources. Historically, the O&G industry is subject to heavy state regulation and characterised by state ownership through public enterprises. In Brazil, Petrobras played a central role in sectoral development and, through its particular relationship with the government, grew to become a major global energy player. Hence, the O&G sector is today one of the main drivers of the Brazilian economy; its contribution to national GDP increased substantially from 3% in 2000 to 13% in 2014.[4] Echoing Ovadia and Wolf in this volume, scholars need to look beyond traditional sectors if we are to seek for emerging developmental strategies outside of the East Asian region. Brazil is an exemplar of a developmental state that has successfully industrialised in the recent past, but is also attempting to make important strides to seek new comparative advantages and promote alternative ways of doing industrial policy. Our paper, then, offers an initial evaluation as regards the gains and shortcomings of its strategy.

What we know about developmental states

The idea of government intervention in developing countries has a long intellectual history that privileged the state as the prime entrepreneur in the context of uneven development.[5] However, the necessary empirical evidence supporting the viability of state intervention did not come until the successful industrialisation of East Asian countries. The concept of the 'developmental state' emerged, and became 'a shorthand for the seamless web of political, bureaucratic, and moneyed influences that structure economic life in capitalist Northeast Asia'.[6] But as global market integration narrows the spaces for national industrialisation, the purpose and significance of state action in directing growth-enhancing sectors in a new international context requires asking what sort of intervention enhances productivity and generates structural transformation, how this intervention occurs and for what purpose.[7]

Historically, states have intervened in many ways to initiate economic development. In order to enhance productivity and initiate structural transformation, states used a variety of direct and indirect instruments. Such instruments ranged from subsidies, tariffs, incentives and direct credit to monetary policies, to name a few.[8] Driven by the need and intent to industrialise, they sought to expand the size of their domestic markets through political centralisation, creation of domestic demand through backward linkages and improvement in labour productivity and supply by removing barriers to mobility as well as development of human capital.[9] These policy objectives were achieved through the mobilisation of resources aimed at promoting the import and adaptation of foreign technology. In other words, states implemented a series of interdependent policies aimed at responding to the multiple bottlenecks of late development.

In the literature on developmental states, there are three important elements that have been identified as *necessary preconditions* for successful industrialisation: (1) a high degree of administrative capacity of the professional bureaucracy – or state capacity (developmental structures) – combined with relative political autonomy from rent-seeking interests to carry out a development programme; (2) the presence of a developmental vision or guiding ideology that proffers coherence in policy paradigm (developmental role);[10] and (3) the presence of a governing coalition between states and industrial elites bound by discipline and mutual interdependence – a relationship that is crucial for the exchange of information, effective policy implementation and the creation of a shared developmental vision.[11] In contrast to the regulatory state often associated with Anglo-Saxon capitalism, where bureaucratic administrative capacity is focussed on rules and procedures, the bureaucracy in developmental states uses administrative discretion to establish economic goals and set targets – in other words, guide business through a number of instruments, such as preferential credit and subsidies.[12]

However, the DS literature has oftentimes come across as almost prescriptive and have been criticised for having unrealistic expectations about the actual workings of states outside East Asia.[13] In exploring the case study of Brazil, we highlight some of the assumptions of the theory that require further elaboration. Even when states bear the key characteristics that constitute a developmental state, the nature of domestic political coalitions and the historical conditions that shaped national firms and their relationship with governments co-vary across space and time. For example, South Korea is more successful than Taiwan and Singapore in mobilising financial resources for industrialisation because the Korean state was more disciplined with capital and labour.[14] Conversely, in the case of Brazil, the developmental state is not as cohesive as its East Asian counterparts and, given its economic size and territorial space, is historically fraught with political challenges of state centralisation.[15]

Brazil and a reappraisal of the developmental state

We draw out three elements of the theory to explain the changing Brazilian DS model. Firstly, we emphasise the *political* nature of state-building. Although 'pockets of state efficiency' and insulated bureaucrats were fundamental in crafting cohesive development plans, such bureaucracies are neither truly depoliticised nor completely technocratic. In Japan, MITI's bureaucratic autonomy was constrained and its decisions often followed the electoral strategy of the ruling party; in Taiwan, in turn, party bosses often shifted bureaucrats across top government agencies and ministries.[16] While bureaucratic selection in East Asian developmental states was based on merit, promotions were based on seniority and performance was assessed according to rule compliance.[17] For Haggard, it is 'misleading to think that bureaucrats enjoyed independence' in East Asian authoritarian regimes. Instead, bureaucracies are rightly 'interpreted as instruments of authoritarian rulers, reformed not to ensure their independence but to assure their loyalty to the leadership'.[18] The point is not that bureaucracies in East Asian developmental states were never autonomous and insulated; instead, bureaucracies are not completely depoliticised as direction, vision and political will are generated outside.[19] Hence, when we examine Brazil and its network of technocrats found in the ministries, government agencies and SOEs, we need to be aware that their autonomy is bounded within a state rationale guided by party politics, developmentalist visions and competing political objectives. The technocratic capacity of bureaucrats to design and implement industrial planning is, therefore, a necessary but insufficient condition in producing public goods, such as sound macro-economic management and pro-business policies.

Secondly, state–business relations are typically understood as the alliance between politicians, bureaucrats and industrial elites. Through the creation of intermediary institutions and informal channels, developmental states provide the platform to facilitate exchange of information, implement policies that support business interests and create a shared developmental vision between economic and political elites. Bearing this in mind, links to society and informal and formal networks were established to create a stable channel of communication and information exchanges between private and public sectors. For example, in Japan, upon retirement bureaucrats took employment in the private sector.[20] The same practice can be found in South Korea and Taiwan. These permeable ties between the public and private are constitutive of the process of embedding states within societies. Thus, the foundation of successful developmental states lies on the capacity of states to discipline businesses as well as on an alliance between state and businesses – or what Johnson refers as a 'consensus' between industrialists and policy elites.[21] This agreement, or developmental coalition, is more than a generic relationship between states and social forces. In Evans' term, it is the reconstitution of state agents and business actors in a relationship built upon the 'embedded autonomy' of the state.[22]

Yet another way of understanding East Asian state–business relations is through the lens of crony capitalism, wherein state–business alliance is about how money, corruption and rent-seeking were controlled by and through state institutions. Johnson admitted the existence of extensive 'structural corruption' (*kozo oshoku*) in the Japanese model, in which politicians receive funds from people seeking favours and that they have obligations to respond to these requests.[23] While some have dismissed this as an 'Asian way' of doing business, political corruption is integral to decision-making and was, in fact, a *precondition* for rapid growth in East Asia.[24] Prior to initiating the macroeconomic policy regimes associated with rapid growth, the conservative leaders in Japan and South Korea had to find ways to deal with potentially paralysing political battles within the right wing while the ruling Kuomintang (KMT) in Taiwan faced a potentially serious threat from an increasingly alienated majority, many of whom did not fully accept the KMT as a legitimate government. As Wederman sums up, the right turned to machine politics to create stable ruling coalitions, which enabled the bureaucracy to implement an industrial policy that transferred rents from state coffers to the private sector. Politicians served to buffer the technocrats from society and elections became the mechanism to buy-in political support through a network of local politicians and business actors. On the one hand, businesses offered financial resources in order for conservative political leaders to build stable coalitions by 'binding together what would otherwise have been a series of rival and often hostile factions'.[25] On the other hand, government control and policy stability provided the ruling coalition with the capacity to harness state policies aimed at repaying the 'big bosses' in *chaebols* and *keiretsu* while also investing on public and private goods.[26] To put it simply, state–business alliance is effectively a stable, recurring system of redistribution between public and private channels, which meets the mutual obligations of business and the state, leading to a political coalition able to forge a developmental vision and deliver these objectives through developmental structures within the state apparatus.

However, not all close relations between states and businesses lead to positive outcomes; depending on the context, they may degenerate into particularistic predation.[27] An unbalanced relationship may result in penetration and capture, as in the Philippines, or loss of state effectiveness, as in Korea, where reforms led to the fragmentation of the state and strengthening of business groups.[28] In the context of Evan's intermediate states, of which Brazil and India are examples, an unbalanced relationship could lead to clientelism, 'inability to construct joint projects with potential industrial elites' or inconsistency, as 'joint projects may be possible in certain sectors or certain periods but degenerate into clientelism or isolated autonomy in other sectors or other periods'.[29] The key, as Kang outlines, is a relationship built on a *coherent state and concentrated business* ('mutual hostages'), as opposed to dispersed business groups, which would compete for rents, or a fractured state that is incapable of disciplining the industrial elites.[30] In other words, only when neither the state nor business can overpower each other would a developmental alliance work and lead to industrial growth.

Finally, as Nem Singh and Chen argue, state ownership particularly in strategic industries has been relatively undertheorised in relation to the workings of the developmental state. Most DS scholarship focusses on the balance between the state and privately-owned businesses in terms of building an autonomous and equal partnership as the micro-foundation of state-guided high-growth system.[31] However, catching up in the industrialisation race is not a homogeneous or linear process; instead it is a process involving some segments of the economy through specific sectors to harness spill-over effects beyond the industry as well as to establish consumption, fiscal and production linkages over time.[32] The capacity to deliver rapid growth and move into higher value-added activities are not inevitable processes. Both require institutional coordination and state planning and, historically, this was achieved by developmental states through SOEs. In fact, political leaders in East Asia partially relied on state ownership as a means to maximise rents in strategic sectors, either through monopoly or through control over assets via state-backed financing.[33] However, certain states, such as Brazil and China, are far more reliant on SOEs for the development of strategic industries. Throughout Brazil's developmental history, investment in strategic industries was mostly done through direct investments by SOEs or state-owned banks.[34] In the next section, we examine Brazil's DS model, its highly politicised nature and the place of state-owned companies in strategic industries as political elites push for new methods of gaining comparative advantage in the new global economy.

Brazil's oil-based industrial policy, 2003–2016

The O&G industry is of critical importance to the Brazilian economy. In addition to its strategic importance, the discovery of pre-salt oil reserves off the coastline of Rio de Janeiro by Petrobras was momentous for the country. To start, the discovery reflected the *raison d'être* of Petrobras since 1952: to find oil reserves and reduce Brazil's energy dependence. When the PT government came to power, the O&G industry became the focal point of a new development strategy aimed at promoting technological innovation within the O&G supply chain while building sectoral linkages. This strategy became possible only through the integral role of Petrobras in the transformation of the sector. The state enterprise held a monopoly for 45 years and slowly developed the supply chain. Along the way, the SOE found its niche in deep-sea exploration and production technology. Petrobras developed its extensive knowledge of the domestic market, geological expertise of Brazilian onshore and offshore reserves and, through the import substitution (IS) model, had direct political influence in shaping O&G policy. This was consequential to Petrobras' high levels of independence from the state, which meant the firm became 'a state within a state'.[35]

However, the changes towards more open markets in the world economy made it hard for policy elites to sustain the developmental state model.[36] Typical policy instruments, such as subsidies, tax rebates and protectionism, were slowly abandoned during the 1990s. In the O&G industry, the role of the Brazilian state shifted from *direct producer* with monopoly control towards a *regulator*. The Cardoso government (1995–2003) argued that private investment was crucial to bring economic dynamism to the sector. The 1997 Petroleum Law was then passed, with the principal objective of introducing market competition and breaking the state's monopoly. Through the establishment of a regulatory agency, the National Agency of Petroleum, Natural Gas and Biofuels (ANP), Cardoso sought to break tradition from the DS model and the political power of Petrobras.[37] Yet amidst major changes in Brazil's petroleum law, Petrobras has remained the dominant player, exercising control across different segments of the market (see Table 1).

While sectoral policy under Cardoso aimed to introduce private investment in the O&G industry, Lula da Silva (2003–2011) sought to deepen state capitalism, particularly during his second term. To this end, he sought approval of a new legislation, which was realised upon the passage of Law 12.351/2010. The law altered the nature of contracts in the Brazilian O&G sector from a concession contract towards a production-sharing arrangement. Under this new institutional design, the state retains subsoil rights while it also permits private firms to operate in the development of oil fields as service contractors. The Brazilian state reaps the high rewards, as risks of non-discovery in the oilfields are low. The legislation also established a 30% minimum participation share-rule reserved for Petrobras; consortia and joint ventures with international oil companies (IOCs) were allowed under the rules of the 1997 Petroleum Law.

Broadly speaking, da Silva's oil regulatory framework was an attempt at re-industrialisation, which coalesced around state intervention to *strategically* guide national industrial growth. There were two key components in this approach: first, heavy state investment in infrastructure in oil and related sectors to generate new demand in the domestic market;

Table 1. Petroleum and natural gas production in Brazil by operator, 2015.

	Petroleum (in Barrels)		Natural Gas (in Cubic Millimetres)	
TOTAL	889,667,381		35,126,447	
Petrobras	822,051,381.5	*92%*	33,115,158.6	*94%*
Statoil Brasil	26,459,293.4	*3%*	36,773.1	*0%*
Shell Brasil	23,460,667.4	*3%*	265,679.3	*1%*
Chevron Frade	8,500,306.9	*1%*	92,041.3	*0%*
OGX	4,900,627.0	*1%*	15,407	*0%*
Others	4,295,104.8	*0%*	1,601,387.7	*5%*

Note: ANP, *ANP Annuário 2016*, 82 (adapted).

and second, the utilisation of local content requirements to consolidate a local supply-chain while fostering linkages between oil and the wider economy. Lula da Silva sought to take advantage of Petrobras' technological advantage in offshore drilling technology by investing heavily in the O&G sector.[38] In 2007, the government aggressively earmarked funding for infrastructure projects with the objective of creating jobs through public spending. At the back of windfall profits from a commodity boom, da Silva launched a two-phase major infrastructure programme – the Growth Acceleration Program (PAC). An initial US$349 billion (2007–2010) was invested through PAC 1, followed by PAC 2 with an estimated spending of US$526 billion between 2011 and 2014.[39] Public expenditure rose from 0.5% in the 1990s to 5% of the GDP in 2007–2010.[40] Investment under PAC was divided into three categories: (a) logistical infrastructure; (b) energy infrastructure, which includes generation and transmission of electricity, as well as the production, exploration and shipping of petroleum, natural gas and renewable fuels; and (c) social and urban infrastructure.[41] The energy infrastructure projects were concentrated in O&G aimed at exploring the pre-salt oilfields, to which the direct beneficiary was Petrobras.

The second aspect of the government's sectoral policy was focussed on local content requirements. Although it is often assumed that a radical break towards a new form of developmentalism was achieved under Lula da Silva, oil policy is an example of institutional continuity. Although Cardoso de-emphasised industrial policy, seeking to promote macroeconomic stability, privatisation and deregulation, several of his policies might be considered as de facto sector-specific industrial policies. An example of this approach is the establishment of local content (LC) rules and the procurement policy under the ANP in 1999.

Through local content rules, the Brazilian state sought to expand the capacity of the domestic supply chain.[42] This approach to sectoral development is intimately linked to the evolution of Petrobras. The company has a long history of supporting domestic suppliers. During the IS period, its policy of favouring domestic producers was strategically used to develop the capital goods sector. Petrobras successfully created a network of local suppliers, as it worked in enhancing the quality standards of inputs of Brazilian firms into the supply chain. Local content policies were widely used and Petrobras' purchases peaked at 80% in the 1980s. However, local content dropped substantially, falling to about 40% during the 1990s. The policy was then re-established in response to growing business concerns regarding the competitiveness and capacity of the domestic industry to meet the challenges of an open economy. Since 1999, companies taking part in O&G exploration are required to acquire local goods and services. Contracts signed between the ANP and oil firms also required that firms give preference to Brazilian suppliers in cases where prices, quality, and delivery were equivalent to those of international suppliers.[43]

Under Cardoso, there was no minimum or maximum levels of local content; during da Silva's government, LC became obligatory. In 2003, the government imposed a minimum share. In 2005, the ANP introduced a measure of local content, which established a minimum and a maximum level and a certification process through an independent organisation accredited by the regulatory agency. The results were apparent (see Table 2); the average of LC increased from 33.5% in exploration and 42.25% in development phases in the first four rounds to 79.6% and 85.3% respectively in the following bid rounds.

The PT government saw the potential to use local inputs as a way to hasten the development of the local supply chain and develop linkages between the O&G sector and other productive sectors of the economy. The strategy, therefore, was to consolidate and further the vertical integration of the O&G supply chain in Brazil, using Petrobras as the main driver. Given the size of Petrobras and the importance and contribution of the oil sector to domestic GDP, the establishment of a procurement policy, which gives priority to domestic suppliers, has the potential to significantly impact the supply chain and productive structure of the Brazilian industry. For instance, in the pre-salt area, Petrobras alone was expected to invest US$128 billion in exploration and production between 2012 and 2015.[44] In 2014, the government further estimated that until 2020, US$400 billion would be invested in equipment, services, maintenance and production expansion.[45] This would, in theory, facilitate an increase in domestic demand of machinery and equipment, trade and services, as well as oil tankers, support ships and marine services.

The pre-salt exploration and expansion of the O&G industry also opened the possibility for sectoral linkages. An effect of the 1997 Petroleum Law was the revitalisation of the shipbuilding industry. In the 1970s, Brazil's shipbuilding industry ranked among the largest in the world. Since the late 1970s, however, the industry experienced a drastic decline.[46] At the height of liberalisation, the industry decline was intensified as domestic shipyards were exposed to increased global competition. Unable to compete, most firms went bankrupt and employment fell from over 39,000 in 1979 to only 1880 in 1998.[47]

The 1997 Petroleum Law enabled competition (although limited), which in turn yielded to gradual recovery in outputs, and brought forth new demands for drill rigs, support vessels and marine services. The industry was further boosted by Petrobras' programme of modernisation and expansion of its fleet (PROMEF). Part of PAC, the programme called for investment in support vessels, platforms and related services that were expected to reach R$135 billion (approximately US$41.5 billion at current exchange rates) until 2020.[48] In other words, Petrobras was fundamental to the recovery of the shipbuilding industry by retaining its role as the largest contractor of vessels and marine support services in the country. In terms of investment, Petrobras, through its subsidiary Transpetro, shored up purchases and volume of orders that reached up to 80% of sectoral investment.[49]

The local content policy was further extended to the sector and used as the main instrument for the development of local suppliers. The basic rules for local content were no different in the shipbuilding sector as shipbuilders, equipment manufacturers and service providers were required to fulfil LC requirements. According to SINAVAL – the organisation that represents Brazilian shipyards – in 2011, the local industry aimed to supply over 70% of the inputs required for the construction of tankers and over 64% of the inputs for FPSOs.[50] Petrobras demand for new vessels was expected to assure work in Brazilian shipyards up to 2020.[51] As a result of the LC policy and incentives to revitalise the shipbuilding industry, employment in the sector increased significantly – reaching over 82,000 in 2014[52] – as

Table 2. Bidding rounds and percentage of local content, 1999–2015.

	R1	R2	R3	R4	R5	R6	R7	R9	R10	R11	R12	R13
Bidding Rounds	1999	2000	2001	2002	2003	2004	2005	2007	2008	2013	2013	2015
Local Content (%)												
Exploration Phase	25.0	42.0	28.0	39.0	78.8	85.7	74.0	68.9	79.0	61.5	72.6	73.1
Development Phase	27.0	48.0	40.0	54.0	85.6	88.8	81.0	76.5	84.0	75.6	84.5	79.5

Note: Percentages are averages per round. ANP, *ANP Annuário 2016*.

investment, mostly from Petrobras, in upstream segments of the pre-salt area fuelled new demands for ships. However, despite these positive results, there were important shortcomings in the design of PT's sectoral policy, which hindered the effectiveness of the strategy. These are discussed in detail below.

The decline of state-guided growth regimes: Brazil amidst a crisis

During the period marked by the commodity boom, Brazil experienced decent growth rates, an expansion of the middle classes and subsequent increase in consumption and a return to an interventionist state. However, flaws in policy design and the exacerbation of politicisation that consolidated a state-managed rent-seeking system have contributed to what is now a political and economic crisis. In this section, we examine the factors that contributed to the failure of state intervention as a development strategy in Brazil.

Inherent flaws in institutional design of the Brazilian DS

State intervention is an expensive, highly politicised process that requires cohesiveness both in developmental vision and structures. Therefore, any state intervention must be justified by the *objectives of the economic and development policy*. The Brazilian LC policy, however, lacked strategic direction. It failed to take into consideration long-term goals, namely value-creation and diversification of the economy. From the beginning, the 'policy's general objectives were quickly imposed without focused targets' or 'advanced metrics or indicators that could accurately measure its results'.[53] There was no consideration of which segments of the domestic industry had better chances of competing internationally and, therefore, could benefit most of extended protection. It also failed to appreciate the realities and actual production capacity of the domestic industry.[54] By establishing high local content requirements, it created a demand for equipment and services beyond the supply's chain production capacity. Investments in the Brazilian O&G sector increased rapidly, from US$10 billion in 2006 to US$40 billion in 2013. Domestic firms did not have the time and capabilities to adjust to the sudden growth, since to fill the demand of the industry would require substantial investments.[55] The LC requirements became impossible to achieve, which then led to delays, fines and higher prices. In 2013, Petrobras complained to ANP that the local industry could not meet LC requirements to proceed with exploration and development of oil fields auctioned in Round 11. It also announced that it was moving the work on the conversion of four tankers into FPSOs to China because Brazilian shipyards could not keep up with the required construction schedules.[56] Crucially, the lack of international competitiveness of the domestic industry became manifest as prices of domestically produced equipment could be nearly 70% more expensive than its foreign competitors.[57] In other words, domestic content became costly and highly controversial.

The policy further failed to properly consider the capacity of the regulatory agency to monitor the sector. The ANP as a regulatory agency did not have sufficient capacity to enforce the rules given the complexity of the O&G industry and of the LC rules. In an audit carried out in 2012, the Federal Court of Auditors (TCU) concluded that the ANP lacked the structure to adequately supervise the industry. According to the report, the ANP's inspection and monitoring system were flawed since it relied solely on information declared by companies.[58] With the change in the methodology for measuring LC requirements and the adoption of the certification system in 2005, third-party evaluation was established as a requirement. This, in turn, introduced new activities which resulted in accumulation of tasks and limited the agency's coordination capacity and performance.[59]

In addition, the institutional gridlock between ministries coordinating the sectoral policy is also an indication of the weakening state cohesion in Brazil. While the Ministry for Mines and Energy (MME) and ANP are jointly responsible for the formulation and implementation of sectoral policy, these agencies were unable to design a cohesive sectoral approach given their distinctive institutional rationale, objectives and regulatory functions. Unlike in the past, where Petrobras controlled the needs and demands of the sector due to its monopoly position, the ANP faced technocratic deficits to monitor and make Petrobras compliant – a company that trained and hired professional oil engineers and geologists over the past 45 years.[60] As the first ANP Director, David Zylberstajn, puts it, 'the challenge for ANP was to establish itself as a credible regulatory body that can effectively conduct social, environmental, and commercial audits to promote fair competition in the sector'.[61]

Building developmental capacity and technocratic expertise in the O&G sector was challenging in a developmental state model where regulatory bodies do not have similar logics of administrative functions compared to the Anglo-Saxon liberal capitalist model. In Brazil, both ANP and MME did not have the time to develop contacts with their domestic suppliers. Thus, the state had limited understanding and capability to formulate policies that directly responded to the problems and concerns of the industry.[62] By contrast, Petrobras' developed the local supply chain during the IS period through its capacity to transfer information between the market and the state. Furthermore, a key feature of the Brazilian DS model is the reliance on SOEs in promoting its industrial policy. The cornerstone of PT's oil-led strategy assumed that Petrobras would drive both the demands for heavy capital goods and technological learning in the sector. While such dependence worked for Brazil during the IS period, similar approach failed as Petrobras became politicised and the target of a grand rent-seeking scheme.

The creation of a state-managed rent-seeking system

Perhaps what hastened the decline of the state-guided growth regime in Brazil is the extreme politicisation of the bureaucracy combined with the consolidation of rent-seeking centralised around the PT government. The Car Wash (*Lava Jato*) scandal is the most evident example of how extensive structural corruption has led to the weakening of the Brazilian state's developmental capacity. Petrobras became entrenched in a rent-seeking scheme that involved millions of dollars in kickbacks to officials of the SOE, high-level bureaucrats and elected politicians, particularly members of the ruling PT government. The scheme lasted for at least a decade and was aimed at defrauding Petrobras on contracts upon the discovery of pre-salt oilfields. Contractors organised a cartel and paid bribes to Petrobras senior executives, segments of the bureaucracy and elected politicians. A criminal conspiracy was organised and run from within Petrobras after 2003 – a period when former president Dilma Rousseff was Minister for Mines and Energy and chairman of the company's board of directors as well as chief of staff of Lula da Silva's government. According to the Public Prosecutor's Office (MPF), the prices in the contracts offered to Petrobras were calculated and adjusted in secret meetings.[63] These meetings served for the contractors to agree beforehand which company would win the contract and at what price. Consequently, bribes, which varied from

1% to 5% of the total amount of contracts, were then distributed through financial agents in order to ensure that transactions would go through the state apparatus.[64] Among the directly implicated in the scandal are the CEOs and senior executives of major construction companies, such as Odebrecht Group, OAS, Queiroz Galvão, Andrade Gutierrez SA and Camargo Corrêa.[65]

The damage of the scandal is particularly evident in Petrobras, which quickly eroded its reputation as a highly professional and autonomous state enterprise. Those involved sought to ensure that only members of the cartel would be invited to bid on projects. To do so, Petrobras' employees were co-opted, who then restricted the participation of outsiders, negotiated unnecessary additions to contracts, raised prices at excessive rates and leaked relevant information to favoured bidders.

The scheme, however, goes beyond Petrobras and extends to the wider political system. A second pillar of the Car Wash scheme was the involvement of financial operators who became responsible not only for intermediating the payment of bribes, but also for laundering and distributing the money to key beneficiaries in the legislature and executive branches. In 2015, the Attorney General of the Republic presented to the Federal Supreme Court 28 petitions for the opening of criminal investigations on 55 people, 49 of which were holders of *foro privilegiado* (privileged forum).[66] This is a special status granted to individuals with high positions in the public administration. In practice, these are office holders in the executive, legislative and judiciary branches of government to which only the Supreme Court has the power to prosecute. As the investigation unfolded, most people charged are related to political parties responsible for nominating and maintaining the directors of Petrobras.[67] It is estimated that over US$2 billion were redistributed through the scheme, mostly to the benefit of the scheme's operators and to politicians, mostly from PT and its main coalition partner, the Party of the Brazilian Democratic Movement (PMDB).

The goal of the scheme is very telling about developmental states outside East Asia. Moneyed influence was an effective instrument to grease the political system into buying political support, sustaining electoral victories of politicians in power and consolidating a permanent coalition that would generate institutional equilibrium. On the one hand, construction companies benefitted from lucrative contracts that led them to internationalise and provided stable support to PT's developmental vision. On the other hand, kickbacks and side payments were channelled from big private firms towards public agencies and political parties – a precondition for PT to keep political power intact while promoting its expensive industrial policy. Like structural corruption, the PT sought to create a mutually-beneficial arrangement that would mitigate regional factionalism, clientelism and patronage, and fragmentation resulting from Brazil's democratic multiparty system. At the same time, this scheme is precisely the reason why state-led developmentalism in Brazil has lost its steam today.

Implications of the Brazilian case to developmental state theory

The rent-seeking scheme that began to be uncovered in the Car Wash investigation has important implications for the study of developmental states. To start, Brazil reaffirms the arguments of Kang, Wedeman and Weiss as regards the centrality of political corruption in generating political stability and in the formation of pro-growth coalitions. While industrial policy can be interpreted as the productive allocation of rents leading to state-guided growth, the *manner of* distributing state resources is in fact mediated by money politics and collusion between states and big business. Perhaps more crucially, what Wedeman considers as developmental corruption in East Asia now appears to be more synonymous with predatory corruption given that Brazil's Car Wash scandal dramatically impacted the credibility of Petrobras and weakened the capacity of the state to discipline domestic firms. By early 2015, the new management team of Petrobras announced that the scandal had cost the company US$17 billion, its market value was reduced by half, is burdened by a US$100 billion debt and had to deal with a class action suit and investigations by the US Securities and Exchange Commission (SEC) and Department of Justice. This has led the company to cancel or postpone its investment plans, halting the development of the domestic oil industry.

Taking a comparative perspective, Brazil's structural corruption resembles the process upon which South Korea, Thailand and Indonesia have been crippled by rent-seeking in the face of an economic crisis. In these countries, the developmental state became synonymous with crony capitalism, and the close relationship between states and big business was suddenly blamed as the malaise of development. The same industrial policy that fuelled the expansion of strategic sectors and financed state-guided high growth system began to be perceived as the root cause of corruption and the reason for the on-going political crisis in Brazil. Hence, structural or developmental corruption and wastage of state resources are two sides of the same coin. The question is how far such state intervention and the politicisation of the state apparatus can generate political stability – a precondition for high growth – and under what conditions rent-seeking becomes predatory and damaging to growth.

Secondly, Brazil's industrial policy has produced mixed results, which is partly an outcome of the inherent flaws of its strategy and partially due to political interactions between states and SOEs. While corporate governance reforms were implemented in Brazil to transform SOEs into more efficient firms, this was ultimately not sufficient to insulate the company from being used as an instrument of rent-seeking of political elites. In significant ways, it confirms the long-standing dilemma of state capitalism: how to maintain competitive SOEs and internationally-oriented domestic firms while also avoiding excessive state interference that oftentimes reverse the benefits of development policy.

As Brazil's *Lava Jato* investigation draws to a close, the costs of state interventionist policies and its rent-seeking tendencies are becoming clear. In a sector that was largely dependent on a single SOE for its expansion, Petrobras' reduction in expenses and investment caused the supply chain to dramatically shrink in terms of production, employment and consequent reduction in consumption of goods and services, as well as tax revenues. Crucially, the effects of the scandal spread from the O&G to the construction sector – one of the key sectors directly being investigated – as well as the shipbuilding industry, which was heavily dependent on Petrobras orders. As the company reduced and halted its orders, the industry immediately lost its biggest market. The story of Brazil's developmental approach reflects the tensions inherent in this model of growth. As we argued earlier, developmental states require institutional capacity and developmental vision; their success hinges on the capability of political elites to strike a balance between state discretion over designing industrial policy on the one hand and sustaining a coalitional base without turning into rent-seeking and clientelism. For aspiring developmental states, purposive and pragmatic state action in pursuit of new strategies is important, but this approach bears costs as political interventions can oftentimes lead to rent-seeking, and worse, the creation of predatory capitalism.

Disclosure statement

No potential conflict of interest was reported by the authors.

Notes

1. Leahy, "Brazil's State-Controlled Companies."
2. Schneider, "Developmental State in Brazil."
3. Schneider, "Developmental State in Brazil"; see also Evans, *Embedded Autonomy*; Kohli, *State-Directed Development*.
4. BN Americas, http://www.brasil.gov.br/economia-e-emprego/2014/06/setor-de-petroleo-e-gas-chega-a-13-do-pib-brasileiro.
5. Hirschman, *Strategy of Economic Development*; Nurkse, *Problems of Capital Formation*; Rosenstein-Rodan, *Problem of Industrialization*.
6. Woo-Cummings, *The Developmental State*, 1.
7. Nem Singh and Ovadia, "The Theory and Practice of Building Developmental States."
8. Adelman and Yeldan, "End of the Developmental State," 4.
9. Ibid.
10. For the distinction between developmental structures and roles, see Vu, "State Formation."
11. Amsden, *Asia's Next Giant*; Evans, *Embedded Autonomy*; Johnson, *MITI and the Japanese Miracle*; Wade, *Governing the Market*.
12. Routley, "Developmental States"; Vu, "State Formation."
13. For a reappraisal of this debate, see Chu, *The Asian Developmental State*; Williams, *The End of the Developmental State?*
14. Yeung, "Rethinking the East Asian Developmental State."
15. Chibber, *Locked in Place*.
16. Noble, *Collective Action in East Asia*.
17. Nunberg, "Civil Service Quality."
18. Haggard, "Institutions and Growth," 64.
19. Pempel, "The Developmental Regime," 144; Randall, "Political Parties," 638–9; Routley, "Developmental States," 21.
20. Johnson, *MITI and the Japanese Miracle*.
21. Johnson, *MITI and the Japanese Miracle*.
22. Evans, *Embedded Autonomy*.
23. Johnson, *MITI and the Japanese Miracle*; Vogel, *Japan Remodelled*.
24. Wedeman, *Double Paradox*, 15–16.

25. Ibid., 17–18.
26. Ibid
27. Evans, *Embedded Autonomy*, 53.
28. Wade, "After the Crisis," 158.
29. Evans, *Embedded Autonomy*, 60.
30. Kang, *Crony Capitalism*, 13–18.
31. Johnson, *MITI and the Japanese Miracle*, 195, 309.
32. Hirschman, *Strategy of Economic Development*.
33. On different types of rents, rent-seeking and productive distribution of assets leading to rapid growth, see Amsden, *Escape from Empire*; Amsden, *The Rise of "The Rest"*; Khan, "Rents, Efficiency and Growth"; on Malaysia, see Gomez and Jomo, *Malaysia's Political Economy*.
34. Amsden, *Escape from Empire;* Trebat, *Brazil's State-Owned Enterprises*.
35. For this concept, see Thurber, Hults, and Heller, "Exporting the 'Norwegian Model.'"
36. Nem Singh and Ovadia, "The Theory and Practice of Building Developmental States."
37. Nem Singh, *Building Developmental Capacity.*
38. Nem Singh, *States, Markets and Labour Unions.*
39. SECOM, "Brazil Announces Phase 2."
40. Resende, "Chapter 2.1. Infrastructure," 32.
41. Pardelli, "Appendix 1," 54–7.
42. In a Brazilian context, local content rules refer to the percentage of domestically produced goods and services used in O&G projects.
43. Xavier Junior, "Políticas de Conteúdo Local."
44. BNDES, "Perspectivas de Investimento."
45. PWC, "A Indústria Brasileira."
46. Several factors, such as low worldwide demand, low productivity, macroeconomic instability and overdependence on orders from SOEs, contributed to failing production and employment levels; Araujo, Dalcol, and Longo, "Diagnosis of Brazilian Shipbuilding."
47. Araujo, Dalcol, and Longo, "Diagnosis of Brazilian Shipbuilding."
48. Silva Campos Neto, "Investimentos e Financiamentos."
49. Pires, Gomide, and Amaral, "A Ver Navios?"
50. SINAVAL, "Offshore and Shipbuilding Industries."
51. Ibid.
52. ABENAV, "Dados do Setor," 2016.
53. Narciso Filho, "Brazil's Oil & Gas Local Content Policy," 3–4.
54. Narciso Filho, "Brazil's Oil & Gas Local Content Policy."
55. IBP, "Proposta de Políticas Públicas," 14–15.
56. Offshore Magazine, "Petrobras moves FPSO Conversion Work to China." http://www.offshore-mag.com/articles/2013/02/petrobras-moves-fpso-conversion-work-to-china.html
57. ONIP, "Agenda de Competitividade."
58. TCU, "Relatório de Auditoria Operacional."
59. Ibid.
60. Nem Singh, *States, Markets and Labour Unions.*
61. Author's interview with David Zylberstajn, Rio de Janeiro, August 2010. See also Nem Singh, *States, Markets and Labour Unions,* for complete discussion of this point.
62. CNI, "A Indústria e o Brasil."
63. MPF, "Caso Lava Jato."
64. Ibid.
65. Ibid.
66. Ibid.
67. Ibid. Among those implicated by the scandal were prominent business people and politicians, such as Senator Delcidio do Amaral of the PT, the president of the Senate, Renan Calheiros; the speaker of the House, Eduardo Cunha; and Lula da Silva's former ministers of finance, Antonio Palocci and Guido Mantega; and former Minister for Mines and Energy, Edison Lobão, among others. Later, Lula da Silva, himself was ensnared by the investigation and convicted. The fallout of the scandal also cost Dilma Rouseff the presidency and plunged the country into one of the worst recessions in history.

Bibliography

Adelman, Ilma and Erinc Yeldan. "The end of the developmental state?" Department of Agricultural Resource Economics and Policy Division of Agricultural Natural Resources, Working Paper No. 888. University of Berkeley.

Amsden, Alice. *Asia's Next Giant: South Korea and Late Industrialization*. Oxford: Oxford University Press, 1989.

Amsden, Alice. *The Rise of "The Rest"*. Oxford: Oxford University Press, 2001.

Amsden, Alice. *Escape from Empire*. Oxford: Oxford University Press, 2007.

Araujo, Fernando, Paulo Roberto Dalcol, and Waldimir Pirró e Longo. "A Diagnosis of Brazilian Shipbuilding Industry on the Basis of Methodology for an Analysis of Sectorial Systems of Innovation." *Journal of Technology Management & Innovation*, 6 no. 4 (2011): 151–171.

Brazil's National Oil Industry Organization (ONIP). "Agenda de Competitividade da Cadeia Produtiva de Óleo e Gás Offshore no Brasil," 2010, accessed online on 20 October 2017 at, http://en.braudel.org.br/events/archive/downloads/agenda-de-competitividade-da-cadeia-produtiva-de-oleo-e-gas.pdf

Brazilian Association of Shipbuilding and Offshore Companies (ABENAV) "Dados do Setor," 2016, accessed online on 20 November 2017 at, http://abenav.org.br/web/dados-do-setor/

Brazilian Development Bank (BNDES). "Perspectivas de Investimento na Indústria: 2012-2015." *Visão do Desenvolvimento, No 100* (2012).

Brazilian Federal Court of Auditors (TCU). "Relatório de Auditoria Operacional. Fiscalização de Conteúdo Local," 2012, accessed online on 10 November 2017 at, https://contratospublicos.com.br/tcu-relatorio-de-auditoria-operacional-fiscalizacao-de-conteudo-local-identificacao-de-oportunidades-de-melhoria-determinacoes-recomendacoes-ciencia-aos-interessados-arquivamento/jurisprudencia

Brazilian Petroleum, Gas and Biofuels Institute (IBP). "Proposta de Políticas Públicas. Relatório Final," 2015, accessed online on 2 November 2017 at, https://www.ibp.org.br/personalizado/uploads/2017/01/ESTUDO-DE-POLITICAS-PUBLICAS.pdf

Chibber, Vivek. *Locked in Place: State-building and Late Industrialization in India*. Princeton: Princeton University Press, 2006.

Chu, Yin-Wah (ed.). *The Asian Developmental State: Reexaminations and New Departures*. Basingstoke: Palgrave Macmillan, 2016.

Evans, Peter. *Embedded Autonomy*. Princeton: Princeton University Press, 1995.

Gomez, Edmund Terrence, and K. S. Jomo. *Malaysia's Political Economy: Politics, Patronage and Profits*. Cambridge: Cambridge University Press, 1997.

Haggard, Stephen. "Institutions and Growth in East Asia." *Studies in Comparative International Development* 38, no. 4 (2004): 53–81.

Hirschman, Albert. *The Strategy of Economic Development*. New Haven, CT: Yale University Press, 1958.

Johnson, Chalmers. *MITI and the Japanese Miracle*. Stanford: Stanford University Press, 1982.

Kang, David. *Crony Capitalism: Corruption and Development in South Korea and the Philippines*. Cambridge: Cambridge University Press, 2004.

Khan, Mushtaq. "Rents, Efficiency and Growth," in *Rents, Rent-seeking and Economic Development*, Mushtaq Khan & KS Jomo (eds.). Cambridge: Cambridge University Press, pp. 21–69.

Kohli, Atul. *State-Directed Development: Political Power and Industrialization in the Global Periphery*. Cambridge: Cambridge University Press, 2004.

Leahy, Joe. "Brazil's State-controlled Companies Pursue Reinvention,"*Financial Times*, accessed online on June 8 2017 at, https://www.ft.com/content/9bd21e82-4a95-11e7-919a-1e14ce4af89b

Narciso Filho, Nelson. "Brazil's Oil & Gas Local Content Policy: Lessons Learned," Institute of the Americas Report, 2017, accessed online on 22 October 2017 at, https://www.iamericas.org/documents/energy/reports/Brazil_Oil_Gas_Local_Policy.pdf

National Agency of Petroleum, Natural Gas and Biofuels (ANP). *ANP Annuário 2016*, Rio de Janeiro: ANP, 2016.

National Confederation of the Industry (CNI). "A Indústria e o Brasil," 2012, accessed online on 2 November 2017 at, http://arquivos.portaldaindustria.com.br/app/conteudo_13/2012/08/20/44/20120906112614214901e.pdf

Nem Singh, Jewellord. *States, Markets, and Labour Unions: The Political Economy of Oil and Copper in Brazil and Chile*. PhD Dissertation, University of Sheffield, 2012.
Nem Singh, Jewellord. *Building Developmental Capacity: State-Owned Enterprises and Natural Resources in Latin America*. Mimeograph, Forthcoming.
Nem Singh, Jewellord, and Jesse Ovadia. "The Theory and Practice of Building Developmental States." *Third World Quarterly*, this issue.
Noble, Gregory. *Collective Action in East Asia: How Ruling Parties Shape Industrial Policy*. Ithaca: Cornell University Press, 1998.
Nunberg, Barbara. "Civil Service Quality After the Crisis: A View of Five Asian Cases." *Asian Journal of Political Science* 10, no. 2 (2002): 1–21.
Nurkse, Ragnar. *Problems of Capital Formation in Underdeveloped Countries*. Oxford: Basil Blackwell, 1953.
Pardelli, Guilliana. "Appendix 1: The Growth Acceleration Programme (PAC)", in *Brazil Infrastructure: Paving the Way*, Morgan Stanley Research. Morgan Stanley Blue Paper, May 5 2010, accessed online on 15 July 2012 at http://www.morganstanley.com/views/perspectives/pavingtheway.pdf
Pempel, T. J. "The Developmental Regime in a Changing World Economy." In *The Developmental State*, edited by Meredith Woo-Cumings, 137–181. Ithaca: Cornell University Press, 1999.
Pires, Roberto, Alexandre Gomide and Lucas Amaral. "A Ver Navios? A Revitalização da Indústria Naval no Brasil Democrático," in *Ressurgimento da Indústria Naval no Brasil (2000-2013)*, Carlos Alvares da Silva, Campos Neto and Fabiano Mezadre Pompermayer (eds.). Brasília: IPEA (2014), pp. 69–108.
Public Prosecutor's Office (MPF). "Caso Lava Jato," 2017, accessed online on 20 November 2017 at, http://www.mpf.mp.br/para-o-cidadao/caso-lava-jato
PWC. "A Indústria Brasileira de Petróleo e Gás," 2014, accessed online on 30 November 2017 at, https://www.pwc.com.br/pt/publicacoes/setores-atividade/assets/oil-gas/2014/pwc-oeg-tsp-14-port.pdf
Randall, Vicky. "Political Parties and Democratic Developmental States." *Developmental Policy Review* 25, no. 5 (2007): 633–652.
Resende, Paulo. "Chapter 2.1. Infrastructure: Will PAC Really Accelerate Growth?", in *Brazil Competitiveness Report 2009*, Irene Mia, Emilio Lozoya Austin, Carlos Arruda, Marina Silva Araújo (eds.). Geneva: World Economic Forum (2009), pp. 31–39.
Rosenstein-Rodan, Paul. "Problems of Industrialization in Easter Europe and South-Eastern Europe." *Economic Journal* 53 (1943): 202–211.
Routley, Laura (2012). Developmental States: A review of the literature. Effective States and Inclusive Development (ESID) Working Paper No. 03, University of Manchester.
Schneider, Ben Ross. "The Developmental State in Brazil: Comparative and Historical Perspectives." *Revista de Economia Política* 35, no. 1 (2015): 114–132.
Secretariat for Social Communication of the Presidency of Brazil (SECOM). "Brazil Announces Phase 2 of the Growth Acceleration Programme," March 30, 2010, accessed online on 15 July 2012 at http://blogs.worldbank.org/growth/brazil-announces-phase-two-growth-acceleration-program#secom
Silva Campos Neto,and Carlos Alvares. "Investimentos e Financiamentos na Indústria Naval Brasileira 2000-2013," in *Ressurgimento da Indústria Naval no Brasil (2000-2013)*, Carlos Alvares da Silva, Campos Neto and Fabiano Mezadre Pompermayer (eds.). Brasília: IPEA (2014), pp. 109–150.
SINAVAL. "Offshore and Shipbuilding Industries," May 2012, accessed online on 12 November 2017 at, http://www.bw-i.de/fileadmin/user_upload/redbw-i/veranstaltungen/bw_-_fachthematische_veranstaltungen/informationsveranstaltung_petrobras/pps/sinaval.pdf
Thurber, Mark, David Hults, and Patrick Heller. "Exporting the "Norwegian Model:" The Effect of Administrative Design on Oil Sector Performance." *Energy Policy* 30, no. 9 (2011): 5366–5378.
Trebat, Thomas. *Brazil's State-Owned Enterprises*. A Case Study of the State as Entrepreneur. New York: Cambridge University Press, 1983.
Vogel, Steven. *Japan Remodelled*. How Government and Industry are Reforming Japanese Capitalism. Ithaca: Cornell University Press, 2006.
Vu, Tuong. "State Formation and the Origins of Developmental States in South Korea and Indonesia." *Studies in Comparative International Development* 41, no. 4 (2007): 27–56.
Wade, Robert. *Governing the Market*. Princeton: Princeton University Press, 1990.
Wade, Robert. "After the Crisis: Industrial Policy and the Developmental State in Low-income Countries." *Global Policy* 1, no. 2 (2010): 150–161.

Wedeman, Andrew. *Double Paradox: Rapid Growth and Rising Corruption in China*. Ithaca: Cornell University Press, 2012.

Williams, Michelle. *The End of the Developmental State?* London: Routledge, 2014.

Woo-Cumings, Meredith. *The Developmental State*. Ithaka: Cornell University Press, 1999.

Xavier Junior, Carlos Eduardo. "Políticas de Conteúdo Local no Setor Petrolífero." *IPEA Discussion Paper No. 1775* (2012): http://www.ipea.gov.br/portal/images/stories/PDFs/TDs/td_1775.pdf.

Yeung, Henry Wai-chung. "Rethinking the East Asian Developmental State in its Historical Context: Finance, Geopolitics and Bureaucracy." *Area Development and Policy* 2, no. 1 (2017): 1–23.

The Ethiopian developmental state

Christopher Clapham

ABSTRACT

Ethiopia provides one of the clearest examples of a 'developmental state' in Africa. Drawing on a deeply entrenched experience of statehood, the present Ethiopian regime has embarked on an ambitious programme, depending on the central capture of 'rents', to fund a massive expansion especially in communications, education, and hydroelectricity. High initial rates of growth have been achieved. However, the political setting is tightly constrained and the state has not allowed the private sector freedom of action to generate the required levels of production. Ultimate success will depend on the capacity to transform a state that has itself been central to the development process.

Introduction

The level of economic growth in Ethiopia in recent years has been startling. Over the period from 2000 to 2013, Ethiopia ranked second only to Angola in sub-Saharan Africa (and equal with Equatorial Guinea) with a gross domestic product (GDP) growth rate of 9.5% a year, against Angola's 11.1%, and a sub-Saharan mean of 5.2%; for 2015, Ethiopia's GDP growth rate of 9.6% was the highest in Africa and second highest in the world.[1] And while growth in both Angola and Equatorial Guinea can be straightforwardly ascribed to hydrocarbons, Ethiopia has very little by way of minerals of any kind, 83% of its merchandise exports in 2013 (down from 90% in 2000) coming from agricultural produce. Nor is this a case simply of capital city-centred growth. Though Addis Ababa is now a megalopolis of some four million inhabitants, provincial towns have undergone a similar transformation, and way out into the countryside, gangs can be found at work on the roads and other infrastructural projects. One study shows how a tiny settlement developed over the 10 years to 2010 into a small town, with electricity, cellphones, a greatly improved highway and – not least – changes in the attitudes of the inhabitants themselves.[2] This level of change, moreover, is taking place in a country notorious as a scene of famine and civil war, with an exceptionally rugged landscape, very poor communications, and little by way of natural endowments, and also (since Eritrea's independence in 1991) landlocked.

As a case study in developmental statehood, Ethiopia is therefore both interesting and important. Along with Rwanda, it provides the most significant attempt to implement the idea of a 'developmental state' in sub-Saharan Africa, and a critical example of the applicability of this form of governance beyond East Asia. This paper seeks to provide an overview of the Ethiopian experience, situating it in the *longue durée* of the Ethiopian state, the specific circumstances that gave rise to its introduction, and the ways in which it is proving more and less successful in meeting the massive challenges of 'development' in a country long known as one of the poorest in the world.

Origins

The place to start is that if you are going to build a developmental state, the first thing you need is a state. Ethiopia has a very long experience of statehood, anchored not just in the political forms introduced in most of tropical Africa by European colonialism in the late nineteenth century, but in many centuries as an identifiable political unit, characterised by entrenched habits of authoritarianism on the one hand, and obedience on the other. Ethiopian statehood has certainly been problematic in many respects, notably its historical origins in the northern highland areas of the country, and often-brutal imposition on other areas of the present national territory. The culture of statehood in Ethiopia has long been – and remains – hierarchical and intolerant of dissent, and imposes limitations which are not only responsible for much of the conflict from which the country has suffered, but also constitute a significant barrier (of which more later) to the development enterprise itself. It has nonetheless created an idea of the state, spread much more widely through the society, which makes it possible for Ethiopian governments to conceive and implement projects of transformation to an extent that is difficult to imagine in much of post-colonial Africa. Though Ethiopia shares with other African states the difficulty of projecting authority over sparse populations that Herbst has identified as the key problem of African statehood, it does have a densely populated core. When taken alongside the East Asian developmental experience, which has likewise – in Japan, Korea, China and Vietnam – rested on societies with deeply entrenched projects of statehood,[3] the Ethiopian case raises the question of whether developmental statehood is a plausible option at all in African states where the state itself, and the social foundations on which it rests, are far more weakly established.

The handful of indigenous Asian states that succeeded in maintaining their independence through the colonial era generally emerged from the experience with their state machinery and national self-confidence greatly enhanced by this success, and an intense awareness of their need to 'catch up' with the more developed world. This pressure for 'defensive modernisation' likewise applied to Ethiopia, save that the base from which the 'catch-up' exercise had to proceed was so low that the models of development that Ethiopia sought to emulate were found among early modernisers such as Russia and Japan, rather than in western Europe.[4] In this sense, a developmental project has been present in Ethiopia since the reign of emperor Tewodros (1855–68), though its implementation was impeded by massive physical and cultural obstacles, the weakness of the state machinery, and the demands of more pressing priorities. In a sharp contrast to the normal African experience of state creation by external colonialism, state capacity in Ethiopia has been an indigenous process, driven first by war and subsequently by revolution. It thus corresponds to the pattern made familiar by the work of Tilly and Skocpol.[5] The organisational capacity that enabled the Ethiopian empire to defeat nineteenth-century attempts at colonial conquest was subsequently enhanced by social upheavals that helped to destroy obstacles to state power, starting with the Italian conquest and five-year occupation (1936–41), which enabled the restored government of emperor Haile-Selassie (1941–74) to start a still-rudimentary programme of 'modernisation'. Elements in this programme, such as a belief that lowland areas constituted 'virgin lands' suitable for state-directed development, have persisted to the present day. Much more important, however, was the 1974 revolution, which led to the installation of a Marxist military dictatorship, the *Derg*, heavily backed by the Soviet Union; the nationalisation of rural and urban land; and the creation of a structure of administrative control that reached down to the *kebelle*, or peasants' or urban dwellers' association.

The *Derg* (1974–91) did indeed have a project of transformation, that was pursued with energy and dedication until its demise.[6] This project was, however, fatally undermined by two basic flaws. First, it took over a Soviet blueprint, complete with Leninist party-state, five-year plans and state farms, at precisely the moment that its inadequacy was becoming all too obvious in the USSR itself. Second, it took for granted that its policies could be imposed from the top down (a longstanding Ethiopian failing), and came up against increasingly effective guerrilla opposition movements, which sucked its resources into a desperate struggle for survival, to which it eventually succumbed. The Ethiopian case nonetheless confirms Kohli's findings that the creation of effective states precedes the emergence of industrialising economies, and that patterns of state authority are critical to the development process,[7] and draws attention to the importance of an indigenous, rather than colonial, process of state formation. And although focussed and dynamic leadership is certainly needed to drive this process, as Henley suggests,[8] it is far from clear that this can achieve the desired results without an effective state structure to back it up.

Meles Zenawi and the EPRDF agenda

A development project geared to a more plausible model had to await the advent in 1991 of a new regime, which drew its ideological inspiration from exactly the same student Marxism of the early 1970s as the *Derg*, and derived its origins from a classic Maoist peasant-based insurgency, the Tigray People's Liberation Front (TPLF). Such regimes have characteristically opted for economically disastrous policies of the kind represented by the Khmers Rouges in Cambodia, and indeed the TPLF leader Meles Zenawi had, shortly before coming to power, proclaimed Enver Hoxha's Albania as his model.[9] From this fate, both he and Ethiopia were saved by three factors. First, Soviet-style state-directed socialism had by 1991 very obviously failed as a developmental blueprint. Second, it was necessary to create a new political settlement, not only to replace the dead hand of the ousted Soviet model, but also to address the fundamental weaknesses built into the Ethiopian state, and notably the inequalities created by the dominance of the peoples of the northern highlands over the historically exploited peripheries. And, third, Meles Zenawi was a whole lot smarter than any of his predecessors (or most people worldwide, for that matter), and proved exceptionally capable of articulating an ideology of development that drew heavily on the East Asian model, while adapting it to Ethiopian circumstances. Meles' mindset was fundamentally shaped by Marxism–Leninism all his life, but he was extraordinarily creative and open-minded in applying it to changing conditions, and was able to stand back and appraise his policies, changing them as required, in a way found in very few national leaders. He must qualify as one of the most remarkable leaders and original thinkers in independent Africa.

The political pressures for development, unlike several of the East Asian cases, were domestic more than external. The continental settlement represented first by the Organisation of African Unity and then by the African Union has been extraordinarily successful in protecting weak and artificial post-colonial states against threats to their survival, and Ethiopia has been among its beneficiaries. The internal situation was, however, deeply problematic. Not only was the country riven by divisions that derived essentially from its creation through a process of internal rather than external colonialism, but the TPLF was itself drawn from a small and unrepresentative region at the extreme north of the national territory, and its victory bestowed no entitlement to rule the country as a whole. This obliged it to broaden its political base by creating a federal system based on ethnicity (in emulation, even then, of the USSR), in which the constituent ethnic groups or nationalities were formally accorded a right to 'self-determination, up to and including secession'; it was clear that governance could no longer just be imposed from the top, and the new political settlement, though heavily influenced by the TPLF, took the form of a composite party called the Ethiopian Peoples' Revolutionary Democratic Front (EPRDF) which in principle at least provided an integrative mechanism for the country's major groups.[10] In practice, nonetheless, the regime was widely perceived as controlled by people from the Tigray region from which its initial leadership derived, and this imposed a need to seek 'performance legitimacy' through a project of economic transformation. This need became all the more urgent after the regime held reasonably open and competitive elections in 2005, in response to pressures from donors, and was then shocked by the support revealed for the two major opposition groupings. It secured its survival by announcing election results in its own favour, and then forcibly suppressing the resulting demonstrations. This effectively ended any plausible claim to democracy. Though a number of opposition parties are permitted to exist, these are effectively restricted to a narrow base within the intelligentsia, and it has become abundantly clear since 2005 that no significant challenge to the regime would be permitted. In the subsequent May 2010 elections, only two candidates not affiliated to the ruling EPRDF were elected, and in the May 2015 elections parties associated with the government (whether as full members of the EPRDF, or as recognised affiliates) took every single seat. This is a single-party state in all but name.

Meles' ideas of economic development were first articulated during the liberation struggle, and subsequently adapted.[11] He rejected out of hand the 'Washington consensus' model of development as a 'dead end', arguing that this simply bound developing countries into relations of subservience to already developed states, and that a strong state geared to a purposive development agenda was required in order to break the stranglehold of dependence. An initial emphasis on 'agricultural development-led industrialisation' (or ADLI) was understandable, given the origins of the regime as a guerrilla movement in one of the most impoverished and famine-prone regions of northern Ethiopia, and the commitment to self-reliance that this brought with it. The regime has been thoroughly aware of the importance of increasing the productivity of peasant agriculture to the East Asian development model, which it has sought to emulate.[12] In practice, however, Ethiopian peasant agriculture simply did not produce the surpluses needed to make such a policy work. In the EPRDF's early years (1991–98), the regime's key priority was to establish its political base, an enterprise that called for a decentralisation programme, involving the establishment of regional states for each of the country's major ethnic groups, staffed so far as possible by indigenes of those groups (though always subject to security control by the regime). This was ultimately counter-productive to the development enterprise, and has been significantly modified in economic policymaking, though it remains central to political management. A vicious war in 1998–2000 against Ethiopia's northern neighbour, Eritrea, over disputed territories on the frontier between the two states, then subordinated every other priority, leaving permanently soured relations with Eritrea that prevented Ethiopian access to the Eritrean Red Sea ports, and imposed dependence on a single lifeline to the coast through Djibouti.[13]

The Eritrean war, however, cleared the decks for a more ambitious development policy in several respects. First, it revealed a level of common Ethiopian nationalism, in place of the conception of Ethiopia as a mere conglomeration of different 'nationalities' that had until that point guided much of the government's thinking. Second, it prompted a deep split within the TPLF itself, from which Meles only narrowly emerged as the victor, but which then enabled him to sideline rivals in the party, and direct development policy in a much more personal way than would otherwise have been possible. And third, it drew attention to the need for a national project, transcending ethnic federalism, on which the country's internal integrity and external security would ultimately depend, thus securitising the development process. This last factor was greatly strengthened by the election crisis in 2005, which intensified the attempt to achieve 'performance legitimacy' through the benefits derived from its developmental success. The articulation of a coherent development strategy therefore derives from the early years of the new millennium.

The East Asian model and the search for capital

This strategy drew explicitly on East Asian models, with China as the single most important source of inspiration, but seeking to learn, where appropriate, from other cases, including South Korea, Taiwan and Japan.[14] Although the government continued to promote improved productivity in peasant agriculture, it now placed its greatest emphasis on providing the infrastructural conditions necessary for industrial development at the hands of private entrepreneurs. Though key factors of production, notably land, remain officially in state ownership, it has left its socialist origins far behind. Three elements in the remarkable investment programme that it has put into effect are especially prominent. The first is the expansion of the communications network, long a major hindrance to development in a country much of which is mountainous.[15] The road network has been expanded and improved beyond all recognition, and the century-old line of rail to the port at Djibouti has been reconstructed with Chinese finance. The second is human capital formation, notably the higher education programme, now with 33 universities, and a characteristically top-down allocation of students – 40% to engineering, 30% to other sciences, and 30% to arts and humanities – intended to provide the skills needed for the new economy; such a massive and rapid expansion may well have led to a loss of quality, but I have no information on the actual standards achieved. There has also been a significant expansion in health services. The third is hydroelectricity, the centrepiece of which is the Grand Ethiopian Renaissance Dam (GERD) on the Abbay (Blue Nile) close to the border with Sudan, currently under construction, which after completion (due for 2017) is expected to generate 6000 MW of electricity, making it the largest hydroelectric power plant in Africa, and eleventh largest in the world. Having failed to gain external investment for GERD, the government has made a virtue of necessity by promoting it as a domestically funded initiative. Other hydroelectric dams have been built, notably those on the Gibe River flowing into Lake Turkana on the Ethiopia–Kenya border, which (unlike GERD) have also been designed to provide water for irrigated agriculture. Designed not only to meet Ethiopia's domestic needs, but to export electricity to neighbouring states, these are intended to take advantage of the country's mountainous topography to turn it into the powerhouse of northeast Africa. Electricity exports to Sudan and Djibouti are already operating, with power lines planned to South Sudan, Kenya, Uganda, Tanzania and Rwanda.

Central to the project is the capacity to attract the massive amount of capital required to build this infrastructure, in advance of any revenues that could be used to defray its cost. Since Ethiopia lacks any significant source of mineral exports, it was in no position to benefit from the commodity boom as a potential source of industrial investment capital. It is worth noting, indeed, how *little* the windfall profit from commodities appears to have done to promote industrialisation in Africa. Ethiopia has indeed run a massive balance-of-payments deficit, with merchandise exports at about 20% of imports. The quest for capital has therefore derived from three principal sources, the first of which is domestic savings. This has taken the form of a relentless search for 'rents', which for this purpose can be defined as any source of potential investment income that the government can lay its hands on, and that it is intent on removing from the control of anyone else. Some of these 'rents' would be recognised as such under the standard economists' definition of the term, such as the massive profits that the government is able to extract from its monopoly of telecommunications, which are as a result both substantially more expensive and less efficient than in comparable countries such as Kenya which operate a free market, but which in Ethiopia provide essential capital for infrastructural projects. Further rents are extracted from the private sector, for example by requiring banks to hold a proportion of their deposits in government bonds, which amounts in economic terms to a forced loan to the state, at a rate of interest substantially less than that of inflation. It is likely that much of the speculative building boom, very visible in Addis Ababa and other major towns, represents a haven for savings that would otherwise be vulnerable to state exactions.

It is paradoxical, given the government's own efficiency and success in appropriating rents, that 'rent-seeker' has become a catch-all term of abuse that it used to describe any attempt, whether by private businesses or by associates of the government itself, to retain resources that the state seeks to use to promote its own development agenda. The appropriation of rents is clearly critical in preventing surplus funds from being wasted in excess private consumption or the appeasement of social or political interests, in a way that has been all too evident in those states in Africa and elsewhere that have received massive amounts of money especially from hydrocarbons or mineral extraction, and have entirely failed to provide any remotely equivalent benefits in the form of public welfare or long-term development goals.[16] In the Ethiopian case, nonetheless, the constant excoriation of 'rent-seeking' raises questions about the role of actors beyond the state in bringing about the boost in production that must ultimately be at the heart of the developmental enterprise.

A second source of investment capital, especially for infrastructure projects, has been external development aid and concessional loans, which Ethiopia has been extremely adept at attracting, despite its explicit disavowal of the 'neoliberal consensus' economic policies ostensibly favoured by the principal Western donors, and a very evident failure to meet the 'good governance' criteria, in terms of multiparty democracy and human rights, that many donors likewise claim to insist on. This success derives in part from the skilful way in which Ethiopia has placed itself diplomatically, as a force for 'stability' in an unstable region: as a leading partner in the 'global war on terror', a major supplier of peacekeeping forces to help control conflicts in neighbouring states, and a generally responsible mediator in disputes such as those in Somalia and South Sudan. Ethiopia has also been able to make common cause with Western donors over its poverty reduction programmes, and ability to achieve a high level of success in meeting the 'millennium development goals', which emphasise measures such as the eradication of extreme poverty, primary education, reduction in child mortality, and promotion of gender equality. But, equally, Ethiopia has made a reputation for itself among donors as a reasonably honest and efficient user of the aid that it receives, and this technical 'good governance' in large measure compensates for its shortcomings in political liberalism. Whatever the formal ideologies of donors, which tend to claim that economic liberalism, multi-party democracy, and corruption-free governance are all part of a single package, at an operational level donors are driven largely by 'value for money' criteria that emphasise the visible returns on their investments. As the head of the UK development agency, Department for International Development (DFID), in Ethiopia explained:[17]

> It is all about the efficiency and effectiveness of the assistance. . . . When we looked at Ethiopia, a country with a large yet poor population, we noted that there is a good experience in the expansion of basic services in the last five to ten years. Though the quality of some of these services is still in question, which we are helping to improve, our quantitative analysis has shown that for every pound that we spent we can buy better results. Hence it is good value for our money.

Other donors have reached similar conclusions. As the case of Rwanda also indicates, African states actually enjoy far greater freedom of action in articulating and implementing their own development policies than much of the literature that continues to emphasise African 'dependency' has been willing to concede.

A further important factor has been the emergence of alternative sources of finance to the 'traditional' Western agencies, and notably China. Unlike many African countries in which Chinese investment has been prominent, Ethiopia does not possess significant mineral deposits of a kind that would fuel the Chinese search for raw materials, and its role in the country can most plausibly be explained in terms of its overall importance in the African continent (as its second most populous state, fastest growing economy, and diplomatic centrality as the host country for the African Union and other international agencies), as well as its ideological affinity. China has invested heavily in infrastructure, including telecoms, the modernisation of the critical rail link between Addis Ababa and Djibouti, the Gilgel Ghibe III hydroelectric and irrigation dam in southern Ethiopia, and the Addis Ababa light railway. The Ethiopian government has insisted on an appropriate level of skills transfer as part of these investments – staff for the light railway, for instance, were sent to China for training in everything from ticketing to track maintenance – and China has emerged as Ethiopia's largest trading partner.[18]

The third source of capital has been foreign direct investment (FDI), which has derived from a wide range of sources, though with Asian companies – ranging across the continent from Turkey to Japan – to the fore.[19] Floriculture was one of the earliest sectors, with initially Indian and subsequently Dutch engagement, and was particularly suited to the employment of a large indigenous labour force, mostly women, and to the transfer of expertise to small-scale Ethiopian entrepreneurs.[20] Leather products, notably shoes, are likewise well adapted to the country's massive livestock resources, and provide the most visible case of ADLI; the industry has been able to recover from the initially devastating impact of Chinese competition by concentrating on areas of comparative advantage,[21] and a Chinese shoe manufacturer has established a factory in Ethiopia. Textiles are another obvious area of interest, attracting investments from Bangladesh, China, India, South Korea and Turkey. These have been concentrated in industrial parks, mostly situated near and to the south of Addis Ababa, on which much of the government's industrialisation policy has focused.[22] FDI inflows have increased dramatically, from US$279 million in 2012 to $2168 million in 2015, leading to a doubling of the total FDI stock in just three years.[23] A recent book by the special adviser on industrialisation to the Ethiopian prime minister makes a strong case for an activist industrial policy, with case studies of three of the major industries, cement, floriculture and leather goods.[24] This found that policies were more successful in promoting development in the two new industries, cement and floriculture, than in the leather sector where the country enjoyed the apparent advantages of ample raw materials and a strong indigenous tradition of leatherwork. The problems lay in the fragmentation of the industry among a large number of small businesses scattered widely around the country, and in the path dependencies resulting from established supply chains and modes of operation. In sharp contrast to the picture of organic growth deriving from ADLI that underlay the government's initial industrial policy, it may actually be more effective to start from scratch.

Given the regime's origins in a peasant-based guerrilla insurgency, it is unsurprising that improving productivity in peasant agriculture should be a major priority, but this is extremely hard to deliver. While retaining a smallholder approach to agriculture in areas of historically high-density ox plough-driven agriculture,[25] it has opted for large-scale commercial agriculture in what it continues to regard – like its imperial and *Derg* predecessors – as essentially virgin lands in the south and west, demonstrating in the process a disregard characteristic of the Ethiopian state in all its manifestations for the livelihoods of pastoralists and shifting cultivators. This has been especially marked in the Gambella region adjoining South Sudan in southwest Ethiopia, where large tracts of land have been allotted at minimal prices to foreign agribusinesses from Saudi Arabia, India, Japan and elsewhere.[26] This process provides a classic example of the regime's willingness to override the local self-government ostensibly granted to indigenous peoples under the federal constitution, given that the negotiations with the companies concerned were conducted entirely at federal level, but has actually given rise to extremely limited outcomes. Essentially, the agribusinesses took cheap options on areas supposedly appropriate for mechanised farming, at a time of global concern over food stocks and the availability of agricultural land, without adequate appraisal of the environmental conditions and the massive infrastructural investment required, and little if any significant production has actually resulted. Some investors have been stripped of their concessions, having failed to make the required investments. The massive Kuraz sugar project in the extreme south of the country, intended to develop over 500,000 ha of sugar production irrigated by the Gibe dams on the lower Omo river, has also run into the problems characteristic of large state-sponsored projects.[27] The Ethiopian case supports the view that smallholder agriculture provides a far better base than plantations for securing equitable development.[28]

The state–private sector interface

The critical challenge facing the Ethiopian developmental state is, however, not the ability of the state to meet its own obligations in providing the appropriate infrastructure, but rather the ability of the private sector to provide the productive capacity on which the success of the whole enterprise must depend. The government, in a sharp about-turn from its original socialist inclinations, now recognises that its own role must be limited, and that it needs to encourage both FDI and Ethiopian entrepreneurship if its policies are to succeed. There remains a significant level of direct state ownership, including public utilities of which the telecoms sector is the most controversial, and the extremely successful Ethiopian Airlines. In addition to the state's engagement in infrastructure, with the Grand Ethiopian Renaissance Dam as the flagship project, it is also involved in sugar and fertiliser production. The Metals and Engineering Corporation, Metek, which originated as a supplier of defence equipment to the armed forces, has now expanded its role into civil engineering capabilities, such as building the locomotives for the expanded rail network, which the indigenous private sector is unable to meet. Metek retains its close linkages to the armed forces, providing for example management positions for retired officers, which gives it a certain clout vis-à-vis other areas of government.

Two other major enterprises, though falling into the private sector, retain close links with government that give them a privileged position. The first are the endowment companies, formed in close association with the constituent parties of the EPRDF, by far the most important of which is the Endowment Fund for Tigray, EFFORT, which is examined in some detail by Gebremichael and Vaughan.[29] EFFORT's pre-eminence is explained by its very close links with the TPLF, the dominant party in the governing coalition, and the one that drove the guerrilla war that brought it to power. It is a conglomerate, with 16 companies operating across the range of the modern Ethiopian economy, including transport, cement, construction, agro-processing, textiles, industrial engineering and banking. Several of these, notably cement and construction, are in areas with heavy state involvement, and although government sources insist that EFFORT is legally a private enterprise like any other, it would be implausible to suppose that it did not derive considerable advantage from its political connections. The Amhara region endowment fund, TIRET, has also been growing in importance.[30]

Another potential contender for the role of an Ethiopian *chaebol* is the MIDROC group, owned by the Saudi entrepreneur Mohammed Al Amoudi, whose mother is believed to have been a Moslem Oromo from the Welo region, and who thus qualifies as quasi-Ethiopian. MIDROC owns a range of enterprises, including the Dashen bank, cement, real estate, and commercial agriculture, and is best known for owning Ethiopia's most luxurious hotel, the Addis Sheraton, as well as the country's largest gold mine, at Lega Dembi. It has become rather less prominent since Meles' death in 2012, but whether this reflects a decline in political influence, or simply a relatively lower share of a rapidly expanding economy, I am in no position to say.

Conspicuously lacking, however, is the alliance between government and the domestic private sector that has been identified as a key driver of Asian developmental states. Like China, but unlike other Asian developmental states, the Ethiopian government has looked to FDI more than to domestic entrepreneurs as the main engine for growth, a priority partly explained by the historical weakness of indigenous business, which has been dominated by Moslem small traders and a single small group, the Gurage, who derive from an area southwest of Addis Ababa.[31] One critical constraint facing Ethiopian businesses is a shortage of capital, due not least to the government's success in hoovering up any source of funds within the domestic economy to support its infrastructural drive.[32] Foreign businesses, which bring in external capital, do not face the same problems. The government has also made considerable efforts to attract remittances from the large Ethiopian diaspora community, especially in North America, which have boosted small and medium enterprises within the country, as well as boosting household consumption and helping to relieve pressure on the balance of payments. Remittances increased by 27.7% a year between 2004/05 and 2012/13, from $US400 million to $2500 million.[33] Beyond that, however, and despite the regime's formal recognition of the need for the private sector to assume a dynamic role in expanding the economy, its underlying attitudes remain instinctively statist, and correspondingly suspicious of private businesses, which are subject to an uncertain regulatory environment and readily targeted as 'rent-seekers'. Ethiopia ranks no higher than 114th out of 132 states in the 2016 Global Entrepreneurship Index, though it is slightly above the median for sub-Saharan Africa.[34] At the time of the contested elections of 2005, the indigenous business community tended heavily towards the more nationalist of the two principal opposition parties, the Coalition for Unity and Democracy (CUD), which favoured a markedly more liberal approach to the economy than the EPRDF, and a government still heavily imbued with Marxian attitudes to the relationship between economy and politics can only view it as potentially threatening. Foreign investors are more politically controllable.

The political bases of development

Kelsall has argued that one of the four prerequisites for the long-horizon rent centralisation that must form the basis for a developmental state is a 'constrained yet inclusive political system',[35] on the grounds that the unconstrained political environment created by multiparty democracy makes it virtually impossible to prevent the diversion of rents into political patronage. The Ethiopian political structure certainly exhibits the constraints, but it is far less evident that it provides the inclusivity. The internal operation of the regime is characteristically byzantine, like that of all Ethiopian governments before it, and although there is an evident factional politics, of a kind that is likewise characteristic of closed governance structures, it is not at all clear how, or to what extent, political agendas arising from the base can be transmitted to central decision-making level. At a formal level, the major constituent elements in the EPRDF – the parties for the Amhara, Oromo, Tigrayans and Southern Nations – are not only given extensive control over the government of their own home regions, but are also represented by deputy prime ministers at the central level, working with the prime minister who, under the Ethiopian constitutional system, is the effective head of government.[36] In practice, both the historic trajectories of the Ethiopian state and the conduct of the present regime have been heavily top-down in nature, and it has taken a major shock to the system, of the kind provided by the 1998 Eritrean war and the 2005 elections, to bring the need for change to the attention of central government. Nonetheless, the succession after Meles Zenawi's death in 2012 of his designated deputy, Hailemariam Desalegn, was remarkable, not only in that a peaceful change of leadership has been virtually unprecedented in Ethiopia over the last century and a half, but even more in that Hailemariam is a Welayta from southwestern Ethiopia and a Protestant Christian, strikingly at variance from the historic domination of the state by Orthodox Christians from the Amhara and Tigrayan highlands. He is likewise quite exceptional among the leaders of states derived from a 'liberation struggle', ranging from China to Cuba, in that he has no 'struggle' credentials, and represents an emphasis on technocratic expertise rather than membership of an in-group of former fighters and their descendants. Part of the price to be paid for this is that he evidently does not possess the level of personal authority and control that Meles was able to exercise, at least in his last decade in office, but he has been able to maintain a consensual form of rule that is equally far from the normal 'big man' emphasis of Ethiopian governance. In practice, this has meant that Hailemariam has concentrated on economic policy, while ceding the initiative on security issues to a security establishment in which Tigrayans continue to play a prominent role. How sustainable this will prove to be remains to be seen, but it has at least worked over a period of nearly four years, and does not appear to be under immediate threat.

A further significant consequence of Ethiopia's quest for development has been in its external relations. The Horn of Africa region is justly known for a very high level of external as well as domestic conflict, indicated by civil wars, extensive (if often covert) intervention by governments in support of armed opposition movements in neighbouring states, and the fact that all three of the principal states in the region have been split, as the result of successful secessionist movements establishing states of their own, with the independence of Eritrea from Ethiopia and South Sudan from Sudan, and the 25-year-old but still unrecognised separation of Somaliland from Somalia. Ethiopia has been at the core of all these conflicts, whether as a result of its own internal divisions or of its frequently bad relations with its neighbours. Although Ethiopia's relations with Eritrea remain frozen, as a result of the 1998–2000 border war between the two countries, and are likely to stay that way for as long as President Isayas Afewerki remains in power in Asmara, a remarkable transformation has taken place elsewhere. In perennially fractured Somalia, Ethiopia has maintained good relations with Somaliland and the autonomous Puntland administration, while helping to support the still-feeble regime in Mogadishu. It has worked extremely hard to stabilise and if possible resolve the conflict in South Sudan, albeit without much success, while contributing key peacekeeping forces in the contested Abyei zone between South Sudan and Sudan. And, most significant, it has used the Grand Ethiopian Renaissance Dam, which might have been expected to foster conflict with the downstream states of Sudan and Egypt, as a means of promoting rapprochement with them.[37] These can all be ascribed to the new importance of development as a driver of Ethiopian policy, and the resulting need for good relations with the country's neighbours, not least since the loss of Eritrea's ports has deprived it of direct access to the sea.

This in turn helps to explain the second key question arising from Ethiopia's governance structure: the startling absence of any reaction, especially from Western states, to its very poor democratic and human rights record. While the presence of China as a potential counterweight is obviously one factor, Ethiopia's success in positioning itself as a force for stability in a highly unstable region is also a critical element. With Eritrea locked into an isolated dictatorship, continued domestic conflict in South Sudan, and Islamist movements threatening both Kenya and Somalia to the south, and Yemen across the Red Sea, Ethiopia's capacity both to maintain domestic order (albeit at a cost in repression) and contribute to regional conflict management is extremely welcome, both continentally (where Ethiopia also benefits as the headquarters state of the African Union, and effectively diplomatic capital of Africa), and in the world as a whole.

Conclusion

Ethiopia clearly ranks as one of the clearest examples in Africa of the application beyond East Asia of the idea of the developmental state, and meets Kelsall's criteria for what he terms 'developmental patrimonialism'. The patrimonial elements in the Ethiopian state, though still represented by the continued prominence of individuals associated with the TPLF's liberation war, have been supplemented by the emergence of a technocratic class without evident political connections, most clearly represented by the new Prime Minister. Kelsall's conclusions, which cite Côte d'Ivoire under Houphouet-Boigny, Kenya under Jomo Kenyatta, and Malawi under Kamuzu Banda as cases of long-horizon centralised rent management, suggest, however, that successful development depends on policies that rest essentially in the hands of the leadership, and may therefore be applied to virtually any state, even within a continent in which the imposition of statehood has been as recent, as external, and indeed as partial, as in much of tropical Africa. Although Kelsall's conditions likewise apply to Ethiopia, this is a case that at least raises the question, highly relevant to the East Asian comparison, of whether underlying social and cultural factors, which also reflect a history of independent statehood long preceding colonial rule, are an equally important variable.

It is also important to note that the undoubted successes of the Ethiopian developmental state, up to this point, have been achieved in precisely those areas in which a top-down and at times frankly autocratic state enjoys its greatest advantages: Ethiopia has done the things that a state can do, notably in the maintenance of order and the provision of infrastructure. Even there, it has at times been hindered by its reliance on a directing core with a very limited capacity to listen to alternative voices or take popular reactions into account. The critical challenge that it faces is whether it can make the transition to a very different kind of state, in two key respects: first, to an economy in which the major initiatives come from the private sector, and depend on a level of adaptability that states are inherently ill-equipped to provide; and second, and still more problematically, to a political system in which the state itself becomes liable to a level of accountability that no Ethiopian regime has yet been able to tolerate.

Disclosure statement

No potential conflict of interest was reported by the author.

Acknowledgements

My thanks are due to William Davison, Dereje Feyissa, Elsje Fourie, Tegegne Teka and Sarah Vaughan for commenting on a draft of this paper, and providing very helpful suggestions and information.

Notes

1. World Bank, *World Development Indicators 2015*, table 4.1. African economic statistics are rightly subject to all manner of caveats, and World Bank figures are used where possible; Ethiopian government assessments are generally higher.
2. Harald Aspen, *Rural Land and Urban Aspirations: Future Orientation in a Time of Change*, unpublished ms.
3. See Vu, "Studying the State."
4. This is a theme that I have explored in Clapham, "Ethiopian Development."
5. Tilly, *Coercion, Capital and European States*; Skocpol, *States and Social Revolutions*.
6. See Clapham, *Transformation and Continuity in Revolutionary Ethiopia*.
7. Kohli, *State-Directed Development*.
8. Henley, *Asia–Africa Development Divergence*.
9. This enthusiasm is best accounted for by Albania's role as an example of self-sufficient development independent especially from the USSR (which supported the *Derg* regime against which the TPLF was fighting).
10. Conspicuously excluded from the EPRDF are the pastoralist peripheries of lowland Ethiopia, largely it would seem on the ideological ground that their peoples are not 'peasants', and cannot be fitted into a Marxian class structure; for an excellent survey and analysis of politics in the periphery, see Markakis, *Ethiopia: The Last Two Frontiers*.
11. See de Waal, "Theory and Practice of Meles Zenawi," with subsequent critique by René Lefort and rejoinder by de Waal in *African Affairs*.
12. See Lefort, "Free Market Economy."
13. See Jacquin-Berdal and Plaut, eds. *Unfinished Business*; Negash and Tronvoll, *Brothers at War*; de Guttry et al., *The 1998–2000 War*.
14. Fourie, "China's Example for Meles' Ethiopia." The Chinese example both replicated the central role of the Leninist party-state, and lay outside the Cold War framework that arguably affected the other three East Asian cases.
15. The road network, for example, is reported to have expanded from 36,496 km in 2004 to 85,966 km in 2013; UNDP, *National Human Development Report Ethiopia 2014*, 83, table 6.6. This report provides the most recent comprehensive data on the Ethiopian economy, though it should be noted that it was prepared in collaboration with the Ethiopian government, which is likely to have imposed its own views on the findings: the discussion of democracy and human rights, for example, is notably anodyne. The figures for roads come from the Ethiopian Roads Authority. See also International Monetary Fund, *Federal Democratic Republic of Ethiopia*.
16. For a striking case, see Soares de Oliveira, *Magnificent and Beggar Land*.
17. Cited in Feyissa, "Aid Negotiation"; see also Furtado and Smith, "Ethiopia: Retaining Sovereignty"; and Fantini and Puddu, "Ethiopia and International Aid."
18. See Feyissa, "Aid Negotiation," 808–9.
19. According to United Nations Conference on Trade and Development (UNCTAD) figures, FDI, while varying significantly from year to year, rose from US$135 million in 2000 to $953 million in 2013. See http://unctadstat.unctad.org/wds/TableViewer/tableView.aspx
20. See Kelsall, *Business, Politics and the State*, 108–10; and Melese and Helmsing, "Endogenisation or Enclave Formation?"
21. See Kelsall, *Business, Politics and the State*, 110–1; and Gebre-Egziabher, "Impacts of Chinese Imports."
22. See Rosen, "Made in Africa."
23. UNCTAD, *World Investment Report 2016*, Country fact sheet Ethiopia.
24. See Okubay, *Made in Africa*.
25. See Lefort, "Powers – *mengist*."
26. See Ojulu, *Large-Scale Land Acquisitions*.
27. See Kamski, "Kuraz Sugar Development Project."
28. See Mosley, "Two Africas?"
29. Gebremichael and Vaughan, "Ethiopia: Rent Seekers and Productive Capitalists."

30. Oqubay, *Made in Africa*, 70–2, makes a case for the endowment funds, which should, however, take account of his own position in the Ethiopian government.
31. The Siltie, a largely Moslem group previously included with the Gurage, voted in 2001 to form a separate nationality; see Smith, "Voting for an Ethnic Identity."
32. Ethiopia ranks 132nd out of 189 worldwide in the World Bank's Ease of Doing Business index (www.doingbusiness.org), and 14th out of 47 for sub-Saharan Africa, but much lower, at 165/189, for access to credit.
33. UNDP, *National Human Development Report Ethiopia 2014*, 19, figure 2.5.
34. https://thegedi.org/global-entrepreneurship-and-development-index/
35. Kelsall, *Business, Politics and the State*, 147.
36. This system, unusual in Africa, is probably best ascribed to Meles Zenawi's complete lack of interest in the theatrical elements of power represented by being head of state.
37. See Gebreleul, "Ethiopia's Grand Renaissance Dam."

Bibliography

Amnesty International. 2016/17. https://www.amnesty.org/en/countries/africa/ethiopia/report-ethiopia/.

Clapham, Christopher. "Ethiopian Development: The Politics of Emulation." *Commonwealth and Comparative Politics* 44, no. 1 (2006): 111–121. doi:10.1080/14662040600624536.

Clapham, Christopher. *Transformation and Continuity in Revolutionary Ethiopia*. Cambridge: Cambridge University Press, 1988.

Fantini, Emanuele, and Luca Puddu. "Ethiopia and International Aid: Development Between High Modernism and Exceptional Measures." In *Aid and Authoritarianism in Africa: Development without Democracy*, edited by Tobias Hagmann and Filip Reyntjens, 91–118. London: Zed Books, 2016.

Feyissa, Dereje. "Aid Negotiation: The Uneasy 'Partnership' Between EPRDF and the Donors." *Journal of East African Studies* 5, no. 4 (2012): 788–817. doi:10.1080/17531055.2011.642541c.

Fourie, Elsje. "China's example for Meles' Ethiopia: when development 'models' land." *Journal of Modern African Studies* 53, no. 3 (2015): 289–316. doi:10.1017/S0022278X15000397.

Furtado, Xavier, and W. James Smith. "Ethiopia: Retaining Sovereignty in Aid Relations." In *The Politics of Aid: African Strategies for Dealing with Donors*, edited by Lindsay Whitfield, 131–155. Oxford: Oxford University Press, 2009.

Gebre-Egziabher, Tegegne. "Impacts of Chinese Imports and Coping Strategies of Local Producers: The Case of Small Scale Footwear Enterprises in Ethiopia." *Journal of Modern African Studies.* 45, no. 4 (2007): 647–679. doi:10.1017/S0022278X07002911.

Gebreluel, Goitom. "Ethiopia's Grand Renaissance Dam: Ending Africa's Oldest Geopolitical Rivalry?" *The Washington Quarterly* 37, no. 2 (2014): 25–37. doi:10.1080/0163660X.2014.926207.

Gebremichael, Mesfin, and Sarah Vaughan. "Ethiopia: Rent Seekers and Productive Capitalists." Chap. 4 in *Tim Kelsall, Business, Politics and the State in Africa: Challenging the Orthodoxies on Growth and Transformation*. London: Zed Books, 2013.

Global Entrepreneurship & Development Index. 2016. https://thegedi.org/global-entrepreneurship-and-development-index/.

de Guttry, Andrea, Gabriella Venturini, and Harry H. G. Post, eds. *The 1998–2000 War between Eritrea and Ethiopia: An International Legal Perspective*. The Hague: TMC Asser, 2009

Henley, David. *Asia-Africa Development Divergence: A Question of Intent*. London: Zed Books, 2015.

Henley, David. "Agrarian Roots of Industrial Growth: Rural Development Policy in Southeast Asia and Sub-Saharan Africa, particularly Indonesia and Nigeria."' revised text, December 2008. http://www.institutions-africa.org/trackingdevelopment_archived/resources/docs/Henley-agrarianroots-revised-AbsenFig.pdf

Herbst, Jeffrey. *States and Power in Africa: Comparative Lessons in Authority and Control*. Princeton, NJ: Princeton UP, 2000.

Human Rights Watch. 2016. https://www.hrw.org/africa/ethiopia.

International Monetary Fund. *The Federal Democratic Republic of Ethiopia: 2014 Article IV Consultation*, 2014. https://www.imf.org/external/pubs/ft/scr/2014/cr14303.pdf.

Jacquin-Berdal, Dominique, and Martin Plaut, eds. *Unfinished Business: Ethiopia and Eritrea at War*. Trenton, NJ: Red Sea Press, 2004.

Kamski, Benedikt. "The Kuraz Sugar Development Project, Omo-Turkana Basin Research Network." Briefing Note No.1, June 2016. file:///C:/Users/CSC/Downloads/ksdp_briefing_note_omo_turkana_basin_research_network_1.pdf

Kelsall, Tim. *Business, Politics and the State in Africa: Challenging the Orthodoxies on Growth and Transformation*. London: Zed Books, 2013.

Kohli, Atul. *State-Directed Development: Political Power and Industrialisation in the Global Periphery*. Cambridge: Cambridge University Press, 2004.

Lefort, René. "Free Market Economy, 'Developmental State' and Party-State Hegemony in Ethiopia: The Case of the 'Model Farmers'." *Journal of Modern African Studies* 50, no. 4 (2012): 681–706. doi:10.1017/S0022278X12000389.

Lefort, René. "Powers – mengist – and peasants in rural Ethiopia: the post-2005 interlude." *Journal of Modern African Studies* 48, no. 3 (2010): 435–460. doi:10.1017/S0022278X10000297.

Markakis, John. *Ethiopia: The Last Two Frontiers*. Woodbridge: James Currey, 2011.

Melese, Ayelech Tiruwha, and A. H. J. (Bert) Helmsing. "Endogenisation or enclave formation? The development of the Ethiopian cut flower industry." *Journal of Modern African Studies* 48, no. 1 (2010): 35–66. doi: 10.1017/S0022278X0999O218

Mosley, Paul. *Two Africas? Why Africa's 'Growth Miracle' is Barely Reducing Poverty*. BWPI Working Paper 191. Manchester: Brooks World Poverty Institute, 2013.

Negash, Tekeste, and Kjetil Tronvoll. *Brothers at War: Making Sense of the Eritrean-Ethiopian War*. Oxford: James Currey, 2000.

Ojulu, Ojot Miru. *Large-Scale Land Acquisitions and Minority/Indigenous Communities' Rights under Ethnic Federalism in Ethiopia: A Case Study of Gambella Regional State*. PhD thesis, Bradford University, 2013.

Okubay, Arkebe. *Made in Africa: Industrial Policy in Ethiopia*. Oxford: Oxford U.P., 2015.

Rosen, Jonathan. "Made in Africa: Will Ethiopia's Push for Industrialization Pay Off?" *World Politics Review*. Accessed June 14, 2016. http://www.worldpoliticsreview.com/articles/19057/made-in-africa-will-ethiopia-s-push-for-industrialization-pay-off

Skocpol, Theda. *States and Social Revolutions*. Cambridge: Cambridge University Press, 1979.

Smith, Lahra. "Voting for an Ethnic Identity: Procedural and Institutional Responses to Conflict in Ethiopia." *Journal of Modern African Studies* 45, no. 4 (2007): 565–594. doi:10.1017/S0022278X07002881.

Soares de Oliveira, Ricardo. *Magnificent and Beggar Land: Angola since the Civil War*. London: Hurst, 2015.

Tilly, Charles. *Coercion, Capital and European States, AD 990–1990*. Oxford: Blackwell, 1990.

UNCTAD. 2016. http://unctadstat.unctad.org/wds/TableViewer/tableView.aspx.

UNCTAD. *World Investment Report*, 2016. http://unctad.org/en/pages/PublicationWebflyer.aspx?publicationid=1555.

UNDP. *National Human Development Report Ethiopia*, 2014. http://www.et.undp.org/content/dam/ethiopia/docs/ENDHR_Accelerating%20Inclusive%20Growth%20for%20%20Sustainable%20Human%20Development%20in%20Ethiopia_finalweb.pdf.

United States, State Department. 2013. http://www.state.gov/j/drl/rls/hrrpt/2013/af/220113.htm.

Vu, Tuong. "Studying the State through State Formation." *World Politics* 62, no. 1 (2010): 148–175. doi:10.1017/S0043887109990244.

de Waal, Alex. "The Theory and Practice of Meles Zenawi." *African Affairs* 112, no. 446 (2012): 148–155. doi: 10.1093/afraf/ads081

World Bank. *Ease of Doing Business index*, 2014. www.doingbusiness.org.

World Bank. *World Development Indicators*, 2015, 2016.

An extractive developmental state in Southern Africa? The cases of Zambia and Zimbabwe

Richard Saunders and Alexander Caramento

ABSTRACT
In recent years, an upturn in international commodity markets and the poor development performance of mineral rich African countries have catalysed the resurgence of debate and policy initiatives focused on extractivist models of growth in southern Africa. Beginning with debates on the 'resource curse', the East Asian developmental state and 'developmental patrimonialism', we extend the discussion to consider key unique challenges in contemporary African states: questions of finance and debt leverage, foreign capital domination and the problematic legacy of neoliberal structural adjustment. We consider the cases of Zambia and Zimbabwe, two countries heavily reliant on mining, in which current policy interventions have sought to anchor developmental state ambitions in the restructuring of the minerals sector. These cases illuminate the significance of current developmentalist politics in southern Africa, and underscore their specificity and constraints. Developmentalist projects are unlikely to succeed in the short term, but retain importance as emerging points of critique of neoliberal states in transition.

Introduction

In the wake of a commodities 'super cycle' in the early 2000s, the erosion of neoliberal hegemony following the 2008 financial crisis and rising demands for a more effective and equitable management of natural resources, policymakers and scholars in sub-Saharan Africa have looked increasingly to the East Asian developmental state in exploring alternative paths forward.[1] In recent years, the United Nations Economic Commission for Africa led calls for the establishment of African developmental states built on the foundations of agricultural production and resource extraction.[2] At the African Union, a policy consensus stressing the role the state in steering mining's resurgence emerged around the African Mining Vision (AMV), endorsed by 54 member states in 2009.[3] Meanwhile, scholars and national governments, reflecting some elites' new taste for state dirigisme and rising popular demands for greater state intervention, seized on arguments and concepts associated with the East Asian experience.[4]

While much of the recent comparative literature in sub-Saharan Africa on 'developmental regimes' and 'developmental patrimonialism' stressed the importance of rural transformation under development-inclined elites,[5] the focus in the mineral rich countries of southern Africa fell more narrowly on variations of extractivism.[6] This echoed both the economic significance of mining in the region and the rising wave of 'resource nationalism' there in the 2000s.[7] Minerals have long been a key pillar of southern Africa's leading economies and the commodity super cycle deepened this tendency: at the peak of the commodities surge in 2006, mineral exports constituted 29% of total exports from the region, more than double the continental average of 12%.[8] However, sharp rises in corporate mining earnings were not matched by the growth of fiscal receipts and profit sharing. Together with renewed popular grievances over declining state services and revelations of corruption involving rent-seeking elites, disappointing revenue growth catalysed new thinking linking resources and development; in a period of heightened democratic contestation, this typically took the form of resource nationalist policy prescriptions.

In this paper, we aim to bring greater clarity to current debates around *extractive* developmental states in southern Africa by examining their key constituting conditions and constraints, and assessing the outcomes of recent policy and market interventions. We explore these issues through the emblematic cases of Zambia and Zimbabwe. In both countries, there have been calls for the establishment of robust developmental states. In an editorial praising the resuscitation of the Industrial Development Corporation (INDECO) in early 2014, the former parastatal managing body of Zambia's early post-colonial state, *The Post* proclaimed that 'moving a country's people from poverty requires a strong developmental state' (11 February 2014) – a sentiment shared by many throughout civil society.[9] Meanwhile in Zimbabwe, a leading business group argued that a 'strong developmental state' was required to effectively implement government's Indigenisation and Economic Empowerment (IEE) agenda,[10] and new policy research and debate identified a 'developmental state' path.[11] Mining has been a key component of the national economy, target of foreign investment and source of state revenue in both countries; it was also the focus of extensive restructuring under neoliberalism in the 1990s, elite rent-seeking in the early 2000s and, more recently, the target of resource nationalist politics and policy-making.

While our empirical context is distinctly African, our approach draws on the classical developmental state literature from East Asia. Our case studies both confirm some of the findings of developmental state theory, and underscore and investigate problems largely outside the East Asian experience; including issues of finance and debt leverage, foreign capital domination, democratic contestation (or lack thereof) and the problematic legacy of neoliberal structural adjustment. Methodologically, therefore, these cases studies are *deviant*, uncovering additional variables not previously considered and serving to broaden the scholarly investigation of developmental states beyond East Asia.[12] Through an examination of the political economy of resource extraction and resource nationalism in Zambia and Zimbabwe, this paper argues that the prospects for an extractive developmental state in southern Africa are weak and unconvincing at the current conjuncture, for reasons underscored by classical developmental state scholarship and for political and economic factors that lay outside that paradigm.

Theoretical considerations: moving beyond the 'resource curse', East Asian developmental states and 'developmental patrimonialism'

At the height of economic liberalisation and 'good governance' reforms in the 1990s, the 'resource curse' literature sought to problematise the economic, political and social dimensions of dependence on natural resource extraction.[13] Researchers argued that the volatility of fiscal flows from natural resources (notably due to commodity price fluctuations), and mining's high capital intensity, low value addition and vulnerability to elite rent-seeking and predation, made it difficult to harness extractives for development. In the 2000s, however, a commodities super cycle and the rise of the Latin American New Left raised new questions around key tenets of the 'resource curse'. In this period, several Latin American governments pursued greater control over and capture of more revenue from hydrocarbons, with the aim of deploying the proceeds to finance redistributive reforms.[14] African policymakers and scholars also shifted their developmental focus to minerals in the wake of the commodities super cycle, rising mining investment and increased fiscal flows. Researchers at the Making the Most of Commodities Project explored the potential for resource-linked industrialisation via the nurturing of backward and forward linkages;[15] Ovadia assessed the opportunities for building 'petro-developmental states' through the elaboration of local content policies in oil-producing African countries;[16] and Mosley suggested that inclusive extractive developmental states could be constructed through a judicious mix of fiscal regulation and enabling socio-political arrangements.[17]

If contemporary African and Latin American interventions pointed to opportunities for transcending the 'resource curse', the historical experiences of several East Asian countries provided additional positive benchmarks for the elaboration of new developmental state projects. Here, the East Asian developmental state literature, which underlined the importance of state capacity and autonomy, was particularly instructive for African debates. In East Asia, essential building blocks of developmental states included a professional, well-funded and cohesive bureaucracy;[18] with embedded links to local capital;[19] and a capacity to discipline and coordinate the activities of business in the pursuit of developmental ends.[20] While aspects of these features were present historically in Africa, other important economic and social factors outside of the state were less in evidence, and posed unique challenges to African developmental projects: here, African countries' low savings and tax bases;[21] weak and fragmented indigenous capitalist classes;[22] weak capital markets and reliance on foreign investment flows; and high dependence on commodity exports;[23] eroded the economic and political foundations of developmental capacities. Whereas East Asia benefited from significant military and economic aid and preferential trade concessions from the West during the Cold War, sub-Saharan Africa was burdened with high debt and far less favourable terms of trade and access to manufactures markets.[24] For African countries, spiralling debt in the 1980s and 1990s led to debt peonage, rising vulnerability to donor leverage and a dramatic withering of state capacity.

These weak institutional and economic bases for forging developmental states were reflected in contemporary conceptualisations of Africa's unique developmental challenges. Recent work on 'developmental patrimonialism', for example, acknowledged the shortcomings of institutional capacity, private sector cohesion and domestic capital markets, and placed renewed emphasis on political leadership and the strategic management of rents.[25] Effective management of rents by political elites, it was argued, could compensate for weaknesses of capacity in state bureaucracies, domestic financial markets and indigenous capitalist classes: what might appear at first glance as patrimonial, inefficient, prone to corruption and lacking a developmental outlook, could in reality serve as the foundations for locally-configured, viable and positive development; that is, a new African paradigm of developmentalism.

The approach of this emerging 'developmental patrimonialism' school, however, ignored crucial external influences on African trajectories and endorsed a voluntarist 'developmentalism of elites', without problematising either in their historical context.[26] As Mkandawire observed, the point was not to affirm an authoritarian rentierism which *might* result in an elite developmentalist project, but to ensure greater participation, social bargaining and policy control as a means of embedding developmental processes in political and economic contestation. Here, the question of the 'democratic moment' of political opening in sub-Saharan Africa in the 2000s was critical: its key challenge, to assert the sovereignty of the political electorate over the 'economic sovereignty' of donors and international capital, and the latter's claims on the local state.[27] For Mkandawire, developmental projects which were not underpinned by far-reaching, democratically-driven state restructuring, aimed at addressing the challenges faced by most Africans, stood little chance of being sustained.[28]

Some scholars suggested that Botswana represented such a democratic developmental state.[29] The case of Botswana was particularly germane considering that its sustained economic growth was underpinned by diamond mining. Botswana, it has been argued, possessed a professional bureaucracy with sufficient autonomy from political meddling, effective regulatory bodies including the Botswana Development Corporation and Botswana Meat Commission, and a cattle ranching elite committed to national development; all qualifying the country as a new developmental state.[30] Yet recent debates have called into question Botswana's 'developmental state' *bona fides*.[31] Hillbom held that the country remained heavily dependent on diamond mining, having largely failed to diversify or industrialise its economy; moreover, significant inequality, poverty and unemployment have persisted.[32] Hillbom preferred the term, 'development-oriented gate-keeping state', drawing on Cooper's conception of the African post-colonial state.[33] While there may be certain lessons to be learned from Botswana's institutional achievements, its status as a model extractive developmental state seems questionable.

Some have suggested China could act as a catalyst for African developmental states. Brautigam observed that Chinese investments in, and trade with, sub-Saharan Africa were developmental in nature, rather than exploitative. Key evidence was uncovered in the content and implementation of China's aid, the nature of its African investments and its role in the construction of Special Economic Zones.[34] Similarly, Arrighi speculated that China's rise would provide the economic foundations for a 'new Bandung spirit' of South–South cooperation and mutual prosperity.[35] However, others pointed out that Chinese aid schemes and investors have frequently operated in ways similar to their Western counterparts; Ayers noted, for example, that the bulk of Chinese investment has been directed towards resource extraction – not the promotion of diversification.[36] If the recent emergence of China as an alternative source of finance without lending conditionalities provided new development funding opportunities, it also raised warning flags around the low transparency of such funding. African civil society and social movements, especially, have faced serious challenges in holding to account Chinese investors, trade and aid funding.[37] Questions have also been arisen concerning the scale and overall impact of China's African links: while Chinese activity rose sharply in the past two decades, Africa continued to represent only a small fraction of China's global imports, exports and investment. The West still accounts for most of the continent's stock and flow of foreign direct investment and aid.[38] In the absence of sustained popular contestation and significant reform of African governments' policies, it seems unlikely that China's engagement in the near term will strengthen and diversify African economies, particularly in ways which benefit most Africans.[39]

Against the backdrop of these linked debates, this paper investigates the recent experiences in development policy-making around extractives in Zambia and Zimbabwe. To what extent have these states been 'developmental' in their strategic mobilisation and deployment of resources from mining; by what means, and how successfully, have they engaged with mining capital and various stakeholders in elaborating a new vision and practice; and which obstacles to, and opportunities for, emulating East Asian 'developmentalism' emerge from the conditions and dynamics of these increasingly resource-dependent states?

Zambia

The Zambian economy is heavily dependent on the extraction of copper; it accounted for 78% of the country's exports and 32% of government's revenue in 2014.[40] For five decades, fluctuating international copper prices played a strong role in shaping the country's political trajectory and economic fortunes, resulting in successive waves of resource nationalism. In the 1960s, high market returns, domination of the sector by foreign companies and newly acquired independence led to nationalisation of the mines and the eventual formation of Zambia Consolidated Copper Mines (ZCCM). A subsequent collapse of copper prices in the 1970s initiated a period of economic decline and growing debt, and eventually prompted Zambia's accession to a neoliberal structural adjustment programme in the 1980s. A centrepiece of neoliberal reforms in the 1990s was the dismantling and privatisation of ZCCM under terms spelled out in 'Development Agreements' (DAs) which were seen as highly favourable to new foreign investors.[41] While privatisation brought desperately needed investment to the copper mines, significantly bolstering production levels, some of ZCCM's assets were privatised under dubious circumstances. The subsequent copper price rebound called into question the overly concessionary terms afforded to foreign investors. To make matters worse, the new investors hired part-time and casual workers to avoid paying benefits and pensions, knowingly contributed to the environmental degradation of the Copperbelt, flouted labour safety regulations and eliminated previously funded healthcare and public health services.[42] By the mid-2000s, higher minerals prices, perceived profiteering by foreign companies and continuing popular dissatisfaction with the social consequences of adjustment intersected with increasing democratic contestation and a resurgent civil society, to catalyse a new wave of resource nationalism. Since elections in 2006, when the opposition Patriotic Front (PF) came close to defeating the ruling Movement for Multiparty Democracy (MMD) on a platform of greater state regulation and benefits from copper, mining has remained at the centre of national debates about new post-adjustment paths to development. The Patriotic Front capitalised on popular dissatisfaction with foreign mining investors, securing the support of aggrieved constituencies, the mineworkers of the Copperbelt being prominent among them.[43] Over the past decade, and especially since the PF's election win in 2011, policymakers have responded to these debates and underlying political shifts by focusing on three areas of state developmental intervention: the mining fiscal regime; local content and industrial linkages; and the improvement of regulatory capacity.

Changing policy frameworks

The MMD Government's actions after 2006 were prompted by the rising PF challenge.[44] Initial mining reforms targeted the industry's fiscal regime. When foreign mining companies refused to negotiate their 11 development agreements, government acted unilaterally, legislatively cancelling the agreements and establishing a new taxation regime, including a controversial graduated windfall tax. However, the death of President Mwanawasa, a sharp decline in world copper prices in late 2008 and heavy opposition from mining companies (*Times of Zambia*, 12 February 2008), forced its withdrawal in 2009. With Michael Sata and the PF's ascension to power in 2011, changes to the royalties schedule and income taxes became an important point of contestation. In 2012, copper royalties doubled from 3 to 6%, and in 2015 they rose again to 8% for underground operations and 20% for open pit mines. At the same time, corporate income and variable profit taxes were scrapped. But aggressive opposition by the Chamber of Mines forced a winding back of royalties, albeit alongside the reintroduction of income and variable taxes. More recent changes in 2016 saw the shift from fixed copper royalties to price-based royalties in a move to capture higher value from a low-priced market; a decision, some argued, which risked lower fiscal revenues from copper if its price should rebound in the future (see Table 1).[45] Other measures controlling foreign exchange management put in place in 2012–2013 to curb tax evasion – responsible by some estimates for the loss of $4.9 billion[46] in 2000–2010[47] – were soon withdrawn after depreciation of the Kwacha severely affected mining operations (*Times of Zambia*, 21 March 2014).

Beyond taxation, the Zambian government also sought to empower local suppliers and contractors and encourage backward linkages to mining operations. According to the 2014 Mineral Value Chain Monitoring Project, there existed an 'over dependence on foreign manufactured consumables in the [mining] industry and the absence of significant local manufacturing resulting in most spares and consumables being imported'.[48] Of the approximately $1.75 billion procured by the Zambian mining industry annually, only $87 million (5%) was spent on locally manufactured goods.[49] This was in large part due to the negative consequences of trade liberalisation, with imports outcompeting Zambian produced manufactures and to the privatisation of the mines, with private mining companies moving away from

Table 1. Zambian mineral taxation policies since privatisation.

	DAs	2008	2009	2012	2013	January 2015	July 2015	2016
Mineral Royalty	0.6%	3%	3%	6%	6%	8% Underground 20% Open-Cast	6% Underground 9% Open-Cast	4–6%
Corporate Income Tax	25%	30%	30%	30%	30%	0% concentrate 30% tolling and refining	30%	30%
Windfall Tax	No	Yes	No	No	No	No	No	No
Variable Profit Tax	No	Yes	Yes	Yes	Yes	No	Yes	No
Capital Allowance	100%	25%	100%	100%	25%	25%	50%	50%
Export Duty on Copper Concentrate	0%	0%	0%	10%	10%	10%	10%	10%

Source: Manley, 20 January 2015; Manley, 4 July 2016.

local procurement policies.[50] In 2012, then-Vice President Guy Scott, in cooperation with the Chamber of Mines and the Zambian Association of Manufacturers, championed the Zambian Mining Local Content Initiative (ZMLCI), which was meant to act as a successor to the International Finance Corporation's Copperbelt SME Supplier Development Programme (2007–2010). ZMCLI proposed a series of recommendations to facilitate local supplier development, 'including the establishment of a credit guarantee facility, financial education for micro- and small enterprises, establishment of a central collateral registry, and development of a national MSMEs financing policy'.[51] Unfortunately, the initiative dissipated following President Sata's death in late 2014 and the subsequent departure of Scott from office.[52]

Though less ambitious than the first wave of resource nationalism in the 1970s, initiatives in the 2000s to regulate and secure greater revenue from mining showed signs of waning following the death of President Sata, the changing configuration of the PF under his successor Edgar Lungu, and the onset of the country's economic decline in late 2015. Underlying structural factors compounded the challenge of building an extractive developmental state. Here, key contributing elements included low state capacity, the continuing power and obstructive positions of foreign-owned mining firms and the financial might and policy influence of donors.

State capacity

State technical capacities for regulating and monitoring mining companies were weakened by restructuring in the 1990s and continued to pose challenges in the 2000s.[53] After its privatisation, ZCCM was converted into a state-owned holding company (ZCCM-IH) and tasked with managing the state's minority stake in the mines. In practice, however, this did not lead to the ZCCM-IH assuming an effective monitoring role as a minority shareholder.[54] Cuts to post-secondary education under structural adjustment struck another blow to state capacity, reducing the number and quality of technically trained personnel.[55] Diminished funding to the state bureaucracy was particularly harmful. Two important regulatory bodies, the Mine Safety Department (MSD) in the Ministry of Mines and the Zambian Environmental Management Agency (ZEMA), were underfunded and suffered limited technical capacity, a consequence of having been unable to compete with mining firms in the recruitment of personnel with expertise. Both were often obstructed by political interference.[56] A subsequent strengthening of capacity at MSD only came as a result of a serious accident at a metallurgy plant in Chambishi. While Zambia's mine safety record improved,[57] the MSD's overall capacity remained below optimum.[58] Recognising the need to bolster state capacity, the Patriotic Front government moved to reform state regulatory and revenue collection institutions; for example, in 2011 the ZRA established the Mining Tax Unit with Norwegian assistance, with the aim of strengthening fiscal inflows from minerals.[59] While there was evidence of modest improvements in performance, officials at both the ZRA and the Ministry of Mines pointed to continuing institutional shortfalls. Poor inter-agency coordination further fragmented state capacity, with bureaucrats lamenting that state bodies operated in 'silos', hampering efforts to effectively regulate the mining sector.[60]

The state's relationship with mining capital

Zambia's dependence on copper exports and on foreign mining investment gave foreign firms substantial leverage, often stunting efforts to regulate them. Mining capital pursued three strategies to protest efforts to increase taxation or counter transfer pricing: they threatened to place operations under care and maintenance or to lay off mineworkers; they imposed investment boycotts; and they held out the possibility of appealing to international arbitration mechanisms. Two examples underscored the effectiveness of these strategies. In response to the abrogation of the DAs in 2008, firms threatened to bring the cases to the International Centre for Settlement of Investment Disputes (ICSID), a provision for which was included in many of the DAs. Although such threats did not result in the repeal of the Mines and Mineral Development Act of 2008, they arguably contributed to the decision to remove the graduated windfall tax. With the announcement of the 2015 budget and the proposed hikes to the mineral royalties, Barrick threatened to place Lumwana mine under care and maintenance, and First Quantum Minerals (FQM) suspended the smelter expansion at Kansanshi. The threat of placing a mine under care and maintenance or retrenching mineworkers was particularly effective, since the Patriotic Front was so dependent on the electoral support of mineworkers and their families.

Mining firms' resistance to regulation resulted in a number of reversals, as seen in the oscillating royalty rates under the PF (see Table 1) and the revocation of measures designed to counter transfer pricing. This intransigence extended to the state's local content initiatives, which also failed to bear fruit: the absence of robust local content legislation and the failure to enforce existing legislation[61] stunted the potential of Zambian industrialisation and indigenous capital formation. Low state capacity also meant efforts to monitor and regulate mining capital were severely constrained. This combination of policy reversals and limited regulatory capacity meant the Zambian state sought to utilise pressure tactics and legal action as way of drawing concessions from mining capital. For example, in an effort to prevent Konkola Copper Mines (KCM) from laying off mineworkers in 2013, President Sata deported KCM CEO Kishore Kumar and threatened to revoke the company's mining licence (*Wall Street Journal*, 5 December 2013). However, these measures only served to maintain the status quo, not secure substantive concessions. Similarly, following failed efforts to raise the royalty rates in 2015, ZCCM-IH filed a lawsuit against FQM in late 2016, claiming the company had illegally used $2.3 billion of Kansanshi's profits as cheap financing for its other operations without the express consent of ZCCM-IH. However, after extensive lobbying efforts by FQM, the case was subsequently dropped on President Lungu's orders and the parties agreed to settle the dispute out of court (*The Mast*, 3 June 2017). Arguably, FQM's structural position in the Zambian economy, accounting for 37% of its copper production in 2014 and over 50% of total government mineral revenues, meant that the mining firm could not easily be strong armed.[62]

Debt and technical dependency

The resurgence of resource nationalism was significantly enabled by debt relief. Following the completion of the HIPC debt relief programme in 2005–2006, Zambia's external debt decreased substantially. In 2005, Zambia reached the HIPC Completion Point whereby its debt stock was reduced from $7.1 billion to $4.5 billion. In 2006, under the Multilateral Debt Relief Initiative (MDRI), the IFIs provided those countries that had already reached the HIPC Completion Point an additional write-off without having to undergo further structural adjustment. As a result, Zambia's total debt was further reduced from $4.5 billion to approximately

Table 2. Zambia's sovereign bond issues.

Issue Date	13 September 2012	14 April 2014	23 July 2015
Amount (million)	750	1,000	1,250
Coupon Rate	5.375%	8.5%	8.97%
Tenor	10 years (2022)	10 years (2024)	11 years (2026)

Source: Nalishebo and Halwampa, *A Cautionary Tale*; "Zambia succeeds in getting $1.2bn Eurobond," *Daily Mail* (Zambia), 25 July 2015.

$600 million.[63] A lower debt load and sustained economic growth prompted positive sovereign credit ratings, permitting government to tap into international bond markets to finance infrastructure expansion. However, these sovereign bonds carried increasingly high interest rates and raised the spectre of resurgent indebtedness (see Table 2). A recent UNDP discussion paper estimated that if a 6% royalty and 30% corporate tax rate had been applied in the DAs during the 1997–2012 period, government would have earned an additional $1.6 billion; or the equivalent of 3.7% of annual GDP for the period. Greater resource mobilisation through taxation, the paper concluded, would have enabled government to avoid the costly sovereign bond market.[64]

In recent years, weakened copper prices and ballooning debt fuelled by rising interest rates severely constrained the state's financial autonomy. New bailout negotiations with the IMF were initiated after the 2016 elections, and will likely have important implications for policy formulation and implementation in the near future. This financial vulnerability runs parallel to a dependency on donor technical assistance. After the previous round of structural adjustment, limited bureaucratic capacity compelled the state to seek donor technical assistance, which has continued to shape mining governance. Under these conditions – increasingly reminiscent of the turbulent time of the 1980s and 1990s – it is unlikely that state policy-making will forcefully pursue the kind of robust local procurement measures and comprehensive developmental regulatory regime which had been heralded for the mining sector in the recent past.

Zimbabwe

Mining has been an important contributor to Zimbabwe's foreign exchange earnings, foreign direct investment, GDP and employment since before independence in 1980, and became increasingly prominent in the 2000s as commercial agriculture and manufacturing declined. During 2000–2008, mining's share of total exports doubled from 27 to 53%, with value increasingly concentrated in a narrow range of minerals produced mostly by large-scale operations dominated by foreign miners.[65] Underpinning the sector was a relatively diverse infrastructure inherited from colonial and white-ruled Rhodesia's import substitution strategy. This had bestowed modest capacities for beneficiation through upstream and downstream linkages, and state-led training, research and support services. Despite lingering elements of enclavism and heavy dependence on foreign capital, mining seemed to offer promising foundations for a programme of industrial expansion.[66] Therefore, when the ZANU-PF government announced a new framework for indigenisation, empowerment and development in the mid-2000s, attention turned to mining as a key pillar of expanded fiscal gains, rejuvenated industrial linkages and new investment. However, coming in the wake of the withering of state institutions by neoliberal reforms in the 1990s and emerging forms of militarisation and intensive elite rent-seeking in the 2000s, the promise of new developmental-oriented policies around mining was dampened just as the commodities super cycle generated favourable market conditions for its success. State institutional weakening, resurgent nationalism and elite predation, combined with continuing deep dependence on foreign capital, called into question the prospects of a refashioned developmentalism.[67]

State capacity and autonomy under attack

With the end of white minority rule in 1980, government established new mining and marketing entities and extended state technical and research support services. The aim was to expand production, support a broader range of mining and encourage employment and beneficiation. But the large part of production remained in foreign hands, and would continue to be dominated by expatriate investors for the next three decades.[68] Downturns in commodities markets and rising local production costs in the 1980s, along with constraints on state budgets, saw stagnating or declining mineral production.[69] Market-oriented reforms in the 1990s, including special concessions negotiated to attract new large mining investment,[70] catalysed a revival of activity in exploration and subsequent investment; some reports suggested that Zimbabwe was on the cusp of a 'mining breakthrough'.[71]

Neoliberal restructuring also sowed the seeds of crisis. A deteriorating macroeconomic environment in 1998–1999 rapidly erased mining gains and contributed to the scaling back of production and sharp declines, notably in the strategic gold sector.[72] Declining investment in public mining entities and a significant weakening of bureaucratic capacity exacerbated the state's ability to manage the crisis. State institutions were further undermined in the early 2000s when ZANU-PF militarised the realm of politics in response to a challenge by the Movement for Democratic Change (MDC), a significant new opposition party (*Zimbabwe Independent*, 15 December 2014). 'State capture' emerged as a key ZANU-PF strategy and sought to reconfigure lines of control within state institutions. Bureaucrats were targeted with violence, threats, harassment and irregular disciplinary interventions by government officials, allied state security agencies and ruling party militants. The mining bureaucracy's professional capacity and integrity were assaulted, and key regulatory and service capacities fell into crisis. The departure of strategic personnel in the ministry, University of Zimbabwe and School of Mines gutted the state's research, training and support services.[73] At the ministry, the disruption of information gathering, policy-making and supervisory oversight was widespread.

At the same time, partisan infiltration of these structures challenged their political autonomy. This helped to facilitate a rapid shift of policy formulation and decision-making outside of the normal bureaucratic chain of command. The resulting decentralisation of mining management was exacerbated by factional divisions within ZANU-PF, whose internal political fault lines were replicated across state institutions as the latter were realigned with the party's internally combative politics. The fragmentation of political authority fuelled multiple claims to policy leadership from different locations inside the state, not only the mining ministry but also other powerful ministries like Finance and IEE.[74]

Indigenisation and development

The obstacles posed by state restructuring in the context of resurgent nationalism and elite rent-seeking were brought into stark relief with ZANU-PF's elaboration of a stridently opportunistic initiative in advance of the national elections in 2008, in which the party faced a strong opposition challenge. The IEE Act of 2007 marked an important shift in ZANU-PF's development vision. Even if the IEE's timing and sloppy drafting suggested it was initially formulated as an anchor for the ruling party's electoral strategy, the framework soon came to underpin government's engagement with business, donors and civil society.[75] IEE policies took on the guise of a new developmental politics.

The IEE's key innovation involved the rapid transfer of majority (51%) equity stakes in companies controlled by non-indigenous interests into indigenous hands. Government argued that asset redistribution would generate new economic activity through a wave of small investment and entrepreneurship, and identified a wide range of prospective indigenous recipients of equity targeted for acquisition. Potential beneficiaries of the programme included public bodies, indigenously-owned businesses, community share trusts and indigenous individuals. In support, the state would promote industrial linkages via new interventions, including a National IEE Fund to hold and manage 'warehoused' shares; a Sovereign Wealth Fund (SWF) for developmental investments; and Employee Share Ownership Schemes (ESOS) and Community Share Ownership Trusts (CSOT) to encourage participation and mobilise resources locally.

However, the IEE approach was soon called into question. New supporting institutions were slow to be established, were inadequately funded and had hazy legal status. ESOSs and CSOTs, which emerged in 2011 against the backdrop of ZANU-PF's campaign for the 2013 elections, were undercapitalised, suffered from partisan interference and had opaque governance and membership criteria.[76] Funding shortfalls plagued the IEE Fund and SWF. Meanwhile, the bureaucracy's authority and autonomy were eroded in the context of state capture and heightened partisan contestation around indigenisation. The IEE granted the responsible minister expansive discretionary power in overseeing equity transfers,[77] but failed to specify developmental criteria to guide ministerial decisions and denied the bureaucracy a mandate to steer the new strategy. In practice, the IEE functioned most effectively as a patronage mechanism – 'racketeering by regulation', in the words of a veteran observer – with 'indigenisation' serving as the legal mechanism for the extraction of short term rents.[78]

Elite predation and business resistance

Mining, a leading profit centre in a crisis-stricken economy, and a sector heavily dominated by foreign ownership, became a primary target of the IEE – and an emblem of indigenisation's flawed, contradictory approach to development.[79] On the one hand, the sector witnessed extreme, destructive elite predation; on the other, it demonstrated the continuing power and influence of foreign mining capital and the vulnerability of state development plans to market conditions.

A particularly egregious case of elite rent-seeking which highlighted state capture and the bureaucracy's compromised capacity, emerged in the Marange diamond fields of eastern Zimbabwe.[80] A world-class deposit revealed in 2006, Marange suffered widespread looting organised by political and security elites under the watch of senior mining ministry and state officials.[81] Rent-seeking was thinly disguised in the form of irregular licencing, transfer pricing and organised smuggling, which at times involved national security elites and agencies.[82] Public oversight of diamond production remained weak even after the formation of a multi-party Government of National Unity in 2009 which brought the MDC into shared-power arrangements; indeed transparency and accountability likely worsened, as partisan conflict among different state agencies generated contrasting policy, regulatory and legislative initiatives.[83] Critically, ZANU-PF retained control of the mining and security portfolios in the new government, which enabled the party to consolidate its powerful presence in Marange even as the state moved to 'normalise' alluvial extraction.

The impact on state revenue and diamonds' development potential was devastating. Experts estimated that at least 25% of Marange diamonds' value was lost through undervaluation and transfer-pricing alone.[84] After a decade of predation, President Mugabe lamented that more than $13 billion of diamond production – equivalent to three years of export earnings – was unaccounted for.[85] A 2013 Parliamentary investigative report, quickly shelved, explained why: the weakening of bureaucratic oversight and flouting of management norms by senior mining officials had facilitated, if not encouraged, systematic looting.[86]

Beyond Marange, the mining industry's response to the IEE highlighted the structural obstacles faced by government in reforming large-scale mining; above all, capital's enduring economic power and policy influence. The collapse of domestic finance markets in the early 2000s, severe foreign exchange shortages and an effective boycott of development lending to Zimbabwe, placed foreign mining capital in a privileged position. In the 2000s, foreign players would dominate leading mining mergers, acquisitions and new projects (see Table 3); domestic capital involvement, with the exception of state involvement in the problematic diamond sector in Marange, remained negligible.

With their power to invest new capital – or withhold it – large-scale foreign mining firms exerted considerable influence in the unfolding policy debates and practices around indigenisation at a time when commodity prices were soaring. Alternative proposals for indigenisation and local empowerment were championed by domestic business with the tacit support of larger foreign capital. An influential 2011 business report warned against elite-focused indigenisation and argued for a 'strong developmental state' modelled on East Asian and European experiences. The aim should be to enhance market opportunities, the paper argued: the way forward involved the nurturing of sound business practices, not the facilitation of rent-seeking through the forced takeover of productive assets.[87] Large-scale mining firms pressed the state on reform of the mining fiscal regime, security of title and the

Table 3. Mining investment in the 2000s (key deals).

Investment	Source Company	Source Country	US$ (million)	Year
Unki Platinum Mine	Anglo Platinum	SA	300	2003
Zimplats Selous Mine	Implats	SA	225	2002–2005
Zimplats (Expansion)	Implats	SA	340	2007
Zimasco	Sinosteel	China	200	2007
Murowa Diamonds	Rio Tinto plc	UK	61	2004
Mimosa Platinum Mine	Implats, Aquarius	SA, Australia	30	2001
Independence Gold Mines	Metallon	SA	15	2002
Bindura Nickel Corporation	Mwana Africa	UK/SA	8	2003
Eureka Gold Mine	Mmakau Mining	SA	6	2005
Freda Rebecca Gold Mine	Mwana Africa	UK/SA	2.5	2005

Source: BusinessMap SADC FDI Database (Johannesburg) and Media, Mining House, Chamber Reports.

elaboration of alternative paths to domestication of control in the sector.[88] With these counter-proposals came an unambiguous warning: Zimbabwe's chronically weak capital markets and high foreign debt meant new mining investment was dependent on foreign capital, and state concessions around indigenisation would be required to unlock it.

Donors also played a role in encouraging a rethink of indigenisation through the lens of market priorities. Re-engaging with government after an extended lending boycott, they facilitated critical new policy research and specified the need for greater transparency and market-enabling policy approaches in mining management.[89] A draft Mining Policy (the first since 1980),[90] a Cabinet-approved Diamond Policy and moves to amend the Mines and Minerals Act, echoed many of the demands of business, donors and civil society – even if these policy interventions contained flawed, uneven and ambiguous concessions to regulatory 'best practices'.[91]

By 2016, ZANU-PF's preferred route to mining indigenisation had effectively stalled in the face of business resistance, donor leverage and state vulnerability. Wholesale asset transfers envisioned by the IEE did not happen. Acknowledging this reality, a revised indigenisation framework included a government levy – effectively a fine – for non-compliance.[92] The relaxed enforcement of indigenisation buoyed investment into the country's leading foreign exchange earner: for most of 2009–2013 mining led all sectors in annual investment and remained an important target for capital thereafter, even as mineral earnings declined with falling prices.[93] Yet at the same time, the mutual accommodation of miners and government around indigenisation fell short of generating a new hybrid model that was actively supported by both. In practice, the state's re-engagement of business was limited, hesitant and slow to produce constructive collaboration: engagement around a Mining Policy withered; diamond sector legislation was abandoned; and, after a decade of consultations, critical amendments to the Mines and Minerals Act remained in limbo in 2017.

This failure of the state to chart a new path forward underlined continuing elite power in policy-making, and the persistence of its short-term, partisan, contradictory and sometimes predatory imperatives. Potentially constructive policy interventions borrowed from the AMV (for example, initiatives around beneficiation and upstream/downstream linkages) were repeatedly disrupted by senior officials, who undermined bureaucratic authority and called into question the state's practical commitments to the 'best practices' it officially endorsed. In reality, elite interventions were repeatedly focused on short term priorities driven by fiscal emergencies, opportunistic cash grabs and the need to shore up political promises. This unsteady equilibrium of state concession to business power and state disruption at the hands of diverse elite interventions both enabled continuity in mining production alongside modest investment and dampened the developmental potential of the sector.

Comparative assessment and lessons

A critical feature of developmental states in East Asia involved the capacity, autonomy and cohesiveness of state bureaucracies. Technocratic capacity and bureaucratic coherence were important components for states which sought to direct, discipline and coordinate markets. Bureaucratic relative autonomy in the formulation and execution of policy served to insulate the bureaucracy from politicised, partisan and rent-seeking behaviour; and the emergence of pilot agencies helped consolidate and champion developmental strategies.

Our cases suggest that some African developmental projects faced multiple challenges in this context. In Zambia and Zimbabwe, state mining institutions and capacities were hollowed out through a succession of neoliberal austerity, chronic under-investment in state institutions and skills and, in the case of Zimbabwe, state capture in a period of heightened political contestation. Institutional competition and fragmentation of jurisdiction and policy engagement nurtured low coherence and cohesiveness in Zimbabwe. This compounded a situation of overall low state bureaucratic capacity, for which capacity-building investments appeared to have, at best, minor impacts on state developmental interventions in the mining sector. In both cases, without strengthened state institutions, the likelihood of maximising fiscal returns and beneficiation from minerals was diminished. Low state capacity led to a paradoxical inversion of the coordinating dynamics seen in East Asia: in Zambia and Zimbabwe, business and donor interests often played important, if not dominant, roles in policy research and formulation.

In East Asia, collaborative state–business relations were a key factor in developmental successes. East Asian states worked to harness the capacities of the private sector to specified national goals. This implied both good state capacity and a business sector which was open to and capable of effective engagement. Our case studies reflect significant differences with these East Asian experiences, and raise critical questions about the viability of constructive state–business relations under conditions of uneven power. On the one hand, Zambia's and Zimbabwe's mining state bureaucracies demonstrated little capacity to engage productively with key players in the sector due to state actors' low competence, willingness or practical authority to act on agreed terms. While both countries saw extensive interaction between the state, mining capital and donors, these engagements often reflected mistrust nurtured by contradictory signals on both sides; notably, regulatory inconsistency generated by an unpredictable and incohesive set of state institutions and threats made by mining capital. On the other hand, the problems of trust and accommodation were exacerbated by the structure of mining sector ownership: in Zambia and Zimbabwe (as in many resource-rich African countries), large-scale mining was overwhelmingly dominated by foreign-owned firms and national players remained insignificant outside of the small-scale sector. Moreover, mining capital retained an effective veto over policy due to foreign firms' continuing structural power. Legislation and regulatory initiatives hostile to the interests of these firms were either subverted or aggressively challenged; for example, companies threatened to shutter operations, retrench personnel, suspend investment or slow down and deflect state demands for ownership restructuring.

The skewed pattern of mine ownership increased tension and mistrust between the state and companies. In Zimbabwe, mining policies focused more on targeting foreign-owned firms in the domestication of asset control than on leveraging systematic developmental contributions from leading players. In Zambia, mining policies aimed to secure greater revenue and, to a lesser degree, nurture backward linkages to locally-based manufacturing firms. In both cases, the absence of significant domestic large-scale miners deprived the state of 'natural' developmental partners, opening the way for policy initiatives like royalty hikes and indigenisation measures that served to both consolidate state legitimacy and rattle established foreign mining firms. Prospects therefore seemed dim for the 'embedding' of policy-making in a domestic sector whose dominant foreign investors held the state's intentions in suspicion (if not hostile regard), and whose local prospective newcomers were mostly seen as rent-seeking, predatory and antagonistic to a wider developmental approach.

The implications of foreign investor hesitancy were profound in light of the weakness of local finance markets and the high capital costs of mining. East Asian developmental states succeeded partly due to geopolitical factors that enabled access capital on concessionary terms, and partly by mobilising domestic savings. Neither of these conditions existed in our case study countries. Instead, thin local finance markets, set in the context of high levels of debt, continuing fiscal fragility and growing exposure to volatile commodity markets, rendered new developmental initiatives dependent on inflows of private foreign capital and aid. One result was the 'fiscal embeddedness' of new mining development in offshore finance and credit, which significantly empowered large foreign mining houses due to their unrivalled capacity to mobilise resources; another was the buttressing of donor influence, leveraged through debt management and aid, and complemented by the provision of technical support to state institutions, business groups and independent think tanks. Both outcomes raised questions over the feasibility of financing developmental projects from offshore, especially as business and donors emphasised the central role of private finance in new hybrid approaches to development. With both Zambia and Zimbabwe beleaguered by weak state finances, investor and donor boycott threats proved effective in deflecting policy thrusts.

Recent African contributions to the developmental state literature have suggested that, despite capital constraints, limited bureaucratic autonomy and the presence of a clientelist political elite, a path forward is feasible in the form of 'developmental patrimonialism'. Our case studies call into question the viability of such a model. Centralisation of rent and the elaboration of a developmental vision did not result in either country in substantial progress in the achievement of developmental outcomes; instead, distilled forms of rent seeking, clientelism and corruption were in evidence, and there was a tendency for the state to revert to short term visions and politically expedient forms of resource deployment. In the notable case of Zimbabwe, occasionally extreme centralisation of rents fuelled profoundly *anti*-developmental elite behaviour and outcomes, even as an elaborate developmental vision and accompanying policy frameworks were put in place by the political leadership. Beyond the more exceptional instances of elite predation, including the state's notoriously irregular exploitation of the Marange diamond fields, there was little evidence of centralised and efficient rent-seeking leading to sustainable, transparent developmental interventions by the state; moreover, it was not clear how and why these rent-seeking arrangements would be shifted in a developmental direction by their main beneficiaries – an entrenched, predatory political elite.

Critics of the developmental patrimonial approach, and other contributors who have speculated about the possible developmental benefits of democratisation, have been sceptical of the outcomes of developmental models that are in part dependent on the voluntarism of political elites. They question the 'developmental' content and durability of projects which are hinged on elite accumulation projects and the decisive participation of external structural interests. Some have argued for the deepening of democracy with the aim of leveraging greater transparency, accountability and participation in developmental state projects. While our cases underscore the importance of the democratic moment in fuelling the rise of resource nationalist politics in the 2000s, they also point to the real limitations of democratic institutions with regards to the formulation, implementation and supervision of developmentalism in practice. Beyond helping to place developmentalist politics on the national agenda by means of regime change (Zambia) or in response to an opposition challenge (Zimbabwe), 'the democratic turn' left little imprint on the arc of developmentalism in practice, in either country. Instead, policy processes reflected the relatively weak and ineffective participation of popular classes, shallow democratic oversight by representative institutions and continuing poor accountability of political and economic elites.

If some have held that authoritarian regimes were occasionally functional in the building of developmental states in East Asia, in Zimbabwe – and, to a lesser extent, Zambia – increasing autocratic and authoritarian tendencies tended to undermine the state's legitimacy and developmental capacities, and shield the political elite's rent-seeking activities from close inspection. Following our case studies, democratisation was an important element in the popularisation of the *idea* of the developmental state; but for the idea to be *realised* there was need to democratise policy processes through the enabling of key social constituencies' participation in policy research, formulation, implementation and monitoring. By extension, our case study evidence suggests that understanding the practical content, likely outcomes and political viability of a developmental strategy requires the rigorous assessment of the forces and interests which shape and champion it – as well as those excluded from these constitutive processes.

Notwithstanding the disjuncture between East Asia's historical and structural conditions and those in contemporary Africa, and the unlikelihood of a viable parallel industrialisation model taking shape in Africa, the East Asian model has nonetheless served as an important conceptual and political *point of departure* for African researchers and policy makers in a period when neoliberal orthodoxy has come under increasing pressure. While some African debates have focused – problematically, in our view – on unique African incarnations of developmental patrimonialism in which the prominent role of elites is featured, we argue that understanding the dynamics of African developmental projects requires greater attention to their structural and class features. This is an observation which also applies to the wider international literature on contemporary extractive developmental state projects, where structural and class conditions corresponding to those in southern Africa frequently occur. These include vulnerabilities to international commodity markets, weak domestic finance markets and thin consolidation of domestic capacity in the mining sector. Such factors threaten to inflect state-capital alliances around developmentalism with specific internationalised features. There is need for greater research and theoretical attention to the capacities and interests of states, domestic capital and civil society in steering the restructuring of international investment, finance and productive linkages.

Our cases also suggest the need to refresh thinking on new developmental state projects by incorporating more nuanced, context-specific understandings of the terrain of state-society political relations. The autonomy and relative isolation of state policy-making from popular domestic social forces in many African cases underscore the importance of deepening our understanding of policy and political processes, and the ways in which they have scuttled or enabled the building of public–private consensus in support of aspirant developmental state projects. If state legitimacy and its consolidation have been critical factors explaining the rise of resource nationalism and developmentalist politics, popular claims on the African state – and its capacity to manage and engage with them – are deserving of greater attention. In the East Asian cases, focus fell on state institutions and business; in Africa, experiences suggest the critical need to include institutional conditions, capacities and dynamics *outside* of the state. Are there lead agencies in *civil society,* for example, which can play key roles in elaborating and implementing a social consensus in support of an emergent developmental state project? New theorisation, research and political intervention around the developmental state in Africa – and further afield – will need to incorporate these kinds of questions in coming to terms with the evolving terrain of developmental project beyond East Asia.

Conclusion

The resurgence of debate in southern Africa in the 2000s around 'developmental state' projects marked an important benchmark in the distancing of policy makers, leading social constituencies, donors and researchers from the neoliberal orthodoxy of the 1990s. While the absence of key institutional and market conditions which underpinned the East Asian developmental states raised questions about the possible duplication of the 'tiger' experience by aspiring 'lions', recent African initiatives nonetheless reflected new political energy and creativity in addressing the developmental shortfalls of recent decades. Indeed, in their contributions, African researchers challenged the feasibility, desirability and objective of reproducing East Asian-styled industrial growth in Africa, and called instead for the elaboration of local developmental models informed by, but not conforming to, the East Asian experience. From this perspective, African developmentalism required a judicious mix of economic growth and democratically-driven redistribution, mediated by a state with enhanced capacity and legitimacy. In mineral rich countries, it was argued, opportunities existed for overcoming the challenges of weak domestic capital markets and technological gaps; however, successful strategies depended heavily on the supervisory and disciplinary power of the state, and its ability to nurture the rehabilitation and expansion of private and public infrastructure and enabling institutions.

Our case studies of the Zambian and Zimbabwean mining sectors and their uneven contribution to new developmentalist initiatives broadly concur with the arguments of critical African scholarship on the contemporary local developmental state. In both countries, weaknesses of key state institutions – the result of their erosion under neoliberal reforms, continued under-investment, deskilling and, in some instances, political capture by elites – undercut important opportunities represented by new policy initiatives which were broadly developmentalist in outlook. Chronically weak domestic finance markets, sharp constraints on access to foreign capital and the capital-intensive nature of medium and large-scale mining compounded the fragility of developmental strategies based on extractive resources. Compounding these structural challenges, the state instrumentalised, rather than included and reflected, the interests of key national constituencies like domestic capital and popular social forces. In contrast, large-scale foreign capital maintained a powerful influence in state regulatory practices, despite the resurgence in both countries of resource nationalist rhetoric. As a result, the commodities super-cycle of the 2000s had limited lasting impacts in supporting a new developmental model focused on minerals, despite a policy mobilisation in this direction.

Our cases also point to a changing political and economic environment in sub-Saharan Africa and evolving thinking around developmental state opportunities. Together these suggest that further empirical and historical work is required to support the wave of policy initiatives now underway. We need to better understand the political and economic frailties of recent developmental projects, drawing on important features of the East Asian cases while recognising the uniquely African contexts of evolving states, markets and powerful social constituencies. In this regard, few contemporary national case studies have been undertaken; more are urgently needed to support policy interventions inside and outside the state around re-imagined national developmental projects.

Disclosure statement

No potential conflict of interest was reported by the authors.

Acknowledgements

The authors would like to thank the Special Issue Guest Editors, Jesse Ovadia and Jewellord Nem Singh, and three anonymous reviewers for their very helpful feedback.

Notes

1. Routley, "Developmental States In Africa?"
2. UNECA, *Economic Report on Africa 2011*.
3. African Union, *African Mining Vision*.
4. Zenawi, "States and Markets."
5. Kelsall, *Business, Politics and the State in Africa*; Kelsall and Booth, "Developmental Patrimonialism?"; Henley, *Asia-Africa Development Divergence*.
6. Edigheji, *Constructing a Democratic Developmental State in South Africa*; Ovadia, *The Petro-Developmental State in Africa*; Kanyenze et al., *Towards Democratic Developmental States in Southern Africa*.
7. For an closer mapping of resource nationalism see Wilson, "Understanding Resource Nationalism" and Andreasson, "Varieties of Resource Nationalism."
8. 'Southern Africa' being represented by the countries of the Southern Africa Development Community; see Twerefou, "Mineral Exploitation, Environmental Sustainability," 5.
9. See for example the doctoral dissertation of notable Zambian scholar-activist Charity Musamba, *The Developmental State and Poverty Reduction in Africa*.
10. Business Council of Zimbabwe, *Indigenization and Economic Empowerment in Zimbabwe*, 23.
11. Kanyenze et al., *Towards Democratic Developmental States in Southern Africa*.
12. Lijphart, "Comparative Politics and the Comparative Method," 692.
13. Auty, *Sustaining Development in Mineral Economies*; Sachs and Warner, "The Curse of Natural Resources."

14. Rosales, "Going Underground"; Burchardt and Dietz, "(Neo-)Extractivism."
15. Morris, Kaplinsky, and Caplan, "One Thing Leads to Another."
16. Ovadia, *The Petro-Developmental State in Africa.*
17. Mosley, *Fiscal Policy and the Natural Resources Curse.*
18. Johnson, *MITI and the Japanese Miracle*; Chang, "How to 'Do' a Developmental State."
19. Evans, *Embedded Autonomy.*
20. Amsden, *The Rise of "the Rest"*; Chibber, *Locked in Place.*
21. Sindzingre, "Financing the Developmental State."
22. Taylor, *Business and the State in Southern Africa*; Handley, *Business and the State in Africa.*
23. Saul and Leys, "Sub-Saharan Africa in Global Capitalism."
24. Arrighi, "The African Crisis."
25. Kelsall, *Business, Politics and the State in Africa*; Kelsall and Booth, "Developmental Patrimonialism?"; Henley, *Asia-Africa Development Divergence.*
26. Mkandawire, "Neopatrimonialism and the Political Economy of Economic Performance in Africa," 596–7.
27. Mkandawire, "Aid, Accountability, and Democracy in Africa."
28. Mkandawire, "From Maladjusted States to Democratic Developmental States in Africa."
29. Taylor, "Ditiro Tsa Ditlhabololo"; Samatar, *An African Miracle.*
30. Taylor, "Botswana as a Developmental State"; Samatar, *An African Miracle.*
31. Hillbom "Botswana: A Development-Orientated Gate-Keeping State"; Taylor, "Botswana as a 'Development-Orientated Gate-Keeping State'"; Hillbom, "Botswana: A Response to Ian Taylor."
32. Hillbom "Botswana: A Development-Orientated Gate-Keeping State"; Hillbom, "Diamonds or Development?"
33. Cooper, *Africa Since 1940.*
34. Brautigam, *The Dragon's Gift.*
35. Arrighi, *Adam Smith in Beijing*, 384–5.
36. Ayers, "Beyond, Myths, Lies and Stereotypes."
37. Martin, "Africa's Futures," 351.
38. Ayers, "Beyond, Myths, Lies and Stereotypes," 230–2.
39. Carmody, "An Asian Economic Recovery in Africa?," 1204.
40. BDO, *Seventh Report of the ZEITI.*
41. Conditions stipulated included reductions in corporate taxation, duty-free capital imports, lower royalties and extension of loss carry-forward provisions, among others. See Lungu, "Copper Mining Agreements in Zambia."
42. Fraser and Lungu, *For Whom the Wind Falls?*
43. Caramento, Interview with Charles Muchimba, Director of Research, Mineworkers Union of Zambia (MUZ), 10 July 2015; Caramento, Interview with Branch Officials MUZ Nkana Branch, 5 October 2015; Interview with Branch Officials of MUZ Mpatamatu and Roan Branches, 8 October 2015.
44. Caramento, Interview with a member of Mwanawasa's Cabinet, 17 June 2015.
45. This is the view of David Manley, a former ZRA economist, http://www.resourcegovernance.org/blog/zambias-new-mining-tax-regime-may-fail-test-time.
46. Unless otherwise stated, all figures are in US dollars.
47. Kar and Frietas, *Illicit Financial Flows from Developing Countries*, 2001–2010.
48. Zambia Revenue Authority, *Mineral Value Chain Monitoring Project (MVCMP) Report*, 11.
49. ICMM, *Enhancing Mining's Contribution to the Zambian Economy and Society*, 66.
50. Fessehaie, Rustomjee, and Kaziboni, "Can Mining Promote Industrialization?"
51. Kragelund, "The Making of Local Content Policies," 63.
52. Caramento, Interview with Roseta Mwape, President of Zambian Association of Manufacturers and Managing Director of ZAMEFA, 11 August 2015.
53. Zambia Revenue Authority, *Mineral Value Chain Monitoring Project (MVCMP) Report*, 16–17.
54. Caramento, Interview with Hon. Wylbur Simuusa, former Minister of Mines, 14 October 2015.
55. Hakumona, *Survey and Analysis of Demand*; Fessehaie, Rustomjee, and Kaziboni, "Can Mining Promote Industrialization?," 15–17.

56. Haglund, *Policy Evolution and Organisational Learning in Zambia's Mining Sector*; World Bank, *Zambia Mining Investment and Governance Review*.
57. Mineworkers Union of Zambia data provided by Webby Mushota, 28 September 2015.
58. Caramento, Interview with Mooya Lumamba, Director of Mines, Ministry of Mines, 30 June 2015.
59. Caramento, Interview with Gilbert Kalyandu, Embassy of Norway in Zambia, 9 June 2015.
60. World Bank, *Zambia Mining Investment and Governance Review*, 13.
61. Both the Mines and Mineral Development Bills of 2008 and 2015 included provisions giving preference to 'materials and products made in Zambia' and 'contractors, suppliers and service agencies located in Zambia and owned by citizens or citizen-owned companies'; Government of the Republic of Zambia (GRZ), "Mines and Minerals Development Act 2008," 13:1; GRZ, "Mines and Minerals Development Act 2015," 20:1.
62. BDO, *Seventh Report of the ZEITI*.
63. Fraser, "Zambia: Back to the Future?," 308.
64. Simpasa et al., *Capturing Mineral Revenues in Zambia*.
65. During this period, the share of the top five minerals rose from 24 to 49% of exports, and in 2014 to more than 90%; Hawkins, *The Mining Sector in Zimbabwe*, 1. For 2014 figure, see Nu Times Innovations, *State of the Mining Industry Survey*, 9.
66. Kanyenze et al., *Beyond the Enclave*.
67. For a detailed account of evolving elite rent-seeking and diminishing developmental outcomes, see Dawson and Kelsall, "Anti-Developmental Patrimonialism in Zimbabwe."
68. Some estimated that 90% of mining was under foreign ownership in 1981, a ratio of foreign concentration far higher than other productive subsectors; Davies and Burdette, "The Zimbabwe Economy," 78.
69. Jourdan, "The Non-ferrous Metal Industry in Zimbabwe."
70. Notably 'Special Mining Licences', enacted in 1994 for projects over $100 million, which provided for long-term minerals leases, lower rates of corporate tax, the holding of offshore operational accounts and other incentives; Mupamhadzi, Mlambo, and Kwesu, "A Critical Review of the Mining Fiscal Regime in Zimbabwe."
71. BusinessMap, *Mining in SADC*.
72. Kanyenze et al., *Beyond the Enclave*, 178.
73. Saunders, Interview with Lyman Mlambo, Director of Institute of Mining Research, University of Zimbabwe, 13 March 2014.
74. Saunders, "Crisis, Capital, Compromise."
75. Matyszak, *Everything You Ever Wanted to Know*.
76. Matyszak, *CSOTs in Zimbabwe's Mining Sector*; Mawowa, *Community Share Ownership Trusts*; Parliament of Zimbabwe, *Thematic Committee on Indigenisation and Empowerment, First Report*; "Govt to initiate employee share ownership schemes," *The Herald*, October 19, 2011.
77. Matyszak, *Everything You Wanted To Know*.
78. Matyszak, *Racketeering by Regulation*; Matyszak, *Digging up the Truth*.
79. Government of Zimbabwe, Indigenisation and Economic Empowerment Act. Specific IEE related regulations for mining were introduced in 2011; see, General Notice 114 of 2011 (GN 114; Government of Zimbabwe, "General Notice 114 of 2011."
80. Saunders and Nyamunda, *Facets of Power*.
81. Partnership Africa Canada, *Reap What You Sow*. One of Africa's largest sources of alluvial diamonds, in 2009 Marange represented as much as 30% of the global rough diamond supply.
82. Partnership Africa Canada, *Diamonds and Clubs*; Towriss, *Buying Loyalty*; Global Witness, *Diamonds: A good deal for Zimbabwe?*; Sibanda and Makore, *Tracking the Trends*; Sibanda, *Analysis of ZMDC's Audited Financial Statements*.
83. For example, the Diamond Revenue Bill of 2011 (promoted by the Ministry of Finance) and amendments to the Precious Stones Trade Act (developed by the mining ministry); Dhliwayo and Mtisi, *Towards the Development of a Diamond Act in Zimbabwe*.
84. Biti, "2011 Mid-Year Fiscal Policy Statement," 30–1; Timba, "Statement Made at the Reception for the EITI Conference"; "Anjin remits US$30 m to fiscus," *The Herald*, 28 June 2012.

85. "The President @92," interview with Robert Mugabe broadcast by Zimbabwe Broadcasting Corporation, 3 March 2016.
86. Parliament of Zimbabwe, "First Report on Diamond Mining."
87. Business Council of Zimbabwe, *Indigenisation and Economic Empowerment*, xxxvi.
88. Chamber of Mines, "Issues of Concern"; Chamber of Mines, "Untitled Discussion Document"; Deloitte Zimbabwe, *Zimbabwe Mining Tax Study*; Mupamhadzi, Mlambo, and Kwesu, "A Critical Review of the Mining Fiscal Regime." Key civil society organisations broadly agreed; see, ZELA, *An Outline of the Mining Taxation Regime*.
89. Hawkins, *The Mining Sector in Zimbabwe*; Jourdan et al., *Mining Sector Policy Study*; McMahon et al., "Zimbabwe: From Economic Rebound to Sustained Growth."
90. Government of Zimbabwe, *Draft Minerals Policy*.
91. Government of Zimbabwe, *Mines and Minerals Amendment Bill, 2010 (Draft)*; Government of Zimbabwe, *Zimbabwe Diamond Policy*; Hawkins, *Mining Policy in Zimbabwe*; Mtisi, "Civil Society Perspectives on the Draft Minerals Policy"; CNRG, *An Analysis of Zimbabwe's Diamond Policy*.
92. The 'Indigenisation Compliance and Empowerment Levy' offered scaled rebates of levies for investments with empowerment and indigenisation impacts; Government of Zimbabwe, "Frameworks, Procedures and Guidelines for Implementing the Indigenisation and Economic Empowerment Act."
93. In 2009 mining accounted for more than 93% of approved investment, and retained top spot in 2011–2013 (2011: 55%; 2012: 74%; 2013: 31%); see Zimbabwe Investment Authority, *Annual Reports*.

Bibliography

African Union. *African Mining Vision*. Addis Ababa: African Union, February 2009.

Amsden, Alice H. *The Rise of 'the Rest': Challenges to the West from Late-Industrializing Economies*. Oxford: Oxford University Press, 2003.

Andreasson, Stefan. "Varieties of Resource Nationalism in Sub-Saharan Africa's Energy and Minerals Markets." *Extractive Industries and Society* 2, no. 2 (2015): 310–319.

Arrighi, Giovanni. "The African Crisis: World Systemic and Regional Aspects." *New Left Review* 15 (May/June 2002): 5–36.

Arrighi, Giovanni. *Adam Smith in Beijing: Lineages of the Twenty-First Century*. London: Verso, 2009.

Auty, Richard. *Sustaining Development in Mineral Economies: The Resource Curse Thesis*. London: Routledge, 1993.

Ayers, Alison. "Beyond, Myths, Lies and Stereotypes: The Political Economy of a 'New Scramble for Africa'." *New Political Economy* 18, no. 2 (2013): 227–257.

BDO East Africa and BDO Zambia. *Seventh Report of the Zambia Extractive Transparency Initiative (ZEITI) for the Year Ended 31 December 2014*. Lusaka: ZEITI, December 2015.

Biti, Tendai. "2011 Mid-Year Fiscal Policy Review Statement." Statement Issued by the Minister of Finance, 2011.

Brautigam, Deborah. *The Dragon's Gift: The Real Story of China in Africa*. Oxford, UK: Oxford University Press, 2009.

Burchardt, Hans-Jurgen, and Kristina Dietz. "(Neo-)Extractivism – A New Challenge for Development Theory from Latin America." *Third World Quarterly* 35, no. 3 (2014): 468–486.

Business Council of Zimbabwe. *Indigenisation and Economic Empowerment*. Harare: BCZ, 2011.

BusinessMap. *Mining in SADC: The Market's Mixed Messages for the Future*. Johannesburg: BusinessMap, June 1999.

Carmody, Pádraig. "An Asian Economic Recovery in Africa? The Zambian Case." *World Development* 37, no. 7 (2008): 1197–1207.

Centre for Natural Resource Governance (CNRG). *An Analysis of Zimbabwe's Diamond Policy*. Harare: CNRG, April 2013.

Chamber of Mines of Zimbabwe. "Untitled Discussion Document for Consultation with Government." July 2012.

Chamber of Mines of Zimbabwe. *Issues of Concern to the Mining Industry*. Harare: Chamber of Mines, 2012.

Chang, Ha-Joon. "How to 'Do' a Developmental State: Political, Organisational and Human Resource Requirements for the Developmental State." In *Constructing a Democratic Developmental State in South Africa: Potentials and Challenges*, edited by Omano Edigheji, 82–96. Johannesburg: HSRC, 2010.

Chibber, Vivek. *Locked in Place: State-Building and Late Industrialization in India*. Princeton, NJ: Princeton University Press, 2003.

Cooper, Frederick. *Africa since 1940: The Past of the Present*. Cambridge, UK: Cambridge University Press, 2002.

Davies, Rob, and Marcia Burdette. "The Zimbabwe Economy: Prognostications and Realities after Six Years." *Zambezia* XIV (1987): 73–83.

Dawson, Martin, and Tim Kelsall. "Anti-Developmental Patrimonialism in Zimbabwe." *Journal of Contemporary African Studies* 30, no. 1 (2012): 49–66.

Deloitte Zimbabwe. *Zimbabwe Mining Tax Study*. Commissioned by the Chamber of Mines of Zimbabwe, 2012.

Dhliwayo, Mutoso, and Shamiso Mtisi. *Towards the Development of a Diamond Act in Zimbabwe: Analysis of the Legal and Policy Framework on Diamonds and Zimbabwe's Compliance with the Kimberley Process Certification Scheme (KPCS) Minimum Requirements*. Harare: ZELA, 2012.

Edigheji, Omano, ed. *Constructing a Democratic Developmental State in South Africa: Potentials and Challenges*. Johannesburg: HSRC, 2010.

Evans, Peter. *Embedded Autonomy: States and Industrial Transformation*. Princeton, NJ: Princeton University Press, 1995.

Fessehaie, Judith, Zavareh Rustomjee, and Lauralyn Kaziboni. *Can Mining Promote Industrialization? A Comparative Analysis of Policy Frameworks in Three Southern African Countries*. Helsinki: UNU-WIDER. UNU-Wider Working Paper 2016/83, June 2016.

Fraser, A., and J. Lungu. *For Whom the Windfalls? Winners and Losers in the Privatisation of Zambia's Copper Mines*. Lusaka: CSTNZ & CCJDP, 2007.

Fraser, Alastair. "Zambia: Back to the Future?" In *The Politics of Aid: African Strategies for Dealing with Donors*, edited by Lindsey Whitfield, 299–328. Oxford, UK: Oxford University Press, 2008.

Global Witness. *Diamonds: A Good Deal for Zimbabwe?* February 13, 2012.

Government of the Republic of Zambia. "Mines and Minerals Development Act." [13:1], 2008.

Government of the Republic of Zambia. "Mines and Minerals Development Act." [20:1], 2015.

Government of Zimbabwe. "Frameworks, Procedures and Guidelines for Implementing the Indigenisation and Economic Empowerment Act [Chapter 14:33]." January 4, 2016.

Government of Zimbabwe. "Draft Minerals Policy." October 2013.

Government of Zimbabwe, Ministry of Mines and Mining Development. *Zimbabwe Diamond Policy*. 2012.

Government of Zimbabwe. "General Notice 114 of 2011. Indigenization and Economic Empowerment (General) Regulations: Minimum Requirements for Indigenization Implementation Plans Submitted by Non-Indigenous Businesses in the Mining Sector." 2011.

Government of Zimbabwe. *Indigenisation and Economic Empowerment Act*. Chapter 14:33, 2007.

Government of Zimbabwe. *Mines and Minerals Amendment Bill, 2010* (*Draft*) Chapter 21:05. November 2007.

Hakumona, Passmore. *Survey and Analysis of Demand for and Supply of Skilled Workers in the Zambian Mining Industry*. Lusaka: Ministry of Mines & Minerals Development, 2011.

Haglund, Dan. "Policy Evolution and Organisational Learning in Zambia's Mineral Sector." Unpublished Doctoral Dissertation, University of Bath, Bath, UK, 2010.

Handley, Antoinette. *Business and the State in Africa: Economic Policy-Making in the Neo-Liberal Era*. Cambridge, UK: Cambridge University Press, 2008.

Hawkins, Tony. "Mining Policy in Zimbabwe." Unpublished Draft of Commentary, 2014.

Hawkins, Tony. *The Mining Sector in Zimbabwe and Its Potential Contribution to Recovery*. Working Paper 1, Working Paper Series. Harare: UNDP, 2009.

Henley, David. *Asia-Africa Development Divergence: A Question of Intent*. London: Zed Books, 2015.

Hillbom, Ellen. "Diamonds or Development? A Structural Assessment of Botswana's Forty Years of Success." *Journal of Modern African Studies* 46, no. 2 (2008): 191–214.

Hillbom, Ellen. "Botswana: A Development-Orientated Gate-Keeping State." *African Affairs* 111, no. 442 (2012): 67–89.

Hillbom, Ellen. "Botswana: A Development-Orientated Gate-Keeping State – A Response to Ian Taylor." *African Affairs* 111, no. 444 (2012): 477–482.

International Council of Mining and Metals (ICMM). *Enhancing Mining's Contribution to the Zambian Economy and Society*. London: ICMM, 2014.

Johnson, Chalmers. *MITI and the Japanese Miracle: The Growth of Industrial Policy, 1925–1975*. Stanford, CA: Stanford University Press, 1982.

Jourdan, Paul. "The Non-Ferrous Metal Industry in Zimbabwe." *Minerals & Energy - Raw Materials Report* 4, no. 2 (1986): 12–31.

Jourdan, Paul, Gibson Chigumira, Isaac Kwesu, and Erina Chipumho. *Mining Sector Policy Study*. Harare: ZEPARU, 2012.

Kanyenze, Godfrey, Herbert Jauch, Alice Kanengoni, Masego Madzwamuse, and Deprose Muchena, eds. *Towards Democratic Developmental States in Southern Africa*. Harare: Weaver Press, 2017.

Kanyenze, Godfrey, Timothy Kondo, Prosper Chitambara, and Jos Martens, eds. *Beyond the Enclave: Towards a pro-Poor and Inclusive Development Strategy for Zimbabwe*. Harare: Weaver Press, 2011.

Kar, Dev, and Sarah Freitas. *Illicit Financial Flows from Developing Countries: 2001-2010*. Washington, DC: Global Financial Integrity, 2012.

Kelsall, Tim, and David Booth. *Developmental Patrimonialism? Questioning the Orthodoxy on Political Governance and Economic Progress in Africa*. Africa, Power & Politics Working Paper, No. 9. London: ODA, 2010.

Kelsall, Tim. *Business, Politics, and the State in Africa: Challenging the Orthodoxies on Growth and Transformation*. London: Zed Books, 2013.

Kragelund, Peter. "The Making of Local Content Policies in Zambia's Copper Sector: Institutional Impediments to Resource-Led Development." *Resources Policy* 51 (2017): 57–66.

Lijphart, Arend. "Comparative Politics and the Comparative Method." *American Political Science Review* 65, no. 3 (1971): 682–693.

Lungu, John. "Copper Mining Agreements in Zambia: Renegotiation or Law Reform?" *Review of African Political Economy* 35, no. 117 (2008): 403–415.

Manley, David. "Zambia Votes for President, but What Will the Winner Do about Copper?" *Natural Resource Governance Institute*, January 20, 2015. https://resourcegovernance.org/blog/zambia-votes-president-what-will-winner-do-about-copper.

Manley, David. "Zambia's New Mining Tax Regime May Fail the Test of Time." *Natural Resource Governance Institute*, July 4, 2016. http://www.resourcegovernance.org/blog/zambias-new-mining-tax-regime-may-fail-test-time.

Martin, William. "Africa's Futures: From North-South to East-South?" *Third World Quarterly* 29, no. 2 (2008): 339–356.

Matyszak, Derek. *CSOTs in Zimbabwe's Mining Sector*. Harare: ZELA, 2013.

Matyszak, Derek. *Digging up the Truth: The Legal and Political Realities of the Zimplats Saga*. Harare: Research and Advocacy Unit, April 19, 2011.

Matyszak, Derek. *Everything You Ever Wanted to Know (and Then Some) about Zimbabwe's Indigenisation and Economic Empowerment Legislation but (Quite Rightly) Were Too Afraid to Ask*. 2nd ed. Harare: Research and Advocacy Unit, May 2011.

Matyszak, Derek. *Racketeering by Regulation*. 2nd ed. Harare: Research and Advocacy Unit, May 2011.

Mawowa, Showers. *Community Share Ownership Trusts (CSOT) in Zimbabwe's Mining Sector: The Case of Mhondoro-Ngezi*. Harare: ZELA, 2013.

McMahon, Gary, Rene Hochreiter, Robinn Y. Kearney, and Brandon Tracy. "Zimbabwe: From Economic Rebound to Sustained Growth." Growth Recovery Notes, Note IV: Zimbabwe's Current Potential for Mining Growth, 2012.

Mkandawire, Thandika. "From Maladjusted States to Democratic Developmental States in Africa." In *Constructing a Democratic Developmental State in South Africa: Potentials and Challenges*, edited by Omano Edigheji, 59–81. Johannesburg: HSRC, 2010.

Mkandawire, Thandika. "Aid, Accountability, and Democracy in Africa." *Social Research* 77, no. 4 (2010): 149–1182.

Mkandawire, Thandika. "Neopatrimonialism and the Political Economy of Economic Performance in Africa: Critical Reflections." *World Politics* 67, no. 3 (July 2015): 563–612.

Morris, Mike, Raphael Kaplinsky, and David Kaplan. "'One Thing Leads to Another' – Commodities, Linkages, and Industrial Development." *Resources Policy* 37, no. 4 (2012): 408–416.

Mosley, Paul. *Fiscal Policy and the Natural Resources Curse: How to Escape from the Poverty Trap*. London: Routledge, 2017.

Mtisi, Shamiso. "Civil Society Perspectives on the Draft Minerals Policy." Paper presented at Stakeholder Consultation Meeting on the Draft Minerals Policy, Ministry of Mines and Minerals, Harare, May 23, 2013.

Mugabe, Robert. "The President @92." Interview Broadcast by Zimbabwe Broadcasting Corporation, March 3, 2016.

Mupamhadzi, David, Lyman Mlambo, and Isaac Kwesu. "A Critical Review of the Mining Fiscal Regime in Zimbabwe: Towards an Optimal Structure." Paper for Chamber of Mines of Zimbabwe, March 2014.

Musamba, Charity. "The Developmental State and Poverty Reduction in Africa: The Case of Zambia." Unpublished doctoral dissertation, Universität Duisburg-Essen, Duisburg, Germany, 2009.

Nalishebo, Shebo, and Albert Halwampa. *A Cautionary Tale of Zambia's International Sovereign Bond Issuances*. Working Paper no. 22. Lusaka: ZIPAR, March 2015.

Nu Times Innovations. *State of the Mining Industry Survey: Report on Findings*. Harare: Study commissioned by the Chamber of Mines of Zimbabwe, 2015.

Ovadia, Jesse. *The Petro-Developmental State in Africa: Making Oil Work in Angola, Nigeria and the Gulf of Guinea*. London: Hurst, 2016.

Parliament of Zimbabwe, Committee on Mines and Energy. *First Report on Diamond Mining (with Special Reference to Marange Diamond Fields) 2009–2013*. Presented to Parliament, June 2013.

Parliament of Zimbabwe, Thematic Committee on Indigenisation and Empowerment on the Operations of the Community Share Ownership Trusts and Employee Share Ownership Schemes. *First Report*. Presented to Parliament, February 2015.

Partnership Africa Canada. *Reap What You Sow: Greed and Corruption in Zimbabwe's Marange Diamond Fields*. Ottawa: PAC, November 2012.

Partnership Africa Canada. *Diamonds and Clubs: The Militarized Control of Diamonds and Power in Zimbabwe*. Ottawa: PAC, June 2010.

Rosales, Antulio. "Going Underground: The Political Economy of the 'Left Turn' in South America." *Third World Quarterly* 34, no. 8 (2013): 1443–1457.

Routley, Laura. "Developmental States in Africa? A Review of Ongoing Debates and Buzzwords." *Development Policy Review* 32, no. 2 (2014): 159–177.

Sachs, Jeffrey, and Andrew Warner. "The Curse of Natural Resources." *European Economic Review* 45, nos. 4-6 (2001): 827–838.

Samatar, Abdi Ismail. *An African Miracle: State and Class Leadership and Colonial Legacy in Botswana Development*. London: Heinemann, 1999.

Saul, J. S., and Colin Leys. "Sub-Saharan Africa in Global Capitalism." *Monthly Review* 51, no. 3 (1999): 13–30.

Saunders, Richard, and Tinashe Nyamunda. *Facets of Power: Politics, Profits and People in the Making of Zimbabwe's Blood Diamonds*. Harare/Johannesburg: Weaver Press/Wits University Press, 2016.

Saunders, Richard. "Crisis, Capital, Compromise: Mining and Empowerment in Zimbabwe." *African Sociological Review* 12, no. 1 (2008): 67–89.

Sibanda, Mukasiri, and Gilbert Makore. *Tracking the Trends: An Assessment of Diamond Mining Sector Tax Contributions to Treasury with Particular Reference to Marange Diamond Fields*. Harare: ZELA, 2013.

Sibanda, Mukasiri. *Analysis of ZMDC'S 2012 Audited Financial Statements*. Harare: ZELA, 2014.

Simpasa, Anthony, Degol Hailu, Sebastian Levine, and R. J. Tibana. *Capturing Mineral Revenues in Zambia: Past Trends and Future Prospects*. UNDP Discussion Paper. New York: United Nations Development Programme, August 2013.

Sindzingre, Alice N. "Financing the Developmental State: Tax and Revenue Issues." *Development Policy Review* 25, no. 5 (2007): 615–632.

Taylor, Ian. "'Ditiro Tsa Ditlhabololo': Botswana as a Developmental State." *Pula – Botswana Journal of African Studies* 17, no. 1 (2003): 37–50.
Taylor, Ian. "Botswana as a 'Development-Orientated Gate-Keeping State': A Response." *African Affairs* 111, no. 444 (2012): 466–476.
Taylor, Scott. *Business and the State in Southern Africa: The Politics of Economic Reform*. Boulder, CO: Lynne Rienner, 2007.
Timba, Jameson. "Statement Made at the Reception for the EITI Conference." Statement Issued by the Minister of State in the Prime Minister's Office. Paris, 1 March, 2011.
Towriss, David. "Buying Loyalty: Zimbabwe's Marange Diamonds." *Journal of Southern African Studies* 39, no. 1 (2013): 99–117.
Twerefou, D. K. "Mineral Exploitation, Environmental Sustainability and Sustainable Development in EAC, SADC and ECOWAS Regions." *African Trade Policy Centre (ATPC) Work In Progress*, no. 79 (2009).
United Nations Economic Commission for Africa (UNECA). *Economic Report on Africa 2011: Governing Development in Africa – The Role of the State in Economic Transformation*. Addis Ababa: UNECA, 2011.
Wilson, Jeffrey D. "Understanding Resource Nationalism: Economic Dynamics and Political Institutions." *Contemporary Politics* 21, no. 4 (2015): 399–416.
World Bank. *Zambia Mining Investment and Governance Review*. Washington, DC: World Bank, 2016.
Zambia Revenue Authority (ZRA). *Mineral Value Chain Monitoring Project Report*. Lusaka: ZRA, January 2014.
Zenawi, Meles. "States and Markets: Neoliberal Limitations and the Case for a Developmental State." In *Good Growth and Governance in Africa: Rethinking Development Strategies*, edited by A. Norman, K. Botchway, H. Skin, and J. E. Stiglitz, 140–174. Oxford: Oxford University Press, 2012.
Zimbabwe Environmental Law Association (ZELA). *An Outline of the Mining Taxation Regime in Zimbabwe*. Harare: ZELA, 2012.
Zimbabwe Investment Authority. *Annual Reports (2008–2016)*. Harare: ZIA, 2008–2016.

East Asia's new developmentalism: state capacity, climate change and low-carbon development

Christopher M. Dent

ABSTRACT
This paper argues that to understand the relevance of developmental states in East Asia and elsewhere, we need to focus on the changing development agenda in the early twenty-first century, especially how this connects with the global challenge of climate change and thereby sustainable, low-carbon development. It combines theories on state capacity and ecological modernisation to form the 'new developmentalism' concept. This is applied to study revitalised and refocused forms of state capacity aimed at realising the transformative economic objectives associated with sustainable development. New developmentalism helps us understand not only current state capacity practice in a climate challenged world but also how we have moved beyond original conceptions of developmental statism. It may be understood in the wider context of the sustainable development agenda and climate interventionism. As is argued, new developmentalism is most clearly evident in East Asia but can be applied in a wider geographic sense where strong forms of developmental state capacity are exercised towards meeting transformative sustainable development goals.

1. Introduction

The East Asia region[1] is the original source of the ideas, concepts and theories on the developmental state. These first began to emerge in the 1980s, based on historical overviews of, initially, Japan's industrialisation from the late nineteenth century, and then a wider collection of fast-developing East Asian states from the 1960s onwards, most notably Singapore, South Korea and Taiwan. Into the 1990s and 2000s, studies focused on East Asia's developmental statism remained largely preoccupied with evolving forms and patterns of state capacity, including some analyses contending that developmental statism was no longer relevant or had withered in the era of globalisation. Even most recent studies are still mainly concerned with traditional and 'conventionalised' debates on the subject.

This paper argues that to understand the relevance of developmental states in East Asia and elsewhere, we need to focus on the changing development agenda in the early twenty-first century, especially how this connects with the global challenge of climate change and thereby sustainable, low-carbon development.[2] While progressively technological 'industrial development' is still assumed to be the principal pathway that developmental states pursue to realise transformative economic and social objectives, this no longer exclusively concerns the core heavy industries of the late twentieth century. Many of the growth industries of our current age are 'green' industries. Moreover, low-carbon, sustainable development is the aspiration of not just 'advanced' high-income nations but also increasingly lower income, fast-developing economies and societies. Environmental welfare has become a growing socio-political priority, although raising levels of material prosperity and income remain dominant development goals.

What we can thus observe, most clearly in East Asia, is the emergence of a 'new developmentalism', which can be defined as revitalised and refocused forms of state capacity aimed at realising the transformative economic objectives associated with sustainable development. As is discussed, the analytical framework of this new developmentalism is a synthesis of state capacity theory (SCT) and ecological modernisation theory (EMT), the latter broadly entailing how to make capitalism environmentally sustainable by incremental change. These two political economic discourses have developed almost entirely independently of each other. However, over the last decade or so ecological modernisation has strengthened its influence over development policies worldwide, most notably in recent 'green growth' strategies. New developmentalism helps us understand not only current state capacity practice in a climate-challenged world but also how we have moved beyond original conceptions of developmental statism. This may be understood in the wider context of the sustainable development agenda and climate interventionism. As is argued, new developmentalism is most clearly evident in East Asia but is a concept that can be applied in a wider geographic sense where strong forms of developmental state capacity are exercised towards meeting transformative sustainable development goals. Two country case studies, on South Korea and Singapore, provide insights into key issues regarding East Asia's new developmentalism.

2. Developmental statism and state capacity in East Asia

The profound economic transformation experienced by the East Asia region since the 1950s has been both remarkable and incomparable. Accounting then for around 4% of world gross domestic product (GDP), this share had risen to roughly 30% by the early twenty-first century.[3] Developmental statism – a term first coined by Johnson in his seminal historical work on Japan[4] – has become a powerful explanation of how many East Asian states achieved their sustained, dynamic development based on a combination of factors centring on the directive roles played by the government.[5] This should not be confused with Western notions of state interventionism, where policy measures sought to manipulate markets and state-owned enterprises (SOEs) dominated nationalised industries. Developmental statism has crucial relational aspects, where governments form developmental partnerships or pacts with business and society to achieve transformative economic and social goals, traditionally improving income and material prosperity levels. It was founded on strong state institutions with a capacity to develop and implement strategic policies to realise those goals, involving extensive co-ordination of resources among public- and private-sector agencies. Crucially, the East Asian developmental states were not socialist but capitalist economies, where powerful business sectors had over time been nurtured by the state. Economies that had effectively practiced the above may be considered 'hard' developmental states, such as Japan and the first-generation 'tiger economies' of Singapore, South Korea and Taiwan. However, certain features of developmental statism may be practiced less rigorously and effectively in other nations (eg Thailand, Malaysia, Indonesia and the Philippines), and these can hence be viewed as 'soft' developmental states.[6]

Developmental statism is part of a broader state capacity paradigm that includes conventionally classified 'socialist market' states like China and Vietnam. Here, strategic economic planning agencies are also prevalent but heavy state interventionism entails more direct control over markets and the means of production, hence SOE dominance over key areas of the economy.[7] Socialist market economies nevertheless at times co-opt private enterprise to help meet strategic economic objectives, thus distinguishing them from pure socialist or communist economies. The state's capacity to realise transformative economic change links developmental states and socialist market economies. As a rule, the term 'state capacity' has been used as a generic explanation of governments proactively shaping the paths of an economy's development.[8]

The nature and practice of state capacity in East Asia have evolved significantly over time in light of changing economic, business, political and technological realities. For example, the transnationalising forces of globalisation have made the pursuit of state 'national industry' development projects generally less relevant and tenable.[9] Global firms such as Samsung and Sony no longer require state-assisted 'nurturing'. The development agenda, challenges and priorities of East Asian states have changed significantly too. Whilst techno-industrial upgrading and raising levels of material prosperity remain key development objectives in the region, these have had to be increasingly reconciled with environmental sustainability goals. This is mainly due to East Asia's rapid industrialisation making it an environmental victim of its own economic success. Acute air pollution in major cities and many other localised environmental problems have had growing negative impacts on human welfare, creating domestic social and political pressures on East Asia's governments to 'green' their development policies accordingly. This has combined with mounting international pressures on East Asian states to take stronger actions on climate change given the region is by far the largest emitter of carbon dioxide and other greenhouse gases (GHGs). Addressing the challenges of sustainable development has, though, presented more of an opportunity than a threat to state capacity practice in East Asia. This is because it requires new methods of tackling market failure, reformulations of state–business–society relations, and new approaches on industrial policy, eg promoting green energy. Regarding environment-related market failure, this involves firmer state policies to simultaneously address both negative externalities (eg reducing the 'social costs' of pollution and other forms of eco-damage) and positive externalities (eg promoting the 'social benefits' of clean energy).[10] The two case studies on Singapore and South Korea presented later provide insights into this strengthening environmental dimension of developmental statism.

3. Ecological modernisation and development

Ecological modernisation has played an instrumental role in shaping environmental thinking on recent state capacity practice in East Asia. Originating from the ideas and theories of European scholars in the 1980s and 1990s, [11] ecological modernisation proposes how economic growth may be reconciled with sustainable development through gradual rather than revolutionary reform, and the adaption and improvement of existing economic, business and social structures to realise environmental objectives. EMT postulates that state, society and business all have roles to play in 'greening' capitalism, mainly through supporting the drive forward of new eco-industries and environmentally sustainable practices in production, distribution and new technology application.[12] Firms could thus continue to make profit, expand market share and meet other corporate objectives whilst acting 'sustainably'. Financial markets need not be reinvented to fund sustainable development projects, but rather can adjust themselves to exploit new 'green business' opportunities or can be incentivised to do so through government policy.[13] Ecological modernisation thinkers also emphasise the vital importance of policy interventions to address aforementioned environment-related market failures to help realise sustainable development objectives.[14]

After influencing European policymaking from the 1980s, the World Bank soon too began to apply EMT to its development policies, and its influence also grew within policy circles of higher income countries around this time, including Japan, South Korea and Singapore.[15] By the mid-2000s, EMT's influence had become increasingly evident across East Asia and other developing regions.[16] In China, it became closely associated with President Hu Jintao's 'scientific development concept' first proclaimed in 2004, thereafter becoming the official ideological basis for China's future economic and social development when ratified into the national constitution in 2007. In the same year, the Chinese Academy of Sciences published the *China Modernization Report 2007: Study on Ecological Modernization*, when the government also launched its Medium and Long-Term Development Plan for Renewable Energy as well as its National Climate Change Strategy, where in both cases EMT thinking was strongly evident.[17] Ecological modernisation's emphasis on the state's role in promoting green capitalism and environmentally sustainable industries primarily manifested in East Asia through new low-carbon development, 'green growth' and sustainable energy strategies introduced across the region from the early 2000s onwards, as shown in Table 1. Before we examine some empirical details on this in our two case studies, let us explore more specifically how 'new developmentalism' combines both state capacity and ecological modernisation theory and practice into a synthesised analytical framework.

4. New developmentalism as concept and theory

4.1. Outlining new developmentalism

As Wylde explores in his own special issue paper,[18] the term 'new developmentalism' or 'neo-developmentalism' has been used elsewhere to explain new state-active policies (including industrial policies) in Brazil, Argentina and some other Latin American countries in a more or less conventional neo-Keynesian macroeconomic sense, signifying a break from previous neo-liberal policies in this region and with no specified linkage made to low-carbon development, environmental policies or climate interventionism.[19] The 'new developmentalism' concept I deploy here is based on a distinctly different and broader theoretical approach and empirical foundation by combining two hitherto separate scholarly discourses – SCT and EMT. Both are principally concerned with transformative development and emphasise the critical role played by the state and institutions in shaping markets and paths of economic development, working in partnership with business and society. The core goals associated with each theory – progressive techno-industrial upgrading and sustainable development, respectively – have over time been conflated. They are both also interested in how transformative development is governed, the former mainly with industrial policies,

Table 1. New developmentalist plans in East Asia.

	Green energy plan	National climate change action plan	Macro-plan on low carbon (green growth) development
China	Medium to Long-Term Development Plan for Renewable Energy to 2020	National Climate Change Programme (2007)	11th (2006-2010), 12th (2011-2015) and 13th (2016-2020) Five-Year Plans [elements of]
Japan	Innovative Strategy for Energy and Environment (2012)		New Growth Strategy (2010)
South Korea	New Renewable Energy Medium-Term Plan 2010-2015	[integrated into Green Growth Strategy (2009)]	First Green Growth Strategy (2009-2013), Second Green Growth Strategy (2014-2018)
Taiwan	New Energy Policy to 2030	Adaptation Strategy to Climate Change (2012)	Green Energy Industry Sunrise Plan (2009)
Cambodia		National Adaptation Programme of Action to Climate Change (2007)	National Strategic Plan on Green Development 2013-2030
Indonesia	National Energy Blueprint 2005-2025, National Biofuel Roadmap 2006-2025	National Action Plan Addressing Climate Change (2007)	Mid-Term Development Plan 2010-2014
Laos			7th (2011-2015) and 8th (2016-2020) Five-Year National Socioeconomic Development Plans [elements of]
Malaysia	National Renewable Energy Policy and Action Plan, 2011-2015	National Policy on Climate Change (2009)	Green Technology Strategy (2009), 10th (2011-2015) and 11th (2016-2020) Malaysia Plans [elements of]
Philippines	National Renewable Energy Programme 2011-2030	National Framework Strategy on Climate Change (2007)	
Singapore		National Climate Change Strategy (2008)	Sustainable Singapore Blueprint (2007)
Thailand	Alternative Energy Development Plan 2012-2021	National Strategy on Climate Change (2008)	11th National Economic and Social Development Plan 2012-2016 [elements of]
Vietnam	Renewable Energy Master Plan 2011-2015	National Climate Change Strategy (2011)	Vietnam Green Growth Strategy (2011-2020)

Source: Author's research.

strategic plans, targets and outcomes, the latter in reflexive responses and tactical adaption to new, changing environmental realities. To generalise, state capacity practice may be considered more planned and structured in approach whereas ecological modernisation is more incremental and evolutionary, yet these two approaches can be viewed as complementary. Developmental states have always had to adapt to changing domestic and international circumstances. As noted earlier, local (eg acute urban air pollution) and global (eg climate change) environmental imperatives have compelled development policymakers to increasingly promote decarbonisation of their economies with gradually more ambitious plan targets.

All states are under growing pressure to take action on climate change as the principal global challenge and existential threat currently facing all humanity. While this is not exclusively governments' responsibility, global climate governance and diplomacy is primarily an inter-governmental process under the aegis of the United Nations Framework Convention on Climate Change (UNFCCC). The Conference of Parties21 Paris Agreement signed in December 2015 is the latest UNFCCC treaty to reduce GHG emissions through the 'national determined contributions' (NDCs) mechanism, where each signatory government is obliged to set decarbonisation targets and implement policies to meet them. Each country will take its own NDC actions but because fossil fuel combustion accounts for around 80% of world GHG levels, green energy and low-carbon development will be necessary policy priorities. In those countries with strong state capacity, 'climate interventionism' will comprise increasingly ambitious macro-plans on these fronts. Here, climate interventionism refers to state policy actions that address the various market failures that have caused climate change.

As with developmental statism and state capacity practice generally, new developmentalism has relational aspects. Both SCT and EMT stress the importance of effective state–business partnerships to achieve transformative development goals. However, as the special issue paper from Jennifer Hsu explores, (civil) society has become a more proactive and empowered form of agency in the development process. Democratisation, the rise of non-government organisations, and the emergence of new civic institutions have created a more expansive set of development stakeholders. Nevertheless, as our country case studies reveal, a top-down authoritarian state approach to pushing through low-carbon development strategies has often been a political and institutional feature of East Asia's new developmentalism. At the same time, works from both EMT and SCT have highlighted the growing influential role played by civil society and social movements as developmental partners.[20] As we later discuss, decarbonising economic activity involves, *inter alia*, various societal processes. Furthermore, 'stronger society' is able to feed back important intelligence and information on development issues and challenges, and make state authorities more accountable for good development policy and governance.

To summarise, new developmentalism is an analytical synthesis of state capacity and ecological modernisation theories. It has become especially relevant in the last decade or so in East Asia, in the context of growing disenchantment with the contemporary neo-liberal orthodoxy as well as the exigencies of tackling climate change and other critical environmental pressures. New developmentalism can be defined as revitalised and refocused forms of state capacity aimed at realising the transformative economic objectives associated with sustainable development. In terms of its empirical and functional elements, it is concerned with the governance of developmental process, state policy and strategy-making, setting of development targets and objectives, and state–business–society relational dynamics.

East Asia's new developmentalism is intended to synchronously promote sustainable and techno-industrial development within the same state policy and strategy context, but as we discuss there exist some inherent tensions and contradictions regarding its underlying ideas, politico-institutional processes and technical practices, as well as its reconciliation with other development policies.

4.2. Further outlining through conceptual differentiation

Other authors have also focused on the incorporation of sustainable development goals into developmentalist governance and practice in certain East Asian states. Kim and Thurbon's 'developmental environmentalism' centres on South Korea's recent green growth strategies, these being broadly conceived as 'the reimagining of the relationship between the economy and the environment'[21] by the country's policymaking elite, who – as Thurbon explores in a follow-up work – continue to formulate national economic strategies generally with a 'developmental mindset'.[22] Similar to the new developmentalism outlined in this paper, Kim and Thurbon argue that developmental environmentalism entails the simultaneous pursuit of economic growth and environmental protection by 'efforts to develop, commercialize, produce, and export green technologies, products, and processes'.[23] While 'developmental environmentalism' acknowledges the wider ideational and social dimensions to how South Korea's policy elites formulated green growth strategies, it does not explicitly reference the influence of ecological modernisation thinking on these and other policy elites in East Asia and elsewhere.

South Korea is also an empirical focus (others being China and Singapore) of the 'authoritarian environmentalism' concept,[24] which is closely related to, or almost synonymous with, Beeson's notion of 'environmental authoritarianism'.[25] Both concepts fix on top-down, authoritarian state approaches to addressing environmental challenges where civil society stakeholders play very limited policy-influencing roles. According to Gilley, the former is a 'public policy model that concentrates authority in a few executive agencies manned by capable and uncorrupt elites seeking to improve environmental outcomes',[26] where, in Han's words, 'non-participatory environmental governance, autonomous central governments, aided by exclusive groups of scientists and technocrats, dominate the policy process'.[27] In the latter concept, Beeson applies a very similar analysis to China and Southeast Asia and comes to similar conclusions: compared to liberal democratic countries many authoritarian governed states are proving more effective at realising low-carbon development goals, the corollary of this being further legitimisation of continued authoritarianism and heavy 'market correcting' interventionism on tackling climate change and other environmental-related issues.[28]

In contrast with these twin concepts, new developmentalism firstly casts a wider empirical net and a more political economic approach to explain why and how both authoritarian and democratic countries in East Asia have engaged with low-carbon development, where revitalised state capacity is the common denominator. Its incorporation of ecological modernisation thinking into a conceptual synthesis with state capacity theory also presents a new way of thinking about developmental strategies and partnerships on low-carbon development, as outlined in the previous section. While new developmentalism acknowledges that authoritarian exercises of state capacity on low-carbon development may persist in some countries, it contends that over the longer term we can expect civil society and 'localised' actors and agencies to become progressively more important stakeholder partners to the state on efforts to decarbonise the economy and society. This is primarily due to the fundamental nature of low-carbon development itself and the socio-technical revolutions it is already beginning to create. This is perhaps most evident in the 'energy democratising' impact of small-/community-scale renewables and smart energy micro-infrastructure technologies that have created relatively autonomous local 'energy societies' to form in many parts of the world. Such low-carbon technologies combined with social entrepreneurship and community-level initiatives have enabled this process, in most cases with state policy support.[29] Thus, ideal forms of new developmentalism allow for state capacity to be reflexive and responsive to the socio-technical and socio-cultural changes created by the longer term, deepening low-carbon development and the impacts of its pervasive technologies on society.

5. New developmentalism in practice

5.1. *Initial phases and evidence*

States in developing regions began to implement modern sustainable development policies long before ecological modernisation ideas and theories became influential. Perhaps the deepest historical examples of this relate to what we would categorise today as 'green energy', although ironically these policies were not always at the time based on environmental motives. Hydropower dams were used first from the late nineteenth century and throughout the twentieth century to help drive forward industrialisation in the developing world. Even in Japan, hydro-electricity was the country's dominant power generation sector until the early 1960s.[30] China, meanwhile, started to develop its own solar photovoltaic (PV) energy technology in the late 1950s as part of its fledgling space satellite programme.[31] After the 1973/1974 oil crisis, a number of East Asian and other developing-country governments began to introduce new green energy policies but primarily for the energy supply security reasons of diversifying source options, especially indigenously. Furthermore, green energy and green industry sectors generally have long been perceived as emerging strategic industries with high growth potential. For example, the global wind energy sector has been expanding at a rate of around 20% annually, and solar energy at around 35%.[32] These are also dynamic industries from a technological perspective with high rates of innovation and research and development (R&D) investment. The promotion of green industries is thus consistent with the aforementioned industrial policy practice and techno-industrial upgrading motives (ie market growth, high value-added employment, and new enterprise formation) of conventional developmental statism. Moreover, East Asian and other countries that possess strong state capacity on strategic industry policy have the apparatus to promote green industry development. In the meantime, environmental policies have been introduced over time in East Asia, the earliest being typically in response to human health-related problems. Japan introduced emission control policies in the 1950s and 1960s to deal with a series of industrial pollution crises, and South Korea similarly did so in the 1970s. The bustling city-port of Singapore enacted its Clean Air Act in 1971. In 1983, the Chinese government confirmed environmental protection as a basic national policy aim.[33]

Low-carbon development strategies and green energy policies across East Asia began to take firmer shape by the 1990s and early 2000s, when the influence of ecological modernisation began to spread more widely in the region,[34] but these were not yet coherent multi-sector strategies. At this time, sustainable development policy actions in many parts of the region were generally ad hoc and sector specific (principally green energy), or embedded in broader development policy frameworks where carbon-intensive and decarbonising activities were often being simultaneously promoted. However, by the early 2000s, East Asian states began to construct 'first-phase' multi-sector green energy strategies.[35] South Korea (2001 Basic Plan for New and Renewable Energy Development), Malaysia (2001 Small Renewable Energy Programme – integrated into the 8th Malaysia Plan, 2001–2005) and Vietnam (2001 Renewable Energy Action Plan, part of the Master Plan of Power Development, 2001–2010) were the earliest protagonists, soon followed by the Philippines (Renewable Energy Policy Framework, 2003–2013), and Thailand (2004 Strategic Plan for Renewable Energy Development). This was an important precursor of wider low-carbon development macro-plans introduced by the mid-2000s across the region, as well as national climate change strategies, signifying an early formulation of 'green growth' strategies in East Asia.[36] China's 11th Five Year Plan (FYP) (2006–2010) contained elements of new developmentalism, and as Table 1 illustrates there was a gradual spread of new developmentalist practice by the late 2000s, including a 'second phase' of more coherent, ambitious and substantive green energy strategies among a wider set of nations. A key catalyst for this development was the 2008/2009 global financial crisis.

5.2. The global financial crisis and 'green growth'

The 2008/2009 global financial crisis was arguably the biggest shock to the world economy since the end of World War II. This global-scale market failure caused ultimately by poor financial market regulation precipitated a comprehensive re-evaluation of the neo-liberal economic model, globalisation and economic governance generally. As part of international co-ordinated efforts to fix the global financial system, national governments around the world implemented various fiscal and monetary stimulus counter-measures. Many countries decided to combine this with their climate action agenda and new, upgraded EMT-inspired industrial strategies, and this led to a step-change up on 'green growth' strategy-making in East Asia.[37]

The stimulus package incorporated into South Korea's new Green Growth Strategy (2009–2013) – the subject of our first country case study below – accounted for around four-fifths of the government's total post-crisis stimulus measures, and 2% (US$87 billion) of national GDP. Meanwhile, China's own US$219 billion package in response to the 2008/2009 crisis was dedicated to low-carbon development initiatives.[38] Vietnam announced its own Green Growth Strategy in 2011, and Cambodia its National Strategic Plan on Green Development a year later based on an earlier 'road map' formulation devised in 2010. Other East Asian states were more sector specific. Taiwan's Green Energy Industry Sunrise Plan and Malaysia's Green Technology Strategy were both launched in 2009. As will be discussed in our second case study, the Singapore government launched its own Sustainable Singapore Blueprint plan in 2009.

As Table 1 indicates, though, many East Asian governments embedded their low-carbon development strategies within their existing macro-plan frameworks, eg China, Indonesia, Laos, Malaysia and Thailand. Most significantly, a core element of China's 12th FYP (2011–2015) was the Strategic Emerging Industries (SEI) programme, drawing on RMB4 trillion (US$610 billion) of state-directed support to develop seven targeted sectors (environmental protection and energy efficiency, new energy, next-generation information technology, biotechnology, high-tech manufacturing, clean energy vehicles, and new material science) with annual 20% sectoral growth targets set, and to collectively account for 8% of national GDP by 2015 and 15% by 2020. Meanwhile, the prime aim of Japan's New Growth Strategy (NGS) introduced in 2010 was the creation of a low-carbon society.[39] However, with a change of government and ruling party in the country, the original NGS was ditched in favour of another with the same name. Prime Minister Shinzo Abe's own launched NGS (mark II) was not primarily focused on low-carbon development, but rather preoccupied with conventional macro-economic stimulus measures. The following two case studies on South Korea and Singapore illustrate in some depth the evolution and mechanics of new developmentalism in practice, as well as some of its inherent contradictions and tensions. Their combination of similar and contrasting features makes for a useful comparative analysis. Both are renowned 'hard' developmental states but they have different forms of political governance. Both have relatively strong economies and high income levels, but one is a medium-sized nation and the other a small city-state.

5.3. Case study: South Korea

South Korea's dynamic economic development over the last 50 years has been largely based on successful rapid industrialisation and techno-industrial upgrading strategies undertaken by the state and the country's *chaebol* conglomerated firms in close developmental partnership for most of this period. This, combined with high rates of urbanisation and material prosperity, has made it one of East Asia's most carbon-intensive societies. An Environment Conservation Act was ratified in 1977 but ecological modernisation ideas only began to shape South Korea's development strategy-making from the early 1990s under Kim Young-sam's presidency.[40] His successor, Kim Dae-jung, established the Presidential Commission on Sustainable Development in 2000, this being followed by the creation of a National Strategy for Sustainable Development in 2005 under then President Roh Moo-hyun.[41] The new policies arising from these new institutionalised arrangements were, though, largely limited to a series of market-based incentives and regulatory measures to compel firms to adopt more environmentally friendly business practices.[42] President Lee Myun-bak's Green Growth Strategy (GGS) was the first time the country had formulated an eco-oriented development strategy with an activist industrial policy dimension.

Of notable political and institutional significance was how the GGS reconstructed many elements of the developmental state apparatus that had been previously dismantled under the two Kim presidencies during the 1990s and early 2000s. Both the first GGS under Lee Myun-bak and the second that followed under Park Geun-hye were similar in conception and design to the FYPs that had operated from 1962 to 1993, with a structure of layered goals and targets over phase periods, prioritised techno-industrial sectors to develop, governance mechanisms, funding formulas and state support budgets. For Thurbon, this was further proof of the aforementioned 'developmental mindset' philosophy that persisted in South Korea's policymaking elite.[43]

The First GGS was conceived principally as a post-crisis response to revitalise the South Korean economy and create a new developmental path forward into the twenty-first century. Other motivating factors were also relevant. The nation's high fossil fuel import dependency had created growing energy supply security concerns, exacerbated by oil price increases in the years leading up to the global financial crisis: from US$30 per barrel in 2003 to over US$100 by 2007, and then spiking to almost US$150 in 2008. A 28% depreciation of the Korean Won against the US dollar between August and November 2008 compounded the problem.[44] Thus, the GGS included long-term plans to boost renewable and nuclear energy capacities, both involving very few or no import requirements or notable susceptibilities to commodity price volatility. Oil is used mainly for energy transportation purposes, and there was also an ambitious strategy on developing South Korea's electric vehicle (EV) sector, like solar, wind and other renewable energy technologies perceived as a fast-emerging strategic industry. The government allocated US$1.8 billion to support EV and other low-carbon vehicle development, Hyundai and its network of sub-contractor production firms being the state's main developmental partner in this project. The above encapsulates how environmental sustainability, energy security and emerging strategic industry promotion are three key political economic motivations behind East Asia's new developmentalism.[45]

The GGS also presented a politico-institutional opportunity to Lee Myun-bak to concentrate economic policymaking authority around a small, powerful elite group over which he wielded considerable influence. The newly inaugurated president quickly established the National Future and Vision Office in February 2008 within his own presidential Blue House office, appointing close ally Kim Sang-hyup to lead it organisationally and intellectually. The Office was charged with identifying 'strategic growth sectors' to revitalise the economy, and after sounding out advice from prominent think tanks at home and abroad, Kim Sang-hyup made the decision to make 'green growth' the core around which new industrial and development policy ideas clustered.[46] President Lee responded very positively to this proposal, soon thereafter laying political, institutional and policy foundations for his administration's GGS.

The co-ordinating centre or pilot agency of the GGS was the Presidential Commission on Green Growth (PCGG), overseen by President Lee himself, and its 50 members were mainly handpicked technocrats and economists, with very few civil society representatives.[47] The Lee administration also conferred important policymaking and implementation authority to a newly consolidated Ministry of Land, Transport and Maritime Affairs. Lee utilised this new-formed super-ministry to centralise bureaucratic power and push through his flagship GGS scheme, the Four Major Rivers Restoration (FMRR) project. This absorbed over a third of the Strategy's budget, and the project's involved heavy mass construction attracted much public and environmental group criticism.[48] Democratisation from the late 1980s onwards in South Korea had created liberal political conditions for environmental and other civil society groups to flourish, as well as public concerns over environmental degradation to enjoy greater political traction.[49] However, in its resolve to complete the FMRR project to its target objectives, the Lee administration reportedly ignored significant public opposition and took legal-bureaucratic procedural short-cuts.[50]

The First GGS was structured around three strategic approaches: (1) measures for climate change and energy independence; (2) creation of new growth engines, mainly developing green high-tech industries and greening of industrial practices; and (3) contribution to the international community that included externalising South Korea's green growth approach through diplomacy and best-practice sharing. While the Strategy achieved some notable low-carbon development successes, such as the EV project and building the world's largest energy smart grid on Jeju Island, according to evidence examined by Sonnenschein and Mundaca (2016),[51] it had virtually no impact at the end of the 2009–2013 FYP period of reversing South Korea's long-term trend of rising carbon emissions. Its renewable energy targets also lacked ambition compared to other East Asian countries' new developmentalist plans.[52] When Lee Myun-bak was succeeded by Park Geun-hye in 2013, her government replaced the PCGG with the new Prime-Ministerial Green Growth Committee in October that year. The Second GGS launched in 2014 by the Park Geun-hye government and also based on an FYP format (ie 2014–2018) ran concurrently with a policy strategy on 'Creative Economy', and continued to pursue many of the first strategy's initiatives in a revised framework.[53] Yet, as more widely discussed in the conclusion, the future of the Second GGS is unclear after President Park's impeachment in March 2017.

5.4. Case study: Singapore

Since it gained independence in 1959, Singapore has been continually governed by the Peoples' Action Party (PAP), which adopted a developmental statist approach to economic management from the onset. It has overseen the city-state's transformation into one of East Asia's most developed economies and highest income per capita society through an effective multi-dimensional development strategy based on high value-added manufacturing, financial hub services, entrepot port trade, foreign direct investment, human capital and infrastructure investment, and high-tech R&D. In many respects, Singapore could be viewed as a pioneer of East Asia's new developmentalism. Its government was among the region's first to implement recognisable environmental policies (from the early 1970s) and assimilate ecological modernisation ideas on economic development.[54] The government unveiled its first environmental master-strategy in 1992, the Singapore Green Plan (SGP), although this was essentially an economic growth model intended not to compromise the environment.[55] While this and its sequel SGP launched in 2002 included some ventures on preserving certain habitats, a defining feature of Singapore's sustainability approach has been the creation of 'urban garden' areas rather than conserving natural wildernesses. The city-state's motivation behind its socio-technical endeavours to 'green' Singapore's living spaces in ever more imaginative ways is driven by the imperatives of finding new methods for enhancing its citizens' welfare and in turn also their satisfaction with ruling PAP governments. Like in other higher income East Asian nations where certain material prosperity thresholds have been reached, environmental welfare has become an increasing societal priority in Singapore, and thus ever more important to maintaining the PAP's political legitimacy.[56]

Nevertheless, inherent tensions and contradictions exist between Singapore's economic and industrial development plans and its environmental master strategies. For example, in 1995 – just three years after the first SGP's inauguration – the government ordered that the seven naturally formed Jurong Islands just off the south-west coast be terraformed into a single merged landmass as part of its 25-year petrochemical industry development plan.[57] Singapore eschewed setting carbon emission reduction targets around the time of the UNFCCC Kyoto Protocol mainly due to its plans to further develop this and other carbon-intensive sectors. This is a key feature of the East Asia new developmentalism story, where both carbon-intensive and decarbonising activities are promoted within concurrent development strategy contexts.

As with South Korea under President Lee Myun-bak, decision-making authority in Singapore's new developmentalism has been concentrated in a tight circle of state bureaucratic and political elites, who under mono-regime political conditions have consistently pursued a strong anthropological approach to reconciling environmental and economic development goals.[58] Institutionally speaking, development-oriented bureaucratic agencies have remained dominant partners in the formulation of the state's sustainability plans. The original Singapore Sustainability Blueprint (SSB) and its upgraded 2015 version were devised primarily by both the Ministry of National Development and the Ministry of the Environment and Water Resources, with the Prime Minister's Office also closely involved. This was Singapore's most comprehensive environmental or eco-development master plan to date, covering a wide range of policy areas (eg transport systems, waste management, resource efficiency, energy-efficient buildings and environmental standards) backed by a significant budget of S$1.5 billion. The SSB 2015 public document cites around 20 other state agencies that were involved in the consultation and design process.[59] No civil society organisations are listed. However, in its review of the original SSB, the government claims to have considered general public feedback from more than 130,000 people on specific projects (eg Land Transport Master Plan 2013 and Urban Redevelopment Authority's Master Plan 2014), conducted a series of 'focus-group' dialogue sessions with a sample of the populace, and consulted 6000 people in other dialogues and surveys on the SSB generally.[60]

The Singapore government has increasingly sought public feedback in policymaking and implementation processes as a kind of societal intelligence-gathering mechanism. Nevertheless, the Singapore state continues to strictly regulate civil society groups, and their input into development policy formation must still conform to ecological modernisation norms, consistent with past practices.[61] For Han, the Singapore state's top-down, non-participatory governance approach has notable parallels with South Korea's authoritarian environmentalism.[62] In a similar vein, Wong argues that Singapore's core policy elite have placed too much faith in the idea that 'society can modernise itself out of its environmental crisis' by a series of technocratic and technological fixes, where environmental issues are 'too narrowly defined by state and industrial interests', and that civil society needs to be more actively engaged as a policy stakeholder to form more balanced and holistic sustainable development strategies.[63]

In some contrast to most other forms of East Asian new developmentalism, the SSBs have paid relatively little attention to developing new green industry sectors, rather 'greening' existing ones. The strategy did commit Singapore to expand the number of its 'innovation business districts' mainly to promote best corporate environmental practice, and sought to scale up solar and bioenergy power generation through new schemes such as SolarNova. Yet there were again no references to altering the economy's industrial structure, where energy-intensive sectors such as petro-chemicals remain prominent. Singapore's urban-focused new developmentalism can also be understood as part of the eco-city development trend that has become popular across East Asia and other developing-country regions. Cities are where carbon-intensive activity is concentrated and thus they have a key role to play in decarbonising economies and societies.[64] East Asia's new developmentalist strategies all contain city- and provincial-level actions to some degree, varying in accordance with national political structures.

6. Conclusion: the future of new developmentalism

This paper has explored how new developmentalism, by combining state capacity theory and ecological modernisation theory, presents a new understanding of developmental statism in the early twenty-first century, when environmental sustainability and climate action have become increasingly critical in both national and international development agenda settings. In this concluding section, we consider paths ahead for new developmentalism, assessing the key conditions needed for its future success and critiquing areas of state capacity practice that could be improved.

The first condition is that *deeper societal participation and engagement* will be required for new developmentalism to more effectively achieve sustainable, low-carbon development. Both SCT and EMT have stressed the importance of the state co-opting society into transformative development projects. Low-carbon development is as much a societal process as an economic one, encompassing individual lifestyle and choice issues at the micro level as well as macro-level industrial and infrastructural strategies. Civil society is a crucial stakeholder in terms of contributing ideas on strategy design and providing useful societal intelligence feedback on strategy impact.[65] From East Asia's experience we have seen how state planners have at least acknowledged the importance of establishing a low-carbon society and engaging civil society stakeholders in new developmentalist strategy-making. Yet we have to get beyond the planning document rhetoric to analyse how well the state is drawing upon society as an intelligence resource and working in stakeholder partnership. We saw in the case of Singapore – where state capacity is extraordinarily strong – that the government sought public opinion concerning the Sustainable Singapore Blueprint's design, implementation and outcome stages, but was nevertheless criticised for being essentially elite–technocrat-driven and top-down generally. South Korea's recent political leaders – especially President Lee Myun-bak – have also generally adopted a top-down approach in pushing through their own sustainable development agendas. Authoritarian governance of low-carbon development in East Asia may be a persistent feature of new developmentalism for some time yet. However, in the longer term we may expect states to work in closer partnership with civil societal stakeholders because such a partnership is key to realising the most effective and smarter forms of low-carbon society.

The second condition relates to *addressing contradictions and inconsistencies* often evident within new developmentalist plans themselves, and between those plans and other concurrent development policies. For example, the scaling up of green energy applications has been used not only to decarbonise developing countries but also to meet the growing energy and industrial demands of fast-growing economies, as articulated in government green growth strategies. In South Korea, the First GGS co-existed with the then Ministry of Trade, Industry and Energy's parallel industrial strategy of upgrading various stalwart energy-intensive sectors such as shipbuilding and steel.[66] Singapore's aforementioned burgeoning petrochemical complex on Jurong Island remains central to the government's core industrial policy.

Thirdly, *consolidation and continuity of strategy* will prove crucial to new developmentalism's future effective implementation. South Korea's President Park Geun-hye continued with the Green Growth Strategy FYP framework of her predecessor, but her impeachment in March 2017 leaves the future of the country's new developmentalism unclear. We may expect, on the other hand, mono-regime authoritarian states to adhere to long-term new developmentalist strategies and thereby consolidate their gains.[67] Certainly, China has proved more successful, for example at meeting its green energy sector targets, than Japan, South Korea and Taiwan.[68] As long as 'authoritarian environmentalism' delivers results, especially in terms of key welfare measures such as reduced air pollution, this form of new developmentalism may persist for a while yet, although as argued earlier we can expect over the longer term more organic, bottom-up societal influence on shaping future paths of low-carbon development.

The fourth condition is that new developmentalism is *nationally devised and implemented but will become increasingly part of a much larger international climate action project.* Development strategies in East Asia are still being formulated more or less in the same technocratic fashion, most commonly in national year-plan frameworks (Table 1). These plans have always had an international dimension, such as export targets and attracting foreign investment, and today's sustainable development strategies are essentially framed on national economies. However, the core goals of new developmentalism derive ultimately from the global agenda of decarbonising economic activity and international efforts to tackle climate change. The United Nations 'Sustainable Development Goals' (SDGs) launched in 2015 (superseding the previous Millennium Development Goals) are, together with the UNFCCC Paris Agreement, the most important recent attempts by international society to tackle climate change and steer humanity towards a more environmentally sustainable development path. New developmentalist plans and strategies reference their contribution to such wider international endeavours on low-carbon development. The further thickening of global environmental governance and climate action generally is likely to strengthen new developmentalism at the national level as states comply with their international commitments here, as previously mentioned regarding the 'national determined contributions' mechanism of the UNFCCC Paris Agreement. Another interesting development has been South Korea's internationalisation of its national green growth strategy in which it has positioned itself as a green 'middle power' in global climate governance, seeking especially to shape the low-carbon development agenda.[69] For example, it successfully bid to host the new United Nations Green Climate Fund (GCF) that is tasked with raising US$100 billion annually to help fund sustainable development in low-income nations.[70]

The fifth and final condition follows on from the previous one, and concerns the *continued mounting pressures on low-income countries worldwide to adopt new developmentalism.* Governments from these countries are under domestic pressure to devise macro-plans on boosting economic growth in order to deliver higher levels of material prosperity. At the same time, deteriorating environmental welfare at home together with growing international pressures on developing countries to take firmer action on climate change compel them to 'green' their development strategies. Both global development and environmental situations are predicted to get worse before they better. The combination of diverging income gaps in the world economy and persistently rising GHG levels and other ecological problems only serves to strengthen the imperative to find new developmentalist solutions. As most global GHG emission growth is located in developing regions – especially Asia – their own national development policies and strategies have been an important focus of attention to the wider international community. Developing countries have been subject to 'carbon offloading' due to the gradual relocation of many energy-intensive industries from high-cost to low-cost economies for business competitiveness reasons. This fact notwithstanding, East Asia is not the only developing country region where 'green growth' strategies have been pursued and where the twin pressures on states to intervene on development and climate coincide. As has been argued throughout, strong state capacity working in close developmental partnership with business and society is required for effective action on both fronts.

Disclosure statement

No potential conflict of interest was reported by the author.

Notes

1. Comprising the two sub-regions of Northeast and Southeast Asia.
2. Sustainable development and low-carbon development are treated as broadly interchangeable terms in this paper. The latter term has become increasingly synonymous with multiple-level efforts to tackle climate change due to the global ecological impact of rising carbon dioxide levels, and decarbonising economic activity being the prime sustainable development challenge facing humanity.
3. Dent, *East Asian Regionalism*.
4. Johnson, *MITI and the Japanese Miracle*.
5. Amsden, *Asia's Next Giant*; Evans, *Embedded Autonomy*; Pereira, "Whither the Developmental State"; Weiss, *Myth of the Powerless State*; Woo-Cumings, *The Developmental State*.
6. Doner, Ritchie, and Slater, "Systemic Vulnerability."
7. Nem Singh and Chen, this volume.
8. Beeson and Pham, "Developmentalism with Vietnamese Characteristics"; Weiss, *Myth of the Powerless State*; Weiss, "The State in the Economy."
9. Mok and Yep, "Globalisation and State Capacity in Asia."
10. In externality theory, markets 'fail' to account for social costs and social benefits in the private transactions between producers and consumers, for example in energy markets.
11. Hajer, *Politics of Environmental Discourse*; Huber, *Die Verlorene Unschuld der Okologie*; Jänicke, *Umweltpolitische Pravention*.
12. Jänicke, "Okologische Modernisierung"; York and Rosa, "Key Challenges to Ecological Modernization Theory."
13. Buttel, "Ecological Modernisation as Social Theory"; Langhelle, "Why Ecological Modernisation."
14. Buttel, "Ecological Modernisation as Social Theory"; Huber, *Die Verlorene Unschuld*; Jänicke, *Umweltpolitische Pravention*; Murphy and Gouldson, "Environmental Policy and Industrial Innovation."
15. Massa and Andersen, "Special Issue Introduction."
16. Dent, *Renewable Energy*; UNESCAP, *Green Growth @ a Glance*; UNESCAP, *Greening Growth in Asia*.
17. NDRC, *Medium and Long-Term Development Plan*; NDRC, *China's National Climate Change Programme*.
18. Wylde, this volume.
19. Bresser-Pereira, *From Old to New Developmentalism*; Carrillo, "New Developmentalism"; Milanez and Santos, "Topsy-Turvy Neo-Developmentalism."
20. Weiss, "The State in the Economy"; Toke, "Ecological Modernisation, Social Movements."

21. Kim and Thurbon, "Developmental Environmentalism," 227.
22. Thurbon, *Developmental Mindset*.
23. Kim and Thurbon, "Developmental Environmentalism," 215.
24. Eaton and Kostka, "Authoritarian Environmentalism Undermined"; Gilley, "Authoritarian Environmentalism and China's Response"; Han, "Authoritarian Environmentalism under Democracy"; Han, "Singapore, a Garden City."
25. Beeson, "The Coming of Environmental Authoritarianism."
26. Gilley, "Authoritarian Environmentalism and China's Response," 288.
27. Han, "Authoritarian Environmentalism under Democracy," 811.
28. Beeson, "The Coming of Environmental Authoritarianism."
29. Dent, *Renewable Energy*.
30. Ushiyama, "Renewable Energy Strategy in Japan."
31. Yang *et al.*, "Status of Photovoltaic Industry in China."
32. REN21, *Global Status Report*.
33. UNEP, *Green is Gold*.
34. Dent, *Renewable Energy*.
35. Dent, *Renewable Energy*.
36. UNESCAP, *Greening Growth in Asia*.
37. Jacobs, "Green Growth"; Jänicke, "Green Growth"; UNESCAP, *Low Carbon Green Growth Roadmap*.
38. World Bank, *From Growth to Green Growth*.
39. Ministry of Economy, Trade and Industry (METI), *The New Growth Strategy*.
40. Dent, *Renewable Energy*.
41. Cho, "Emergence and Evolution."
42. Kim and Thurbon, "Developmental Environmentalism"; Moon, "Korea's Sustainable Development Strategy."
43. Thurbon, *Developmental Mindset*.
44. Han, "Korea's Pursuit of Low-Carbon Green Growth"; Kim and Thurbon, "Developmental Environmentalism." South Korea spent US$140 billion – around a third of its foreign exchange earnings from exports – on energy imports in 2008.
45. Dent, *Renewable Energy*.
46. Kim and Thurbon, "Developmental Environmentalism."
47. Han, "Authoritarian Environmentalism under Democracy."
48. Han, "Authoritarian Environmentalism under Democracy"; Moon, "Korea's Sustainable Development Strategy."
49. Ku, "Structural Change of the Korean Environmental Movement"; Lee, "Environmentalism in Korea"; Jeong and Seo, "Democratization, Decentralization, and Environmental Governance."
50. Han, "Authoritarian Environmentalism under Democracy."
51. Sonnenschein and Mundaca, "Decarbonization under Green Growth Strategies?"
52. Dent, *Renewable Energy*.
53. Kim, "South Korea Doubles Down."
54. Neo, "Challenging the Developmental State."
55. Singapore Government, *Singapore Green Plan*.
56. Neo, "Challenging the Developmental State"; Wong, "Developmental State in Ecological Modernization."
57. Dent, *Foreign Economic Policies*.
58. Han, "Singapore, a Garden City."
59. Singapore Government, *Sustainable Singapore Blueprint 2015*.
60. Singapore Government, *Sustainable Singapore Blueprint 2015*.
61. Barnard and Heng, "A City in a Garden"; Wong, "Developmental State in Ecological Modernization."
62. Han, "Singapore, a Garden City."
63. Wong, "Developmental State in Ecological Modernization," 95.
64. Delman, "Urban Climate Change Politics," Franzén, "Local Governments as Nodes."
65. Martinelli and Midttun, "Editorial – Introduction."
66. Dent, *Renewable Energy*.

67. Beeson, "The Coming of Environmental Authoritarianism."
68. Dent, *Renewable Energy*.
69. Blaxekjær, "Korea as Green Middle Power"; Han, "Korea's Pursuit of Low-Carbon Green Growth."
70. Relatedly, Cambodia and Vietnam's green growth plans include measures to attract 'green aid' from foreign donors to help realise national sustainable development goals set by those plans.

Bibliography

Amsden, A. *Asia's Next Giant: South Korea and Late Industrialisation*. Oxford: Oxford University Press, 1989.

Barnard, T. P., and C. Heng. "A City in a Garden." In *Nature Contained: Environmental Histories of Singapore*, edited by T. P. Barnard, 281–306. Singapore: NUS Press, 2014.

Beeson, M. "The Coming of Environmental Authoritarianism." *Environmental Politics* 19, no. 2 (2010): 276–294.

Beeson, M., and H. H. Pham. "Developmentalism with Vietnamese Characteristics: The Persistence of State-Led Development in East Asia." *Journal of Contemporary Asia* 42, no. 4 (2012): 539–559.

Blaxekjær, L. "Korea as Green Middle Power: Green Growth Strategic Action in the Field of Global Environmental Governance." *International Relations of the Asia-Pacific* 16, no. 3 (2016): 443–476.

Bresser-Pereira, L. C. *From Old to New Developmentalism in Latin America*. Oxford: Oxford University Press, 2011.

Buttel, F. H. "Ecological Modernisation as Social Theory." *Geoforum* 31, no. 1 (2000): 57–65.

Carrillo, I. R. "The New Developmentalism and the Challenges to Long-Term Stability in Brazil." *Latin American Perspectives* 41, no. 5 (2014): 59–74.

Cho, M. R. "Emergence and Evolution of Environmental Discourses in South Korea." *Korea Journal* 44, no. 3 (2004): 138–164.

Delman, J. "Urban Climate Change Politics in China: Fragmented Authoritarianism and Governance Innovations in Hangzhou." In *Chinese Politics as Fragmented Authoritarianism: Earthquakes, Energy and Environment*, edited by K. E. Brødsgaard, 156–180. London: Routledge, 2016.

Dent, C. M. *The Foreign Economic Policies of Singapore, South Korea and Taiwan*. Cheltenham: Edward Elgar, 2002.

Dent, C. M. *Renewable Energy in East Asia: Towards a New Developmentalism*. London: Routledge, 2014.

Dent, C. M. *East Asian Regionalism*. 2nd ed. London: Routledge, 2016.

Doner, R. F., B. K. Ritchie, and D. Slater. "Systemic Vulnerability and the Origins of Developmental States: Northeast and Southeast Asia in Comparative Perspective." *International Organization* 59, no. 2 (2005): 327–361.

Eaton, S., and G. Kostka. "Authoritarian Environmentalism Undermined? Local Leaders' Time Horizons and Environmental Policy Implementation in China." *China Quarterly* 218 (2014): 359–380.

Evans, P. *Embedded Autonomy: States and Industrial Transformation*. Princeton: Princeton University Press, 1995.

Franzén, M. "Local Governments as Nodes for Greenhouse Gas Abatement: Climate Change Governance in Multi-Level Frameworks." *European Journal of Sustainable Development* 2, no. 4 (2013): 361–372.

Gilley, B. "Authoritarian Environmentalism and China's Response to Climate Change." *Environmental Politics* 21, no. 2 (2012): 287–307.

Hajer, M. A. *The Politics of Environmental Discourse: Ecological Modernisation and the Policy Process*. Oxford: Oxford University Press, 1995.

Han, H. "Authoritarian Environmentalism under Democracy: Korea's River Restoration Project." *Environmental Politics* 24, no. 5 (2015): 810–829.

Han, H. "Korea's Pursuit of Low-Carbon Green Growth: A Middle-Power State's Dream of Becoming a Green Pioneer." *The Pacific Review* 28, no. 5 (2015): 731–754.

Han, H. "Singapore, a Garden City: Authoritarian Environmentalism in a Developmental State." *Journal of Environment and Development* 26, no. 1 (2017): 3–24.

Huber, J. *Die Verlorene Unschuld der Okologie* [The Lost Innocence of Ecology]. Frankfurt am Main: Fischer Verlag, 1982.

Jacobs, M. "Green Growth." In *Handbook of Global Climate and Environmental Policy*, edited by R. Falkner, 197–215. Oxford: Wiley Blackwell, 2013.

Jänicke, M. *Umweltpolitische Pravention als Okologische Modernisierung und Strukturpolitik* [Environmental Policy Prevention as Ecological Modernization and Structural Policy]. Berlin: Wissenschaftszentrum, 1984.

Jänicke, M. "Okologische Modernisierung: Optionen und Restriktionen Praventiver Umweltpolitik." [Ecological Modernization: Options and Restrictions for Preventative Environmental Policy.] In *Praventive Umweltpolitik* [Preventative Environmental Policy], edited by U. Simonis, 13–26. Frankfurt am Main: Campus, 1988.

Jänicke, M. "Green Growth: From a Growing Eco-Industry to Economic Sustainability." *Energy Policy* 48, no. 1 (2012): 13–21.

Jeong, H., and W. Seo. "Democratization, Decentralization, and Environmental Governance in South Korea." In *Democratization, Decentralization and Environmental Governance in Asia*, edited by A. Mori, 12–25. Kyoto: Kyoto University Press, 2012.

Johnson, C. *MITI and the Japanese Miracle*. Stanford: Stanford University Press, 1982.

Kim, S. Y. "South Korea Doubles down on Green Growth." *East Asia Forum* 25 (December 2015). http://www.eastasiaforum.org/2015/12/25/south-korea-doubles-down-on-green-growth

Kim, S. Y., and E. Thurbon. "Developmental Environmentalism: Explaining South Korea's Ambitious Pursuit of Green Growth." *Politics and Society* 43, no. 2 (2015): 213–240.

Ku, D. W. "The Structural Change of the Korean Environmental Movement." *Korea Journal of Population and Development* 25, no. 1 (1996): 155–180.

Langhelle, O. "Why Ecological Modernisation and Sustainable Development Should Not Be Conflated." *Journal of Environmental Policy and Planning* 2, no. 4 (2000): 303–322.

Lee, S. "Environmentalism in Korea." In *Asia's Environmental Movements: Comparative Perspectives*, edited by Y. S. Lee and A. Y. So, 82–101. Armonk: ME Sharpe, 1999.

Martinelli, A., and A. Midttun. "Editorial – Introduction: Towards Green Growth and Multi-Level Governance." *Energy Policy* 48, no. 1 (2012): 1–4.

Massa, I., and M. S. Andersen. "Special Issue Introduction: Ecological Modernization." *Journal of Environment and Policy Planning* 2, no. 4 (2000): 265–267.

Milanez, B., and R. S. P. Santos. "Topsy-Turvy Neo-Developmentalism: An Analysis of the Current Brazilian Model of Development." *Revista De Estudios Sociales* 53 (2015): 12–28.

Ministry of Economy, Trade and Industry (METI). *The New Growth Strategy: Blueprint for Revitalising Japan*. Tokyo: METI, 2010.

Mok, K. H., and R. Yep. "Globalisation and State Capacity in Asia." *The Pacific Review* 21, no. 2 (2008): 109–120.

Moon, T. H. "Korea's Sustainable Development Strategy." *Korea Observer* 40, no. 1 (2009): 85–114.

Murphy, J., and A. Gouldson. "Environmental Policy and Industrial Innovation: Integrating Environment and Economy through Ecological Modernisation." *Geoforum* 31, no. 1 (2000): 33–44.

National Development and Reform Commission (NDRC). *Medium and Long-Term Development Plan for Renewable Energy in China*. Beijing: NDRC, 2007.

National Development and Reform Commission (NDRC). *China's National Climate Change Programme*. Beijing: NDRC, 2007.

Neo, H. "Challenging the Developmental State: Nature Conservation in Singapore." *Asia Pacific Viewpoint* 48, no. 2 (2007): 186–199.

Pereira, A. A. "Whither the Developmental State? Explaining Singapore's Continued Developmentalism." *Third World Quarterly* 29, no. 6 (2008): 1189–1203.

REN21. *Global Status Report on Renewable Energy 2017*. Paris: REN21 Secretariat, 2017.

Singapore Government. *Sustainable Singapore Blueprint 2015*. Singapore: Ministry of the Environment and Water Resources, 2015.

Singapore Government. *The Singapore Green Plan: Towards a Model Green City*. Singapore: Ministry of the Environment and Water Resources, 2016.

Sonnenschein, J., and L. Mundaca. "Decarbonization under Green Growth Strategies? The Case of South Korea." *Journal of Cleaner Production* 123 (2016): 180–193.

Thurbon, E. *Developmental Mindset: The Revival of Financial Activism in South Korea*. Ithaca: Cornell University Press, 2016.

Toke, D. "Ecological Modernisation, Social Movements and Renewable Energy." *Environmental Politics* 20, no. 1 (2011): 60–77.

United Nations Economic and Social Commission for Asia and the Pacific (UNESCAP). *Green Growth @ a Glance*, Bangkok: UNESCAP, 2005.

United Nations Economic and Social Commission for Asia and the Pacific (UNESCAP). *Greening Growth in Asia and the Pacific*, Bangkok: UNESCAP, 2008.

United Nations Economic and Social Commission for Asia and the Pacific (UNESCAP). *Low Carbon Green Growth Roadmap for Asia and the Pacific*, Bangkok: UNESCAP, 2012.

United Nations Environmental Programme (UNEP). *Green is Gold: The Strategy and Actions of China's Ecological Civilisation*. Nairobi: UNEP, 2016.

Ushiyama, I. "Renewable Energy Strategy in Japan." *Renewable Energy* 16, nos. 1–4 (1999): 1174–1179.

Weiss, L. *The Myth of the Powerless State: Governing the Economy in a Global Era*. London: Polity, 1998.

Weiss, L. "The State in the Economy: Neoliberal or Neoactivist?" In *Oxford Handbook of Comparative Institutional Analysis*, edited by J. Campbell, C. Crouch, P. Hull Kristensen, O. K. Pedersen, and R. Whitley, 183–209. Oxford: Oxford University Press, 2010.

Wong, C. M. L. "The Developmental State in Ecological Modernization and the Politics of Environmental Framings: The Case of Singapore and Implications for East Asia." *Nature and Culture* 7, no. 1 (2012): 95–119.

Woo-Cumings, M., ed. *The Developmental State*. Ithaca: Cornell University Press, 1999.

World Bank. *From Growth to Green Growth: A Framework*. Policy Research Working Paper, no. 5872. Washington DC: World Bank, 2011.

Yang, H., H. Wang, H. Yu, J. Xi, R. Cui, and G. Chen. "Status of Photovoltaic Industry in China." *Energy Policy* 31, no. 8 (2003): 703–707.

York, R., and E. Rosa. "Key Challenges to Ecological Modernization Theory." *Organization and Environment* 16, no. 3 (2003): 273–288.

Exporting the developmental state: Japan's economic diplomacy in the Arctic

Aki Tonami

ABSTRACT

Japan remains a developmental state where the state guides and oversees economic development, and the strong bureaucracy and businesses in turn complement each other in leading and shaping policies to achieve developmental goals. Japan retains the institutions deemed necessary to enhance the cooperative behaviour of the bureaucracy, businesses and politicians, and norms about what is important in order for an interventionist state to implement policies aimed at achieving economic development and the autonomy of the state. Externally, Japan has practised economic diplomacy with tools such as development assistance to achieve its economic security and to promote the developmental state model abroad. The process of making foreign policy contextualised and reinforced the norms, for both Japan's domestic and international audiences. Japan today tries to promote science and technology as a main catalyst for creating industries and supporting its domestic, export-oriented economy. This is based on Japan's own interpretation of its historical path and economic success and is also used to justify its engagement in the Arctic, a region where Japan does not have any sovereign territories. Japan's Arctic policy is as an extension of its economic diplomacy and an attempt to export the Japanese developmental state model.

1. Introduction

The concept of the 'developmental state' has made an essential contribution to analyses of the economic success of East Asia's economies since the early 1980s. It has emerged again recently in the context of the failures of the Washington Consensus, especially in emerging market economies. Following publication of Chalmers Johnson's *MITI and the Japanese Miracle: The Growth of Industrial Policy, 1925–1975*, the developmental state became a shorthand for strong interventionist policies that the Japanese government implemented in order to achieve rapid industrialisation and economic development before and after the end of World War II.[1] The term was then used to explain the booming economies of the newly industrialised countries (NICs) of East Asia to extract institutional factors to make a developmental state a success. These analyses were important as states were increasingly required to navigate economic globalisation with astute political-economic strategies. The East Asian

Aki Tonami http://orcid.org/0000-0001-8394-5226

development model has been a template for innovative institution-building across Latin America, Africa and parts of Asia, referred to in order to counter the Washington Consensus orthodoxy.[2]

Previous research investigated the theoretical evolution of the concept or the applicability of the concept to other regions of the world than East Asia.[3] Nonetheless, it is rare to come across a debate about today's Japan as a developmental state. Japan is mentioned in almost every paper as an epithet to the concept, but the analysis rarely goes beyond that point. In addition, studies on developmental states and state-led development have mostly addressed the domestic context, but had relatively little to say about implications for foreign policy.[4] Against this background, this paper tries to address the following questions: Is Japan still a developmental state? If so, how has it transformed itself over time? What are the implications of Japan's experience for the newer developmental states? What does the foreign policy of a modern developmental state look like?

This paper shows that Japan remains a developmental state in which the state guides and oversees economic development, and the strong bureaucracy and businesses in turn complement each other in leading and shaping policies to achieve developmental goals. What has not changed even after three decades since Johnson's first assessment is the existence of strong, shared norms of communitarian capitalism, in which an interventionist state and the private sector collaborate and manage the market economy to achieve economic development and autonomy of the state. There were times the Japanese state pursued state-led development more rigorously, actively trying to govern the market and catch up with the Western industrialised economies, or less so, focusing more on the role of coordinating the state's functions and businesses. Depending on the level of the state's involvement in managing the process of development, the developmental state could be simultaneously both 'strong' and 'weak'.

Externally, Japan, keenly conscious of its position in the global order and regional political economy, has practised economic diplomacy with tools such as development assistance to achieve its economic security and to promote the developmental state model abroad. Japan today tries to promote science and technology as a main catalyst for creating industries and supporting its domestic, export-oriented economy. This concept is based on Japan's own interpretation of its historical path and economic success and is also used to justify its engagement in the Arctic, a region where Japan does not have any sovereign territories. Japan's Arctic policy is as an extension of Japan's economic diplomacy to achieve economic security, as well as an attempt to export the Japanese developmental state model to the Arctic Region using science and technology as a vehicle. This also functions as an attempt for Japan to self-justify its history of political and economic development and to create a feedback mechanism to adjust domestic institutions.

This analysis will take place in four parts. First, by reviewing the existing literature, I will trace the intellectual history of Japan as a developmental state, with the long economic stagnation starting in the 1990s as a dividing line. Second, Japan's foreign policy as a modern developmental state – particularly the segment that shows strong characteristics of the foreign policy of a developmental state – will be outlined. Third, I will refer to Japan's engagement towards the Arctic Region as an empirical case and address characteristics of Japan's developmental foreign policy today. Finally, implications and recommendations based on Japan's experience for the Global South will be discussed.

2. Japan as a developmental state in full bloom

In an attempt to explain Japan's modern economic and political history, Chalmers Johnson introduced the concept of a 'developmental state' to outline the role of the Ministry of International Trade and Industry (MITI) in facilitating collaboration and solving coordination problems between the state and big businesses, thereby achieving Japan's miraculous post-war economic growth.[5] A developmental state is characterised as a state that sets overall targets, for instance redesigning industrial structures or setting standards to enhance the international competitiveness of its domestic firms. By comparison, a regulatory state such as the United States, which according to Johnson lies at the opposite end of a spectrum of the level of a state's involvement in its national economy, may define the form and procedures to facilitate market competition but does not necessarily aspire to lead in order to control the results of competition in any particular direction. In a developmental state, the decision-making power lies in the hands of elite economic bureaucrats (in the case of Japan, MITI), while in a regulatory state it lies in a democratically elected legislative assembly.

The core of Johnson's argument is that the Japanese developmental state had a highly competent bureaucracy devoted to formulating and executing a planned *process* of economic development.[6] In managing this developmental process, one of the key elements as well as a prerequisite is the existence of a 'pilot agency', such as MITI. Johnson pointed out that a developmental state is a system designed for latecomers in international economy, is most effective in handling conventional issues rather than a crisis situation, and requires a broad societal consensus in favour of various economic targets. Johnson emphasised the role of MITI, in particular the manner in which it selected, prioritised, assisted and supervised particular industries to accelerate economic growth. The concept of a developmental state became widely accepted in the West as it managed to propose an alternative model to both the communist-type command economies and the Western (Anglo-Saxon) mixed market economies.

The 1980s, when Johnson's idea was introduced in Japan, was a period when political economy as a scholarly discipline was only emerging in Japan. Japan was experiencing the first period of long-term stable economic growth since the Oil Shock in 1973, and Japanese society began to widely acknowledge that there were negative consequences of rapid economic development, such as acute environmental pollution. In this context, Japanese political scientists read Johnson's book with an interest in understanding Japan's political model rather than its political-*economic* model.[7] It is rather interesting, therefore, that *MITI and the Japanese Miracle* was first found and translated from English to Japanese by MITI officials themselves. MITI then used the book to promote, defend and protect the ministry, its role and its industrial policy both inside and outside Japan.[8]

Nonetheless, Johnson's concept of a developmental state, especially his emphasis on the role of MITI as the sole pilot agency of Japan's miraculous economic growth after its defeat in WWII, was considered rather constrictive. In reality MITI had not always had supremacy over political parties and big business; even inside the government, MITI was certainly one of the most powerful ministries but its activities had been restricted in its relations with the Ministry of Finance and the Bank of Japan (BOJ), as well as with other numerous ministries on economic affairs.[9] Scholars such as Daniel I. Okimoto asserted that what MITI managed to achieve was to set common targets with the private sector through various networks, such as *keiretsu*, a form of corporate structure in which a number of organisations link together, big business that plays a leadership role in a given industry, trade associations or other human networks.[10] Japan was not a strong state, but rather its consensus-building process depended on the private sector's active participation in the policymaking process. While industrial policies in other parts of the world were often considered political interventions leading to inefficiencies, in Japan, thanks to MITI's networking and coordination, industrial policies succeeded in advancing market functionalities.

Similarly, Kent E. Calder shed more light on the role the private sector played in Japan's economic growth.[11] Calder argued that it was private actors, such as the Japanese long-term credit banks that bore risks and provided capital to new businesses or business groups formed around *sogo shosha* (trading houses) as entrepreneurs, that took the initiative in the consensus-building process and coordination of industrial policies. Takeo Kikkawa revisited discussions on Japan's post-war development policy and its relation to businesses and pointed out: (1) that in Japan, the role of the government depends on whether an industry has the capacity to create an order or coordinate amongst themselves; and (2) that Japanese corporations are extremely willing to make investments if deemed necessary to survive competition; if industrial policy can match this behaviour, it becomes successful.[12]

Meanwhile, a parallel literature on 'regulatory capitalism' on Japan emerged, also helped by Japanese scholars' keen interest to identify Japan's political system or its model of capitalism rather than its political-economic model, as Johnson's work had done. Steven K. Vogel focused on the process of regulatory reforms in Japan from the 1970s to the 1990s and concluded that because reforms were carried out by economic-related ministries, they did not inhibit the bureaucracy in realising their inherent desire to maintain and extend authority.[13] Examples could be found in the implementation of a regulation to manage the market competition process while simultaneously loosening regulations in some other sphere, or the maintenance of regulatory authority that those ministries deemed necessary. This promotion of regulatory reforms under a unified, consistent strategy allowed the Japanese state to execute reforms relatively smoothly, avoiding unnecessary politicisation or lawsuits.

Overall, a common and general position of these analyses is that the main factor in the remarkable economic growth of Japan after WWII can be found in close collaboration between the Japanese state and the private sector. Japan as a developmental state is most characterised by the state's role in shaping, directing and promoting the process of development, but the level of the state's interference could vary. There were times the Japanese state pursued state-led development more rigorously, actively trying to govern the market and catch up with the Western industrialised economies, or less so, focusing more on the role of coordinating the state's functions and businesses. In other words, depending on the level of the state's involvement in managing the process of development, the developmental state could be simultaneously both 'strong' and 'weak'.

3. Japan as a developmental state after the 1990s: failure of the developmental state

If the birth of the concept of Japan as a developmental state was based on its economic success after WWII, discussions on the Japanese political-economic system after the 1990s turned to the analysis of reasons for its failure. The Japanese economy experienced the collapse of the so-called bubble economy in the beginning of the 1990s. Scholars contended that Japan's institutional structure or industrial policies that had been considered the major factor in the success could also have constituted the principal cause of the failure.[14] Richard Katz argued that Japan had overlooked the appropriate timing to change its developmental policies. As a result, its economy turned into a deformed 'dual economy', a hybrid of extremely strong exporting industries and extremely weak domestic industries.[15] When Japan achieved industrialisation and graduated from the state of catching up, Japan should have loosened its 'developmentalist' policies, which were to promote as many infant industries as possible. Instead Japan reinforced them and basically maintained the same industrial policies to protect and promote infant industries well into the 1970s and beyond, thereby exempting inefficient but politically connected industries from domestic and international competition.

While a statist paradigm prevailed in social science theory during this period, for Japanese scholars it was a time of introspection and soul searching.[16] Having witnessed the bursting of the bubble economy and the price the Japanese people had to pay for economic development, such as severe environmental problems, political scientists and economists alike asserted Japan's 'first-class economic success' was premised on 'third-class politics', and 'economic superpower' was under the given conditions of the US–Japan alliance.[17] They saw the Japanese system, which was still led by highly skilled technocrats, as a bad example of a society that single-mindedly pursued economic development but could not handle its negative consequences. Tadashi Yamaguchi argued that

> from a view point of political studies, in order for a success of industrial policies to lead to people's happiness, it is necessary for 'politics' (i.e. political parties, a government and a parliament) to coordinate incomes policy, social policy and ecological policy at a much higher level so that we can correspond to numerous positive and negative consequences of economic development.[18]

Meanwhile, the Japanese government was labouring in an attempt to increase Japan's international influence by advancing the idea of the developmental state outside of Japan. It is a well-known fact among policymakers that the Japanese government provided generous financial assistance to the World Bank in order to write a report, *The East Asian Miracle: Economic Growth and Public Policy*, published in 1993.[19] The report became a reference for the Japanese government to advocate its development aid strategy, emphasising the role of a recipient government in resource mobilisation and investment to export-oriented industries, versus European-style aid that focused on social infrastructure and humanitarian aid.

After a long economic stagnation, the so-called 'lost decade' from 1991 to 2002, the Japanese economy managed to recover from 2002 to the end of 2007 albeit at a low level of 2% annual gross domestic product (GDP) growth.[20] This recovery highlighted the limits of theories whose point of departure was binary assumptions that the Japanese political-economic model was bound to either succeed or fail.[21] This was also influenced by the 'institutional turn' that studies of economics and sociology took in the early 2000s. [22] The institutional approach was particularly known via works related to a book edited by political economists Peter A. Hall and David Soskice, titled *Varieties of Capitalism*, which tried to categorise types of capitalist economies.[23]

Marie Anchordoguy introduced a constructivist view on cooperative behaviour in the Japanese socio-economy and called the Japanese political economy a 'communitarian capitalism'.[24] Under communitarian capitalism an interventionist state and the private sector collaborate and manage the market economy in order to achieve economic development and autonomy of the state. Building on Johnson's theory, particularly the state's role in Japan's industrial development, Anchordoguy attempted to fill the gap that the original concept lacked: *how* such policies were developed and pursued. From this viewpoint, the existence of communitarian norms compelled successive Japanese leaders to pursue policies that represented a wider consensus about what was important, rather than 'the self-interested policies of bureaucratic–authoritarian states such as those in Latin America, India, and Indonesia, which were bogged down with demands from wealthy landholders and burdened with the legacies of exploitative colonizers'.[25] The goal of Japan as a developmental state was to raise the nation's level of prosperity but only so long as this did not reduce social stability, autonomy and security.[26] If one follows the logic of communitarian capitalism, however, not only gains but also losses are broadly distributed across society. For instance, during the economic downturn, Japanese workers accepted lower wages in order to maintain the number of people employed. In this regard, the communitarian capitalism of Japan can be a system in which rooting out inefficiency is difficult.[27]

What can be concluded from the discussion on Japan's developmental state after the 1990s is that constant adjustments were required as it faced challenges over time and within the changing global system. Japan as a strong developmental state as in Johnson's model was effective in handling conventional issues such as industrialisation and economic growth, but was ill equipped to manoeuvre within a crisis situation such as the bursting of the bubble economy. Indeed, numerous Japanese scholars regard institutions that formed the basis of Japan as a developmental state as having burgeoned already in the nineteenth century, much earlier than the post-WWII period Johnson captured.[28]

4. Japan's foreign policy as a developmental state

As mentioned earlier, a developmental state is a system designed for latecomers in international economy.[29] Indeed, Japan had been a latecomer to the international system set in place by the early starters of the West.[30] This status of Japan at the international level as well as the constraints and opportunities created by the norms and structures of the international system made Japan appear a 'reactive state'.[31] This relation between the state's international status as a latecomer and reactivity in its international behaviour corresponds to a lack of studies on developmental states and their implications for foreign policy. However, as Japan eventually caught up with the other major industrialised powers through economic development, it became more proactive in its foreign policy as well, in an attempt to seek a new international role.

Okano-Heijmans studied Japan's foreign policy and found that Japan, a country that engages in state-led development as one of the latecomers in an international system, has practised what can be called economic diplomacy.[32] Put simply, economic diplomacy is the pursuit of economic security within an anarchic system. Economic security consists of the economic prosperity and political stability of a nation. To promote and protect these two types of national interest, a government pursues economic diplomacy using a variety of instruments that are relatively more economic or political in character. In particular, Japan used official development assistance (ODA) as a tool of economic diplomacy and as a tool for restructuring Japanese industry after the 1985 Plaza Accord.[33] For Japan, not only a latecomer but a defeated nation allowed to have a military force only for national territorial defence, ODA has been the most important foreign policy tool from the post-WWII period through the post-Cold War era and up to today.[34]

Japan began to provide ODA in 1954 after signing the Colombo Plan, which was originally an effort to battle communist movements in (South-) East Asia after the end of WWII by providing physical capital, technology and skills development assistance to countries that needed them.[35] During the economic boom of the 1980s, Japan became one of the world's largest donors of ODA, and has remained so since. However, Japan's ODA has long been described as too focused on economy with mercantilist motives and on Asia geographically.[36] This regional focus is linked to the origin of Japan's aid as reparations to its neighbouring countries after WWII.[37] ODA given to Asian countries was generally combined with trade and investment from the private sector.[38] Japan's implied economic interests in its provision of aid prevented it from following international norms and the agendas of the Organisation of Economic Co-operation and Development (OECD) Development Assistance Committee (DAC), which has been the predominant player in the field of foreign aid since it was established in 1961.[39]

For Japan, ODA has served a variety of purposes that are not limited to 'development' per se but include diplomatic and economic policy purposes towards other developing and developed countries. Nonetheless, throughout the last 60 years, there have been major changes in the objectives and implementation instruments of Japan's ODA. For instance, the overall goals of ODA changed from economic development and the 'economic take-off' of developing countries to poverty reduction.[40] Foreign aid activities are administered under a much more centralised system.[41] At the same time, there is a common thread in Japan's ODA policy and practices: an emphasis on economic growth through private-sector activities, supported by infrastructure and human resource development.[42]

Curiously enough, these elements of Japan's ODA – a strong belief in economic development through industrialisation and the state's role in mobilising private-sector resources in order to achieve it – closely resemble the path by which Japan achieved its economic success as a developmental state. Indeed, Japan's aid policy is *autobiographic*; it reflects its interpretation of its own development history and position in global politics.[43] The country's past as an industrial latecomer is used as a principal reason for its particular approach, despite criticism from Western donors. Japan considers itself as having a role to lead other developing countries because it can understand what it means to make self-help efforts. Thus, I argue that Japan's foreign policy reflects its political-economic system under communitarian capitalism, where an interventionist state and the private sector collaborate and manage the market economy in order to achieve economic development and autonomy of the state. Japan's foreign policy, particularly tools of economic diplomacy such as ODA, is most indicative of Japan's own, normative interpretation of its developmental path. Japan's economic diplomacy therefore is the foreign policy of a developmental state, which serves to fulfil Japan's interest to secure its economic prosperity and political stability as well as to establish Japan's role in the international system by exporting and promoting the 'Japan Model' – the developmental state model.[44]

5. Japan's foreign policy towards the Arctic region

I have set out the way that Japan considers ODA an important tool of its diplomacy, and that promotion of its domestic technologies and expertise abroad is considered an important mission, backed by its narrative of domestic development success as a developmental state. Japan's foreign policy towards the Arctic provides a picture of its latest venture to increase its international profile by intervening in regions beyond the developing world, where Japan has long exercised its economic diplomacy and endeavoured to export the developmental state model.

The Arctic is the region above the Arctic Circle, which is an imaginary line circling the globe at approximately 66°34′N, with the North Pole at its centre.[45] Since the first explorers reached the North Pole in the beginning of the twentieth century, the Arctic Region has remained a peripheral region of the coastal states. During the Cold War, the Arctic became a strategically crucial region where the two major protagonists of the Cold War, the USA and the Soviet Union, bordered one another and where strategic weapons systems were installed. As the Cold War ended, however, attention to the Arctic Region shifted from the strategic, security-focused role to the growing body of evidence pointing to the effects of global warming and climate change. The Arctic, once a region locked by thick ice, is becoming ice-free for longer periods and over a greater area for each passing year. All of the eight Arctic states (Canada, the Kingdom of Denmark, Norway, Iceland, Finland, Sweden, Russia and the USA) regard increased traffic and regional activities due to melting ice as a positive economic opportunity but also as a potential security and governance challenge.

Japan, along with other non-Arctic, Asian states, took note of these changes in the Arctic and expressed its interest to be more involved through various means. The most recent and significant effort was its successful application to gain observer status at the Arctic Council, a leading intergovernmental forum for cooperation in and about the Arctic Region, in 2013. Japan's interest in the Arctic goes back to the pre-WWII period with a particular interest in exploring the Northern Sea Route (NSR), a shipping route running along the Russian Arctic coast from the Kara Sea, along Siberia, to the Bering Strait, connecting Asia and Europe with a much shorter distance than a traditional southbound route. Following WWII, Japan's general interest in the Arctic faded and did not re-emerge until the beginning of the 1990s. With the end of the Cold War, the Murmansk Initiative was introduced in 1987 to establish the Arctic as a 'zone of peace'. Japan joined the effort by setting up domestic institutions for scientific research such as the Centre for Arctic Research at the National Institute of Polar Research, and a research station in Svalbard, Norway.

After Japan submitted its application to the Arctic Council in 2009, Japan as a non-Arctic state sought to convince the Arctic coastal states of its legitimacy with a variety of initiatives. The Ministry of Foreign Affairs (MoFA) established an Arctic Task Force and eventually assigned an Arctic ambassador. The Ministry of Education, Culture, Sports, Science and Technology (MEXT) introduced nationwide, large-scale research programmes. The Ministry of Land, Infrastructure, Transport and Tourism (MLIT) began special committee meetings with related ministries, private businesses and advisors to investigate the status of current and future policy on the NSR.[46] The Cabinet Office included the Arctic in the government's Basic Plan on Ocean Policy. In 2015, Japan announced its first official Arctic Policy, which lists seven areas that Japan believes must be addressed: global environmental issues, indigenous peoples of the Arctic, science and technology, ensuring the rule of law and promoting international cooperation, Arctic sea routes, natural resource development, and national security. As specific measures, the policy lists three initiatives: research and development, international cooperation, and sustainable use of Arctic resources.

The majority of Japan's diplomatic efforts towards the Arctic are made by the members of the epistemic community using their scientific knowledge gained from nationally funded research projects. Japan uses the Arctic Challenge for Sustainability (ArCS) project as the main vehicle as well as a showcase for Japanese policymakers towards the Arctic region. The ArCS is funded by MEXT and was announced in 2015 as a 5-year project with 500–650 million Japanese Yen (approximately 4–5.3 million USD). Of numerous meetings and conferences on the Arctic, the Arctic Council is regarded as the most relevant forum – in particular Ministerial Meetings where Japan participates as an observer and Working Groups where Japanese experts can be more actively involved.

In Japan's approach towards the Arctic Region, undoubtedly the Japanese state plays the largest role. The Japanese government recognises the sovereignty of the Arctic states in the Arctic Region; therefore, any issues – including economic ones – related to the Region should be taken up in an existing institutional framework such as the Arctic Council. MoFA is mainly responsible for representing Japan at various international meetings, respecting the rule of law. MLIT bears Japan's interest in the development of the new shipping routes such as the NSR. It is worth pointing out that it is MEXT that has the longest history of involvement in the Arctic and has allocated the largest budget among Japanese ministries to the Arctic so far, mostly concentrated around scientific research and building a polar scientist network. This is due to a strong influence from the segment of the ministry that absorbed the Science and Technology Agency in 2001. This agency's duty was to plan and promote policies related to Japan's science and technology, as well as to conduct large-scale projects that Japan 'should uniformly promote as a nation, such as nuclear power, outer space development and maritime development'.[47] The mission of the agency, which was established in 1956, was to catch up with its technological competitors during the Cold War, but this later shifted to supporting basic research.[48] The shift was a reaction to criticism from other developed countries that Japan achieved economic development in the 1980s partly by 'free-riding on basic science and technological research'.[49] This narrative of legitimising the state's involvement in science and technology in order to achieve economic growth is identical to what we have seen in Japan's industrial policies as well as foreign development assistance after WWII.

To complement and enhance the Japanese state's Arctic policy, Japanese business groups have played an informal yet substantial role. The Japanese bureaucracy and business groups are interdependent, particularly in foreign policy; the bureaucracy relies on business groups to gather political information of interest and on their intelligence capacities, while business groups depend on the government for support and guidance on trade-related issues. In the case of the Arctic, various organisations under the umbrella of the Nippon Foundation, most significantly the Ocean Policy Research Institute (OPRI) under the Sasakawa Peace Foundation, has been instrumental in shaping Japan's engagement in the Arctic Region as well as preparing, planning and implementing the formal Arctic Policy. The Nippon Foundation is Japan's largest philanthropic foundation but is based on profits from public speedboat racing, with an annual revenue of 46 billion JPY (approximately 417 million USD) in 2016, and provides financial assistance for maritime shipping activities, welfare projects, and international development.[50] The OPRI is a private think tank and a lobbying organisation for the Japanese shipping industry and related manufacturing industries. Already in 1993, just a few years after the Murmansk Initiative but long before the issue of melting ice captured international attention, the Ship & Ocean Foundation (the precursor to OPRI) in cooperation with two research institutes from Russia and Norway initiated a 6-year research project on the technical feasibility of the NSR as an international commercial sea route. Today the Nippon Foundation reliably supports the Japanese government, research community and business groups by providing financial assistance for their extensive activities. This is a salient example of new strategic sectors for the Japanese economy still being managed under a coordinated market system.

A narrative shared among the bureaucracy, politicians and business groups of Japan is that science and technology is essential in the economic development of Japan.[51] Indeed, in November 1995, the Science and Technology Basic Law was enacted, and this became the basis of Japan's science and technology policy. The law states that its objective is 'to achieve a higher standard of science and technology, to contribute to the development of the economy and society of Japan'.[52] There was a shared understanding that, in order to shake off the long recession and the end of the era of Japan as a nation 'catching up' to the Western developed economies, it was essential to create new industries by developing high-tech scientific technologies.[53] In other words, in order to maintain the status in the world that Japan achieved after WWII with a developmental state approach, science and technology was deemed key. The logic behind this was that, first, science and technology enabled Japan to achieve economic growth and address environmental problems that arose with it; second, this mere science and technology is now 'one of the few internationally viable trump cards held by resource- and energy-poor Japan'.[54]

Japan's Arctic policy, therefore, can be understood as an extension of Japan's economic diplomacy to achieve economic security, as well as an attempt to export the Japanese developmental state model to the Arctic Region using science and technology as a vehicle. Indeed, Japan regards the Arctic as a 'diplomatic challenge that requires scientific and technological knowledge to produce effective solutions'.[55] I have argued that Japan's foreign policy reflects its political-economic system, in which an interventionist state and the private sector collaborate and manage the market economy to achieve economic development and autonomy of the state. In addition, Japan's foreign policy, particularly as it pertains to the economy, such as ODA, exhibits its normative interpretation of the nation's developmental path. Similarly, Japan attempts to engage in the Arctic Region using its scientific and technological knowledge. This is not simply because science and technology are one of the few diplomatic tools available under the existing framework with the Arctic Council at the core, but because it will eventually bring about economic development for the Arctic region and for Japan (and it may even prevent or solve potential environmental problems), in the way that Japan achieved economic development after WWII.

Indeed, because Japan is by nature an outsider in the Arctic Region as a non-coastal state, and in fact has 'little say in decision making at high-level meetings', Japan's Arctic policy is compelled to be less practical and more normative and value-oriented.[56] For Japan the developmental state approach has worked effectively, or at least there is a broad consensus that the path taken by Japan during the seven decades after the end of WWII has been a success. In constructing its narrative to legitimise its participation in Arctic politics, Japan took up on one of the most significant elements of Japan as a modern developmental state: science and technology. In terms of institutions of the political-economic system, Japan may no longer strictly qualify as a strong developmental state as Johnson described, but belief in developmentalism and communitarian capitalism remains strong. Japan's foreign policy towards the Arctic encompasses norms and values derived from these beliefs.

6. Implications and lessons learned for the Global South

In light of questions this special issue attempts to address, such as the role of the state in economic development as well as its evolution and the possibility of referring to the concept of 'developmental states' in understanding the reorganisation of power and capital in the world economy, there are a few implications this paper can provide. The most important precept is that one must be aware of an unconscious bias of looking at a nation's political-economic system from the viewpoint of success or failure. The lesson Japan's experience provides is that it is crucial for a developmental state to remain innovative and assess the appropriate timing to switch from being a strong developmental state to a weaker developmental state. In the case of Japan, it failed to determine that it had already passed the state of 'catching up' by the 1980s, and to make necessary adjustments. In addition, without institutions to enhance the cooperative behaviour of the bureaucracy, businesses and politicians, as well as norms that exist in the wider society about what is important, it is extremely difficult for an interventionist state to implement policies to achieve economic development and the autonomy of the state.

The process of making foreign policy contextualised and reinforced these norms for both Japan's domestic and international audiences. Norm-oriented foreign policy creates a broad framework that communicates a narrative about the vision of a particular circumstance; in the case of development assistance, a normative framework of aid provides the vision of development as progress and how best to achieve it.[57] We saw earlier one of Japan's norms of development assistance (as well as a programmatic focus) was investing in human and economic infrastructure based on a development model that draws on Japan's own experience with industrialisation and reconstruction. Similarly, Japan applies its own understanding of development, based on its past, towards the Arctic region. The most suitable way to achieve sustainable development – a state where there is a sufficient amount of economic growth but potential environmental problems caused by climatic changes are kept at a minimum – in the Arctic is through the full utilisation of science and technology.

For Japan, the institutional structure or industrial policies associated with a developmental state were not necessarily a matter of choice; rather, it was a survival strategy as a war-torn, latecomer country in the international economic system. As it entered the system rather forcefully, however, Japanese policies were contested. Japan's foreign assistance has been contested at home and abroad. Through these contests, Japan became a more rounded aid donor, blending Western principles with concepts of 'self-help', advocating large infrastructure projects that serve both Japan's and recipient countries' interests.[58] These debates around Japan's attempt to export the Japan Model abroad have been particularly important in making Japan's political-economic system as a modern developmental state appealing to international audiences – what might be characterised as the exercising of Japan's soft power. Japan's example of utilising external policies in order to adjust to the changing global system over time, and creating an institutional feedback mechanism by exporting institutions and exposing them to criticism and contestation from the outside world, is a particularly useful lesson for a latecomer state in the Global South.

Japan's experience as a developmental state – and empirical cases from other papers in this special issue – informs us that in a globalised economy today, state intervention in a country's economic direction is a necessity, even if one is an adherent of neoliberalism. Japan's political-economic system may no longer fit the classic model of a developmental state, where there is a strong state leadership guiding the country's rapid industrialisation. However, state–business relations are still strong and a professional bureaucracy remains the basis of institutionalised expertise in modern Japan. Therefore, an assessment of a developmental state should be extended to a long-term performance of institutions. Indeed, as Richard Stubbs pointed out, the idea of the developmental state itself has been resilient or has had a certain 'stickiness' to it.[59] In the case of Japan, this 'stickiness' is guaranteed and enhanced by strong, shared societal norms to raise the national level of prosperity.

Disclosure statement

No potential conflict of interest was reported by the author.

Funding

This work was supported by JSPS KAKENHI [grant number 17K03576].

Acknowledgements

I wish to thank the anonymous reviewers; the participants in the Japan Association of International Relations Conference 2017, Kobe; and the Guest Editors of this special issue for their valuable comments.

Notes

1. Johnson, *MITI and the Japanese Miracle*.
2. See, for example, articles by Ovadia and Gezmis in this special issue.
3. Stubbs, "What Ever Happened to the East Asian Developmental State?"; Routley, *Developmental States: a Review of the Literature*.
4. Okano-Heijmans, "Japan's 'Green' Economic Diplomacy."
5. Johnson, *MITI and the Japanese Miracle*.
6. Beeson, "The Rise and Fall (?) of the Developmental State."
7. Yamaguchi, "Sengo Nippon no Sangyō Seisaku to Ch. Johnson."
8. Johnson, "The Developmental State: Odyssey of a Concept."
9. Wada, "Nihongata Shihon Shugiron No Aratana Shiza."
10. Okimoto, *Between MITI and the Market*.
11. Calder, *Strategic Capitalism*.

12. Kikkawa, "9 Shō Keizai Kaihatsu Seisaku to Kigyō."
13. Vogel, *Japan as No. 1: Lessons for America.*
14. Wada, "Nihongata Shihon Shugiron No Aratana Shiza."
15. Katz, *Japan: the System That Soured.*
16. Wong, "The Adaptive Developmental State in East Asia."
17. Hiwatari, *Sengo Nippon no Shijō to Seiji.*
18. Yamaguchi, "Sengo Nippon no Sangyō Seisaku to Ch. Johnson."
19. See for example Johnson, "The Developmental State: Odyssey of a Concept."
20. Patrick, "The Japanese Economy's Recovery."
21. Wada, "Nihongata Shihon Shugiron No Aratana Shiza."
22. Evans, "Developmental State: Divergent Responses."
23. Hall and Soskice, *Varieties of Capitalism.*
24. Anchordoguy, *Reprogramming Japan.*
25. Ibid., 208.
26. Ibid., 208.
27. Ibid., 218.
28. See for example Kimura, *Japan's Model of Economic Development*; and Sasada, *Evolution of the Japanese Developmental State System.*
29. Johnson, *MITI and the Japanese Miracle.*
30. G. D. Hook et al., *Japan's International Relations*, 68.
31. Calder, *Crisis and Compensation.*
32. Okano-Heijmans, "Japan's 'Green' Economic Diplomacy."
33. Söderberg, *Business of Japanese Aid.*
34. Kato, "Japan's ODA 1954–2014," 1.
35. For the influence of US aid to Japan as well as Japan's experience as an aid recipient after WWII exerted on Japan's attitude as a donor, refer to Higuchi (2013).
36. White, *Japanese Aid*; Koppel and Orr, *Japan's Foreign Aid.*
37. S. W. Hook, *National Interest and Foreign Aid.*
38. Söderberg, *Business of Japanese Aid.*
39. Arase, "Introduction."
40. Kato, "Japan's ODA 1954–2014," 10.
41. Sato, "Benefits of Unification Failure," 88.
42. Kato, "Japan's ODA 1954–2014," 30.
43. Tonami and Müller, "Trajectories of Japanese and South Korean Environmental Aid."
44. Japan's approach to synthesise aid, direct investment and trade is often called the Trinity Development Cooperation.
45. National Snow & Ice Data Center, "What Is the Arctic?."
46. The NSR, also called the Northeast Passage, is a shipping lane between the Atlantic Ocean and the Pacific Ocean along the Russian coast. The distance from Northern Europe to Asia via the NSR is approximately 40% less than that via the Suez Canal.
47. Kiba, "Kagaku Gijutsu Chō No Seisaku Kettei Katei," 26.
48. Ibid., 31.
49. Ibid., 32.
50. Nippon Foundation, "2016 Nendo Shūshi Yosansho."
51. Christopher Dent's paper in this special issue points out that there exists a wider phenomenon in East Asia that the development agenda is changing, and it can be understood as sustainable development agenda and climate interventionism.
52. Cabinet Office of Japan, *The Science and Technology Basic Law (Unofficial Translation).*
53. Akashi, "Notes on the Science-Technology Basic Law Regime [in Japanese]."
54. Council for Science and Technology Policy, *Toward the Reinforcement of Science and Technology Diplomacy (Provisional Translation).*
55. Kamikawa and Hamachi, "Japan's Evolving Efforts toward Sustainable Development of the Arctic."
56. Ibid.

57. Fukuda-Parr and Shiga, *Normative Framing of Development Cooperation*.
58. Jain, "Japan's Foreign Aid."
59. Stubbs, "What Ever Happened to the East Asian Developmental State?"

Bibliography

Akashi, Hiroyuki. "Notes on the Science–Technology Basic Law Regime [in Japanese]." *Journal of Management Faculty, Komazawa University* 40 (2011): 39–88.

Anchordoguy, Marie. *Reprogramming Japan: The High Tech Crisis and Communitarian Capitalism*. Ithaca: Cornell University Press, 2006.

Arase, David. "Introduction." In *Japan's Foreign Aid: Old Continuities and New Directions*, edited by David Arase, 1–19. London and New York, 2005.

Beeson, Mark. "The Rise and Fall (?) of the Developmental State: The Vicissitudes and Implications of East Asian Interventionism." In *Developmental States: Relevancy, Redundancy or Reconfiguration*, edited by Linda Low, 29–40, New York: Nova Science Publishers, Inc., 2014.

Cabinet Office of Japan. *The Science and Technology Basic Law (Unofficial Translation)*, 2015. Accessed April 28, 2017. http://www8.cao.go.jp/cstp/english/law/law.html.

Calder, Kent E. *Crisis and Compensation: Public Policy and Political Stability in Japan, 1949–1986*. Princeton: Princeton University Press, 1988.

Calder, Kent E. Strategic Capitalism: *Private Business and Public Purpose in Japanese Industrial Finance*. Princeton: Princeton University Press, 1993.

Council for Science and Technology Policy. *Toward the Reinforcement of Science and Technology Diplomacy (Provisional Translation)*. Accessed April 28, 2017. http://www8.cao.go.jp/cstp/english/doc/s_and_t_diplomacy/20080519_tow_the_reinforcement_of.pdf

Evans, Peter. "The Developmental State: Divergent Responses to Modern Economic Theory and the Twenty-First-Century Economy." In *The End of the Developmental State*, edited by Michelle Williams, 220–240. New York: Oxfordshire, 2014.

Fukuda-Parr, Sakiko, and Hiroaki Shiga. *Normative Framing of Development Cooperation: Japanese Bilateral Aid between the DAC and Southern Donors*. Tokyo: JICA Research Institute, 2016.

Hall, Peter A., and David Soskice, eds. *Varieties of Capitalism: The Institutional Foundations of Comparative Advantage*. Oxford: Oxford University Press, 2001.

Higuchi, Toshihiro. "How US Aid in the 1950s Prepared Japan as a Future Donor." In *The Rise of Asian Donors: Japan's Impact on the Evolution of Emerging Donors*, edited by Jin Sato and Yasutami Shimomura, 29–48. Oxon: Routledge, 2013.

Hiwatari, Nobuhiro. *Sengo Nihon No Shijō to Seiji [Post-War Japan's Market and Politics]*. Tokyo: University of Tokyo Press, 1991.

Hook, Glenn D, Julie Gibson, Christopher W Hughes, and Hugo Dobson. *Japan's International Relations: Politics, Economics and Security*. 3rd ed. Oxon: Routledge, 2012.

Hook, Steven W. *National Interest and Foreign Aid*. Boulder: L. Rienner Publishers, 1995.

Jain, Purnendra. "Japan's Foreign Aid: Old and New Contests." *The Pacific Review* 29, no. 1 (August 18, 2015): 93–113. doi:10.1080/09512748.2015.1066415.

Johnson, Chalmers. *MITI and the Japanese Miracle: The Growth of Industrial Policy, 1925–1975*. Stanford: Stanford University Press, 1982.

Johnson, Chalmers. "The Developmental State: Odyssey of a Concept." In *The Developmental State*, edited by Meredith Woo-Cumings, 32–60. Ithaca and London: Cornell University Press, 1999.

Kamikawa, Yoko, and Tomoko Hamachi. "Japan's Evolving Efforts toward Sustainable Development of the Arctic." *Science & Diplomacy* 5, no. 3 (September 28, 2016): 1–7.

Kato, Hiroshi. "Japan's ODA 1954–2014: Changes and Continuities in a Central Instrument in Japan's Foreign Policy." In *Japan's Development Assistance Foreign Aid and the Post-Agenda*, edited by Hiroshi Kato, John Page, and Yasutami Shimomura, 1–18, London: Palgrave Mcmillan, 2016.

Katz, Richard. *Japan: the System That Soured. The Rise and Fall of the Japanese Economic Miracle, Oxon*. New York: Routledge, 1998.

Kiba, Takao. "Kagaku Gijutsu Chō No Seisaku Kettei Katei [The Decision-Making Process of the Science and Technology Agency]." In *Inside the Japanese Bureaucracy*, edited by Hideaki Shiroyama and Hosono Sukehiro, 25–44, Tokyo, 2002.

Kikkawa, Takeo. "9 Shō Keizai Kaihatsu Seisaku to Kigyō: Sengo Nippon No Keiken [Chapter 9 – Economic Development Policy and Corporations: Japan's Post-War Experience]." In *The 20th-Century Global System 4 Developmentalism*, edited by Institute of Social Science, The Tokyo University, 276–304. Tokyo: University of Tokyo Press, 1998.

Kimura, Fukunari. *Japan's Model of Economic Development: Relevant and Nonrelevant Elements for Developing Economies*. WIDER Research Paper 2009-22. Helsinki: UNU-WIDER 2009.

Koppel, Bruce, and Robert M Orr. *Japan's Foreign Aid: Power and Policy in a New Era*. Oxford: Westview Press, 1993.

National Snow & Ice Data Center. "What is the Arctic?." *National Snow Ice Data Center*. Accessed April 28, 2017. https://nsidc.org/cryosphere/arctic-meteorology/arctic.html

Nippon Foundation. "2016 Nendo Shūshi Yosansho [FY2016 Income and Expenditure]." Accessed April 28, 2017. http://www.nippon-foundation.or.jp/who/disclosure/financials/img/2016/201604_shushiyosan.pdf

Okano-Heijmans, Maaike. "Japan's 'Green' Economic Diplomacy: Environmental and Energy Technology and Foreign Relations." *The Pacific Review* 25, no. 3 (2012): 339–364.

Okimoto, Daniel I. *Between MITI and the Market: Japanese Industrial Policy for High Technology*. Stanford, California: Stanford University Press, 1989.

Patrick, Hugh. "The Japanese Economy's Recovery." *East Asia Forum*, November 20, 2010. http://www.eastasiaforum.org/2010/11/20/the-japanese-economys-recovery/

Routley, Laura. *Developmental States: A Review of the Literature*. *ESID Working Paper*, February 22, 2012.

Sasada, Hironori. *The Evolution of the Japanese Developmental State System: Institutions Locked-in by Ideas*. London: Routledge, 2013.

Sato, Jin. "The Benefits of Unification Failure: Re-Examining the Evolution of Economic Cooperation in Japan." In *Japan's Development Assistance: Foreign Aid and the Post-2015 Agenda*, 88–102. London: Palgrave Macmillan, 2016.

Söderberg, Marie. *The Business of Japanese Aid: Five Cases in Asia*. London: Routledge, 1996.

Stubbs, Richard. "What Ever Happened to the East Asian Developmental State? The Unfolding Debate." *The Pacific Review* 22, no. 1 (2009): 1–22.

Tonami, Aki, and Anders Riel Müller. "Trajectories of Japanese and South Korean Environmental Aid: A Comparative Historical Analysis." *Journal of Environment & Development* 23, no. 2 (2014): 191–219. doi:

Wada, Hironori. "Nihongata Shihon Shugiron No Aratana Shiza (a New Perspective on the Japanese Capitalism)." *The Hitotsubashi Journal of Law and International Studies* 6, no. 2 (July 2007): 981–1012.

White, John. *Japanese Aid*. London: Overseas Development Institute, 1964.

Wong, Joseph. "The Adaptive Developmental State in East Asia." *Journal of East Asian Studies* 4, no. 2004 (2004): 345–362.

Yamaguchi, Tadashi. "Sengo Nippon No Sangyō Seisaku to Ch. Johnson [Post-war Japan's industrial policy and Ch. Johnson]." *Policy Science* 2, no. 1 (July 25, 2010): 147–155.

Index

Note: Page numbers in *italics* refer to figures.
Page numbers in **bold** refer to tables.
Page numbers followed by "n" refer to notes.

Kolibri 360 GmbH
Ferdinand-Jühlke-Straße 7
99095 Erfurt, Deutschland
produktsicherheit@kolibri360.de